KID GLOVES

Nine Months *of* Careful Chaos

LUCY KNISLEY

:01

First Second
New York

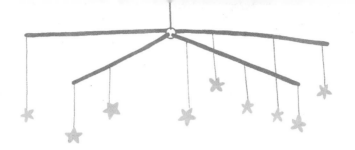

FOR MY TWO K.H.S
ILYYK

First Second

Copyright © 2019 by Lucy Knisley

Published by First Second
First Second is an imprint of Roaring Brook Press, a division of
Holtzbrinck Publishing Holdings Limited Partnership
175 Fifth Avenue, New York, NY 10010

Don't miss your next favorite book from First Second!
For the latest updates go to firstsecondnewsletter.com and sign up for our newsletter.

Library of Congress Control Number: 2018938068

ISBN: 978-1-62672-808-0

Our books may be purchased in bulk for promotional, educational, or business use.
Please contact your local bookseller or the Macmillan Corporate and Premium Sales Department
at (800) 221-7945 ext. 5442 or by e-mail at MacmillanSpecialMarkets@macmillan.com.

First edition, 2019

Edited by Calista Brill and Meg Lemke
Book design by Molly Johanson

Penciled digitally in Photoshop with a Wacom Cintiq 12WX, inked on Canson illustration
paper with Faber-Castell PITT artist's pens, and fondled by a toddler before being scanned.
Flatted by Stephanie Mided and colored digitally in Photoshop.

Printed in China
10 9 8 7 6 5 4 3 2 1

CONTENTS

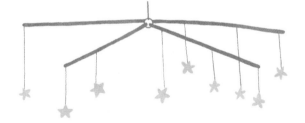

INTRODUCTION

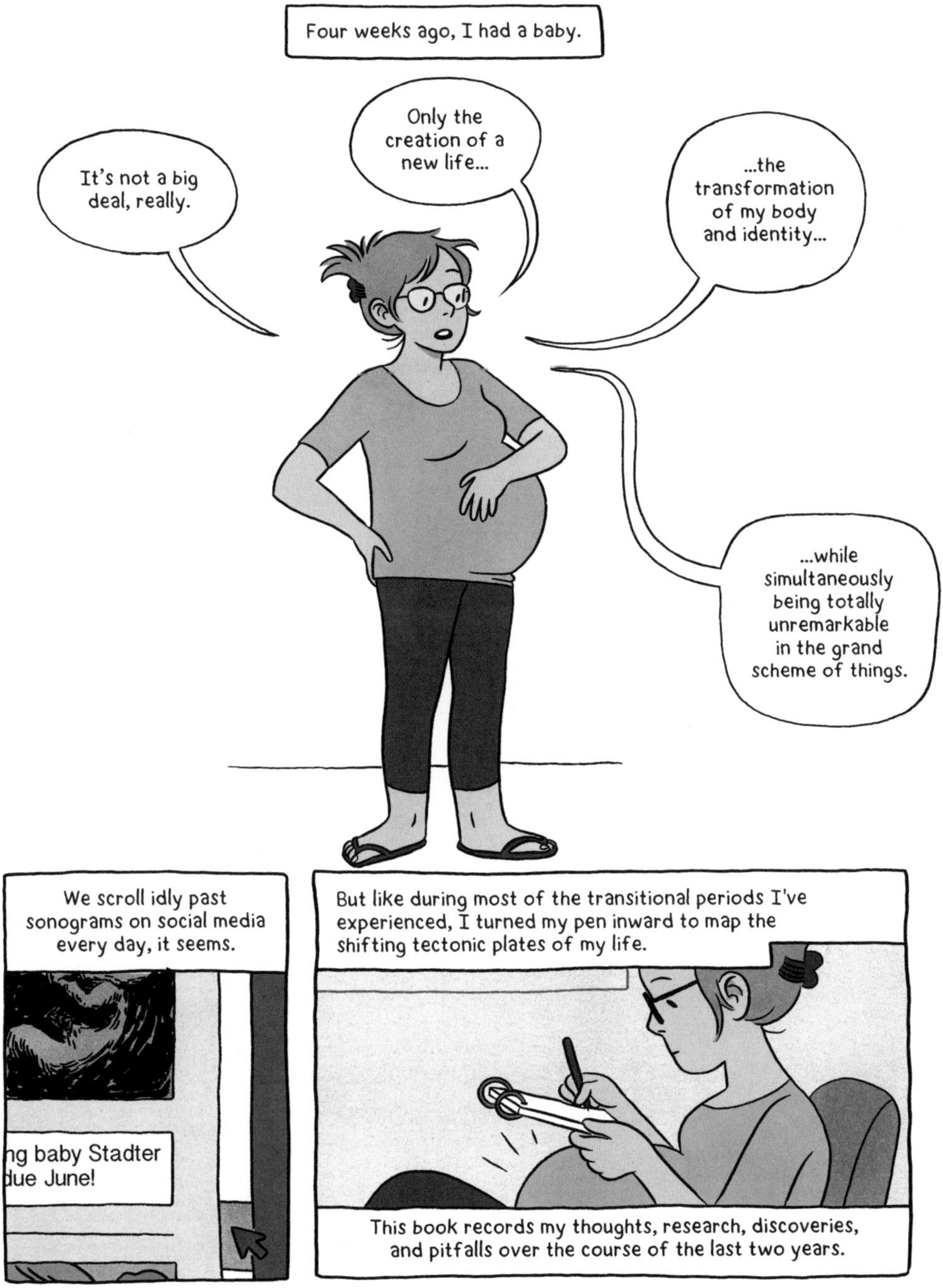
Four weeks ago, I had a baby.
It's not a big deal, really.
Only the creation of a new life...
...the transformation of my body and identity...
...while simultaneously being totally unremarkable in the grand scheme of things.
We scroll idly past sonograms on social media every day, it seems.
ng baby Stadter
due June!
But like during most of the transitional periods I've experienced, I turned my pen inward to map the shifting tectonic plates of my life.
This book records my thoughts, research, discoveries, and pitfalls over the course of the last two years.

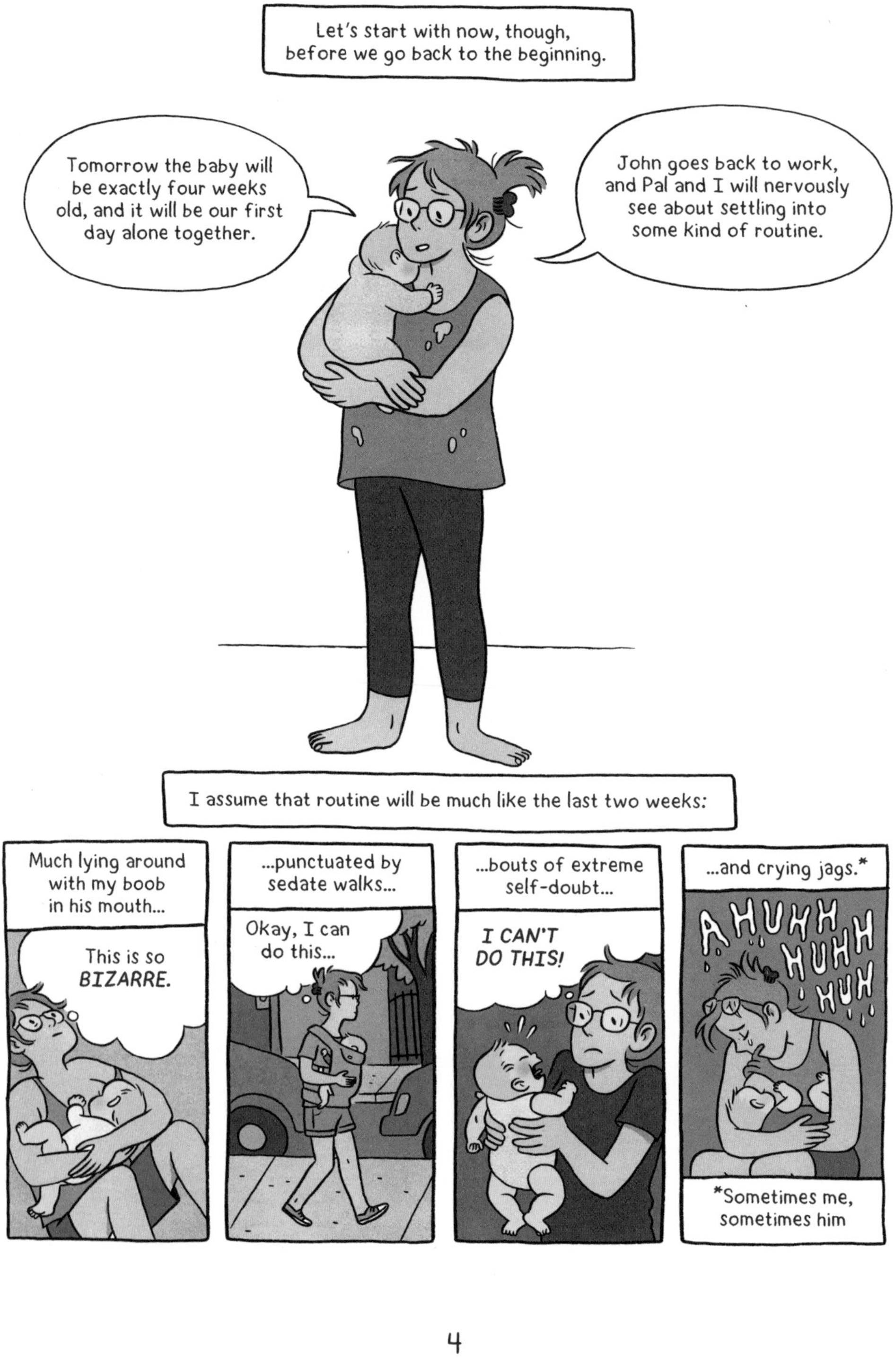

Let's start with now, though, before we go back to the beginning.
Tomorrow the baby will be exactly four weeks old, and it will be our first day alone together.
John goes back to work, and Pal and I will nervously see about settling into some kind of routine.
I assume that routine will be much like the last two weeks:
Much lying around with my boob in his mouth...
This is so BIZARRE.
...punctuated by sedate walks...
Okay, I can do this...
...bouts of extreme self-doubt...
I CAN'T DO THIS!
...and crying jags.*
AHUHH HUHH HUH
*Sometimes me, sometimes him

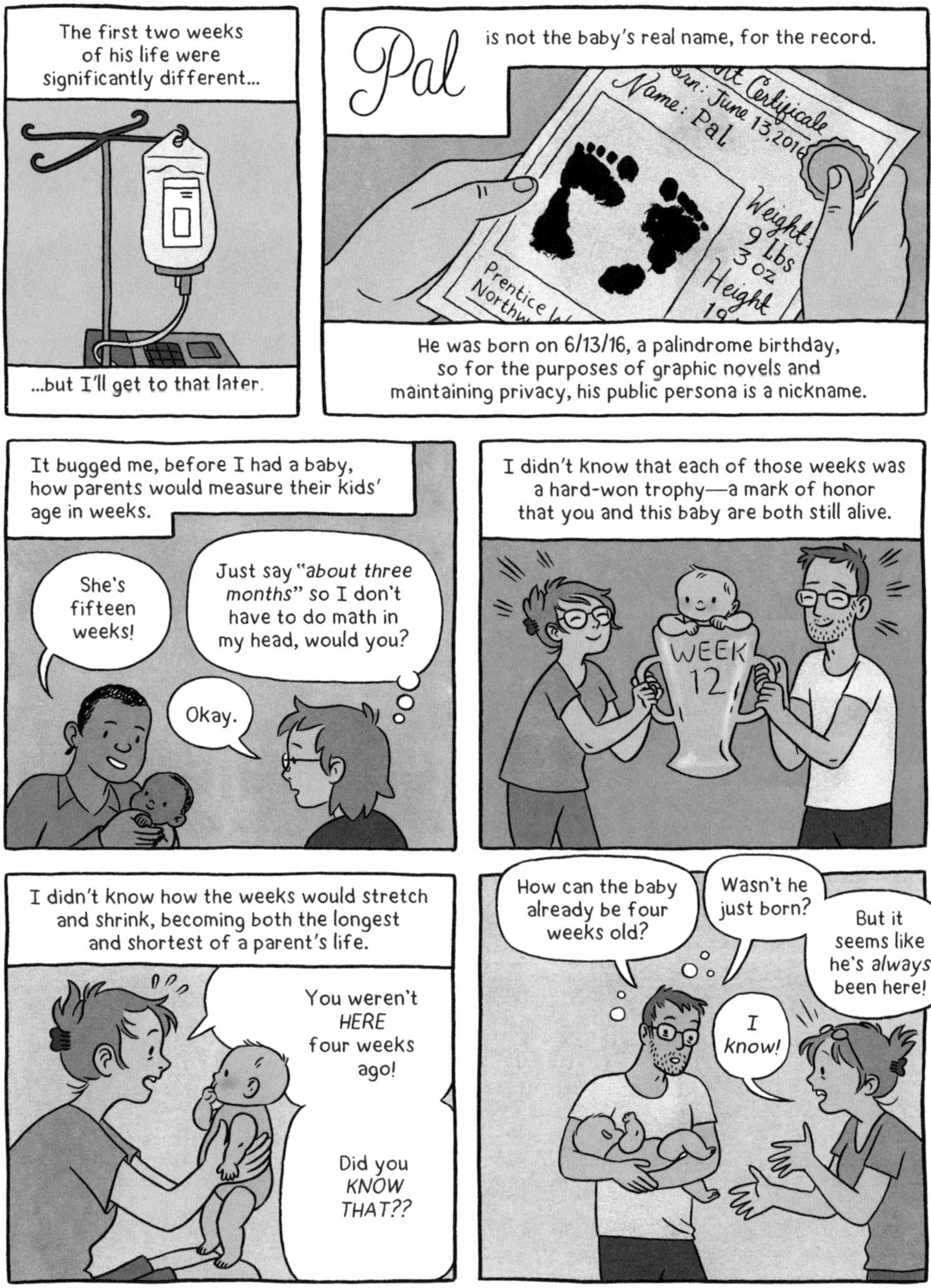
The first two weeks of his life were significantly different...
...but I'll get to that later.
Pal is not the baby's real name, for the record.
Name: Pal
Weight 9 Lbs 3 oz
Height
Prentice
He was born on 6/13/16, a palindrome birthday, so for the purposes of graphic novels and maintaining privacy, his public persona is a nickname.
It bugged me, before I had a baby, how parents would measure their kids' age in weeks.
She's fifteen weeks!
Just say "*about three months*" so I don't have to do math in my head, would you?
Okay.
I didn't know that each of those weeks was a hard-won trophy—a mark of honor that you and this baby are both still alive.
WEEK 12
I didn't know how the weeks would stretch and shrink, becoming both the longest and shortest of a parent's life.
You weren't *HERE* four weeks ago!
Did you *KNOW THAT??*
How can the baby already be four weeks old?
Wasn't he just born?
But it seems like he's *always* been here!
I know!

This is the first time I've set words to page since Pal was born. I think it's the longest stretch I've gone since I learned to write.

Even now, I'm resisting the urge to run upstairs to help John with the squeals I hear from the bedroom that I suspect only my boob will quiet.

WAAHHH!

I'm holding back from opening an internet tab to search "how many poops normal in four-week-old baby?"

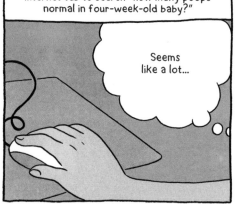

Seems like a lot...

I'm valiantly staying awake past 8 PM.

There are still tabs open from months ago, because this is how I organize my computing.

elephant birth video

pregnancy symptom normal or sign of impending death?

shoes that grow with foot swelling

how many poops n|

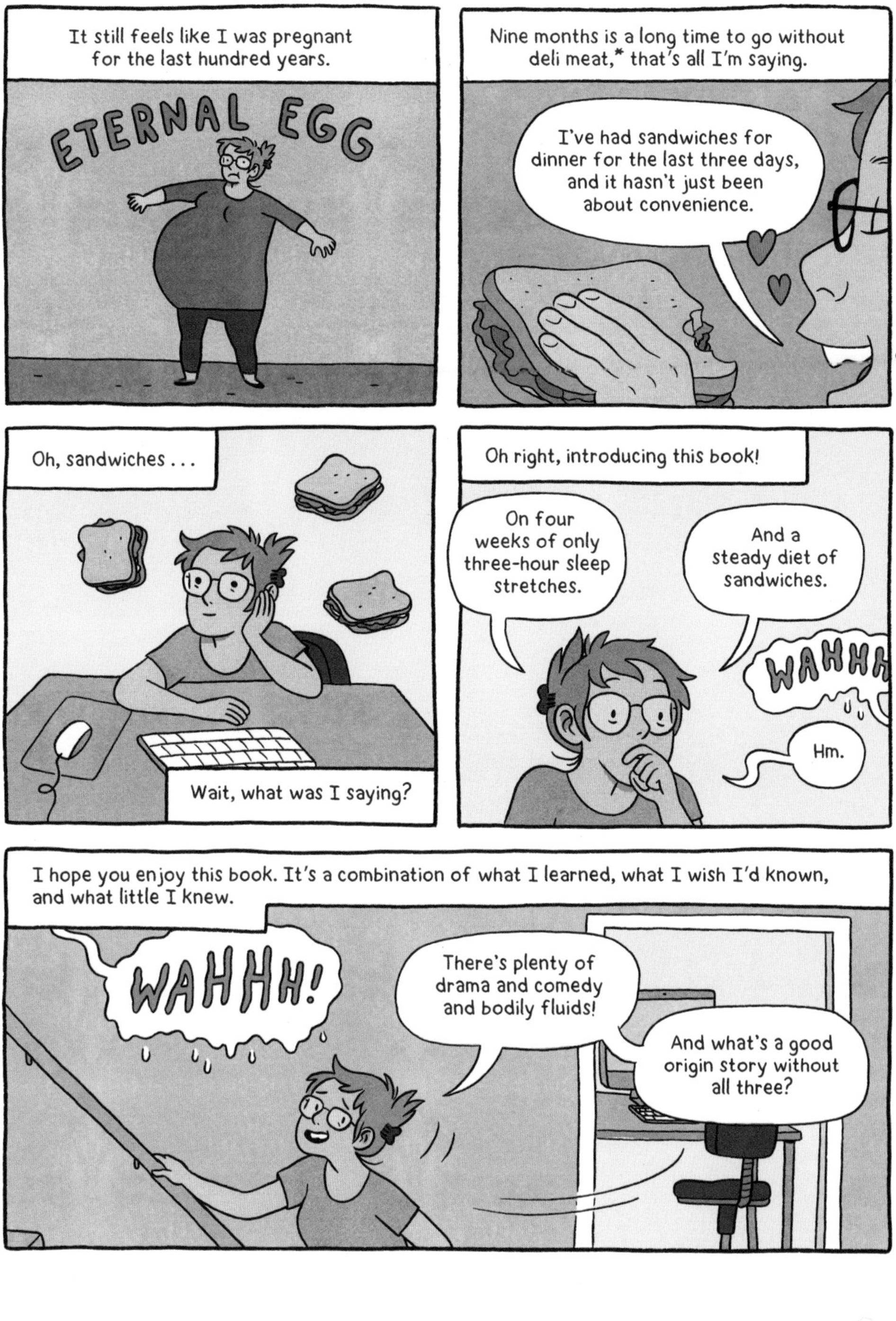

It still feels like I was pregnant for the last hundred years.
ETERNAL EGG
Nine months is a long time to go without deli meat,* that's all I'm saying.
I've had sandwiches for dinner for the last three days, and it hasn't just been about convenience.
Oh, sandwiches . . .
Wait, what was I saying?
Oh right, introducing this book!
On four weeks of only three-hour sleep stretches.
And a steady diet of sandwiches.
WAHHH
Hm.
I hope you enjoy this book. It's a combination of what I learned, what I wish I'd known, and what little I knew.
WAHHH!
There's plenty of drama and comedy and bodily fluids!
And what's a good origin story without all three?

*Pregnant women run the risk of contracting listeria from deli meat and are cautioned to avoid it.

A LITTLE HISTORY

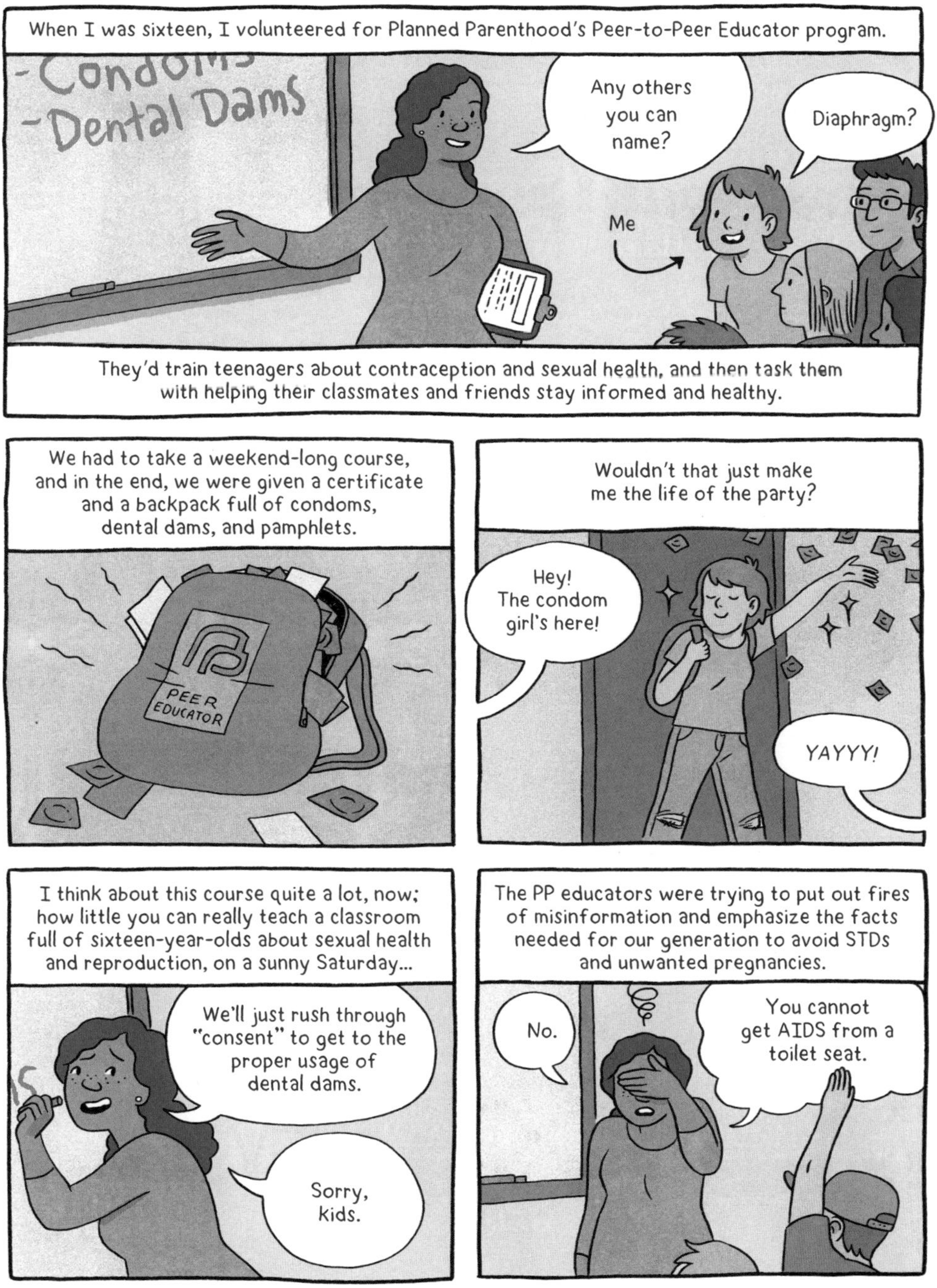
When I was sixteen, I volunteered for Planned Parenthood's Peer-to-Peer Educator program.
-Condoms
-Dental Dams
Any others you can name?
Diaphragm?
Me
They'd train teenagers about contraception and sexual health, and then task them with helping their classmates and friends stay informed and healthy.
We had to take a weekend-long course, and in the end, we were given a certificate and a backpack full of condoms, dental dams, and pamphlets.
PEER EDUCATOR
Wouldn't that just make me the life of the party?
Hey! The condom girl's here!
YAYYY!
I think about this course quite a lot, now; how little you can really teach a classroom full of sixteen-year-olds about sexual health and reproduction, on a sunny Saturday...
We'll just rush through "consent" to get to the proper usage of dental dams.
Sorry, kids.
The PP educators were trying to put out fires of misinformation and emphasize the facts needed for our generation to avoid STDs and unwanted pregnancies.
No.
You cannot get AIDS from a toilet seat.

In college, I went back to PP to get myself fitted for a diaphragm.

Small!

I was starting my first serious relationship with someone who had the ability to get me pregnant.

Here goes...

It took nearly a year before I realized that I was mildly allergic to the latex in diaphragms and condoms, which was why I'd been getting so sick.

Urinary tract infections would lay me up for days.

Am I being *punished*?

UTIs are very common in sexually active young women, which nobody ever bothered to tell me.

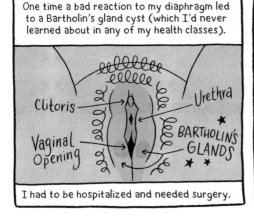

One time a bad reaction to my diaphragm led to a Bartholin's gland cyst (which I'd never learned about in any of my health classes).

Clitoris

Urethra

Vaginal Opening

BARTHOLIN'S GLANDS

I had to be hospitalized and needed surgery.

This possibility had never been suggested in any of my pamphlets in my backpack of condoms.

Let me tell ya 'bout the birds and the bees and the scalpel to your genitals!

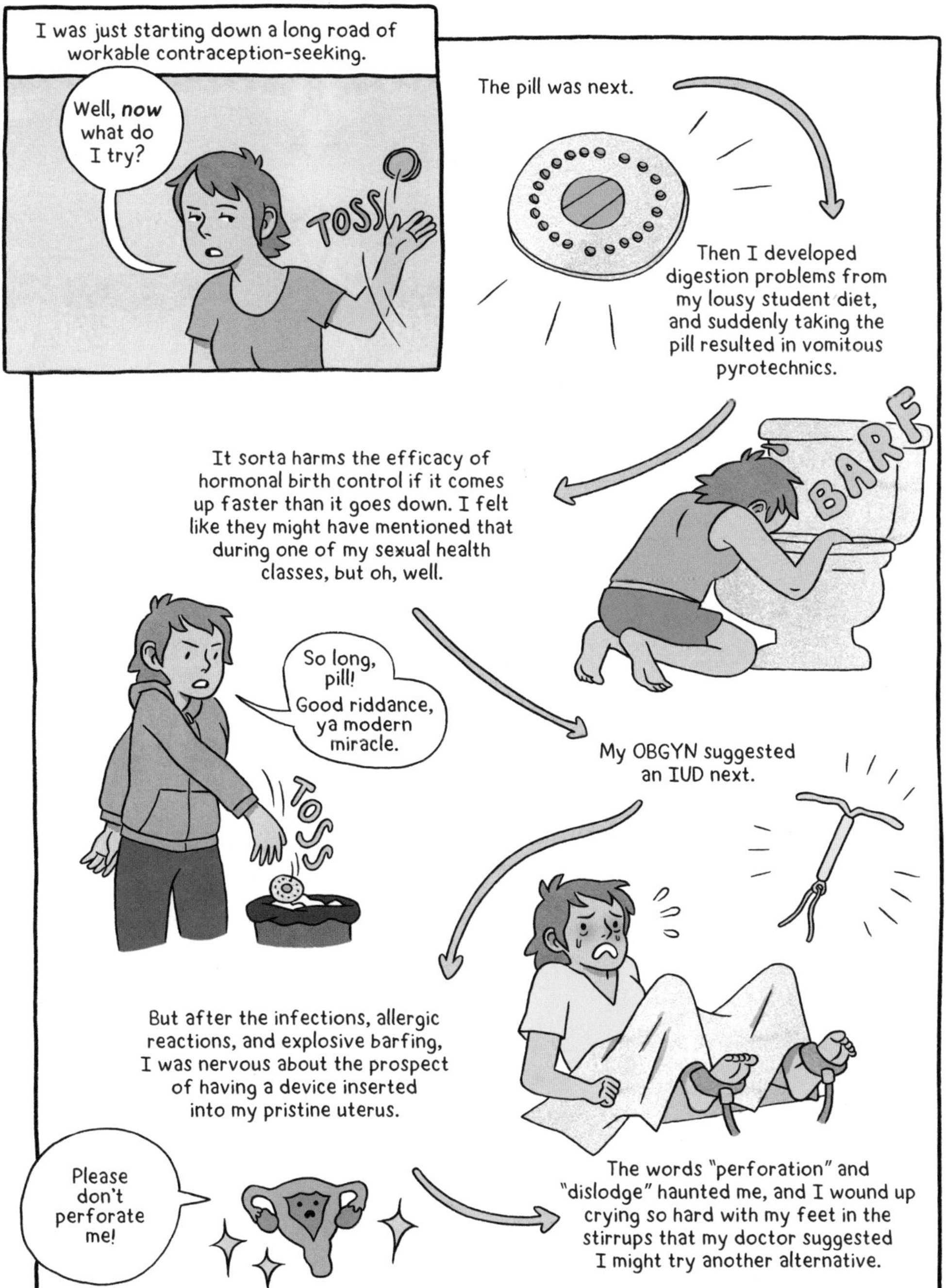

I was just starting down a long road of workable contraception-seeking.
Well, *now* what do I try?
TOSS
The pill was next.
Then I developed digestion problems from my lousy student diet, and suddenly taking the pill resulted in vomitous pyrotechnics.
BARF
It sorta harms the efficacy of hormonal birth control if it comes up faster than it goes down. I felt like they might have mentioned that during one of my sexual health classes, but oh, well.
So long, pill! Good riddance, ya modern miracle.
TOSS
My OBGYN suggested an IUD next.
But after the infections, allergic reactions, and explosive barfing, I was nervous about the prospect of having a device inserted into my pristine uterus.
Please don't perforate me!
The words "perforation" and "dislodge" haunted me, and I wound up crying so hard with my feet in the stirrups that my doctor suggested I might try another alternative.

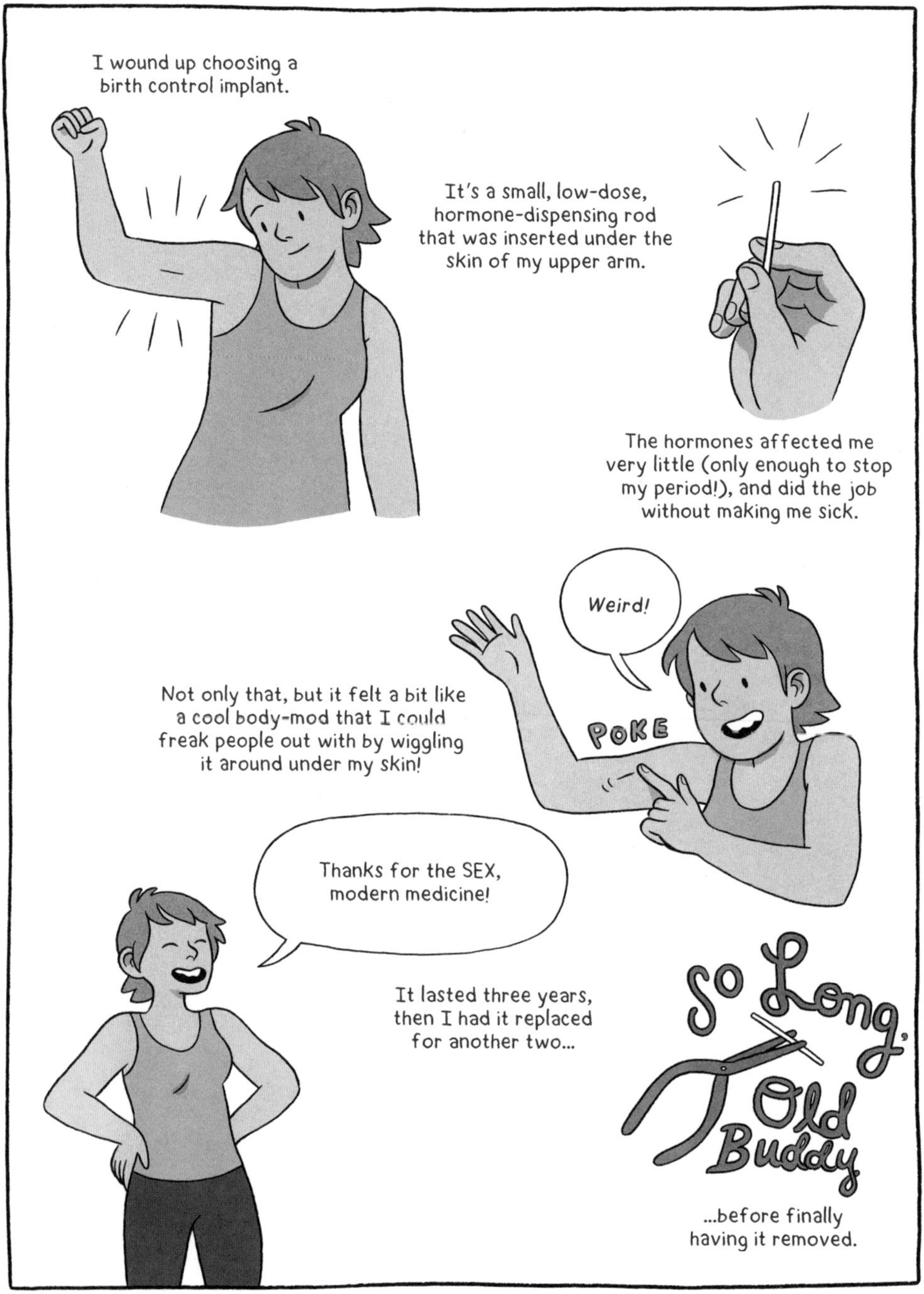

I wound up choosing a birth control implant.
It's a small, low-dose, hormone-dispensing rod that was inserted under the skin of my upper arm.
The hormones affected me very little (only enough to stop my period!), and did the job without making me sick.
Not only that, but it felt a bit like a cool body-mod that I could freak people out with by wiggling it around under my skin!
Weird!
POKE
Thanks for the SEX, modern medicine!
It lasted three years, then I had it replaced for another two...
So Long, Old Buddy
...before finally having it removed.

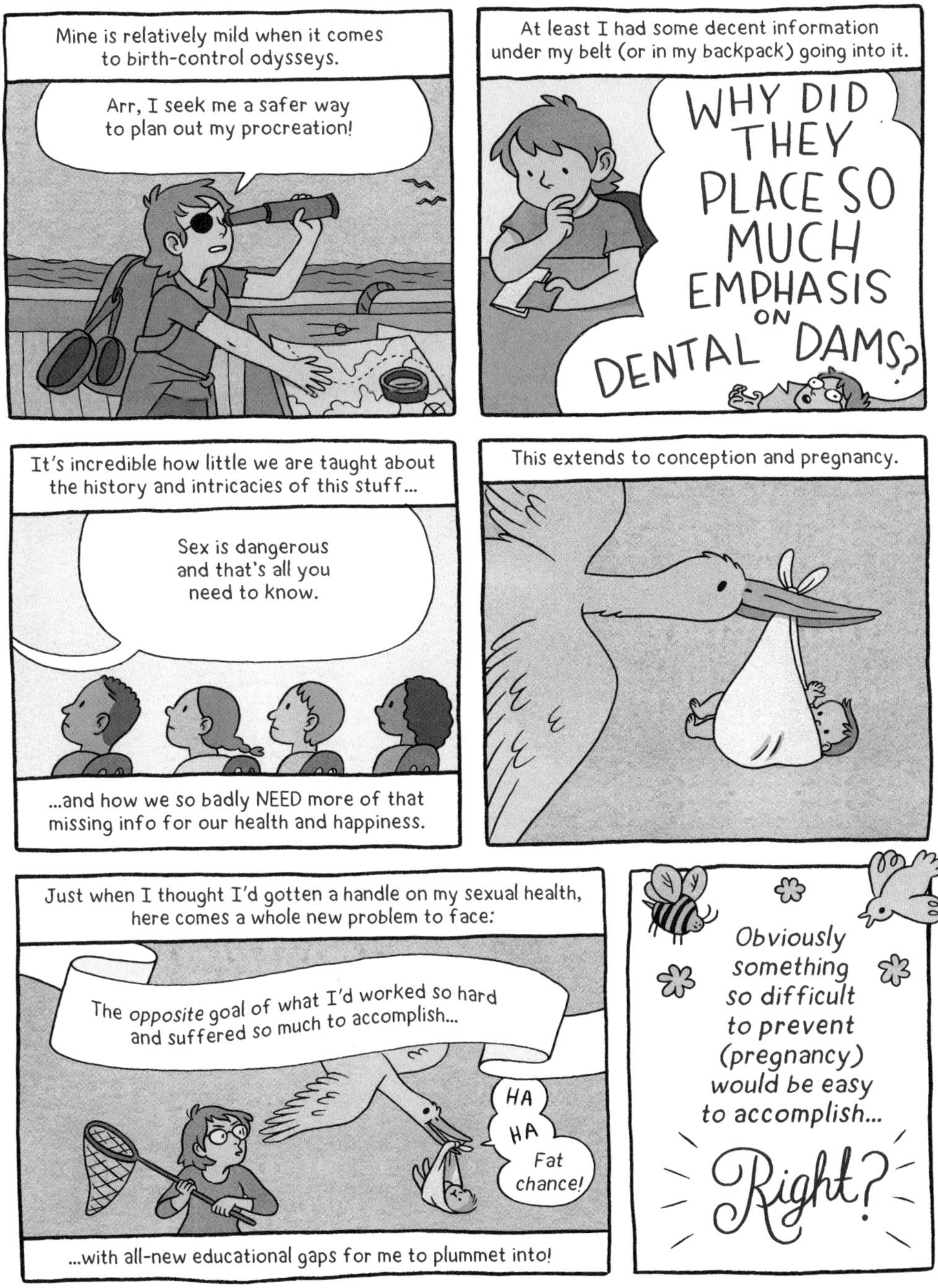

Mine is relatively mild when it comes to birth-control odysseys.
Arr, I seek me a safer way to plan out my procreation!
At least I had some decent information under my belt (or in my backpack) going into it.
WHY DID THEY PLACE SO MUCH EMPHASIS ON DENTAL DAMS?
It's incredible how little we are taught about the history and intricacies of this stuff...
Sex is dangerous and that's all you need to know.
...and how we so badly NEED more of that missing info for our health and happiness.
This extends to conception and pregnancy.
Just when I thought I'd gotten a handle on my sexual health, here comes a whole new problem to face:
The *opposite* goal of what I'd worked so hard and suffered so much to accomplish...
HA
HA
Fat chance!
...with all-new educational gaps for me to plummet into!
Obviously something so difficult to prevent (pregnancy) would be easy to accomplish...
Right?

NOW FOR SOME PREGNANCY RESEARCH

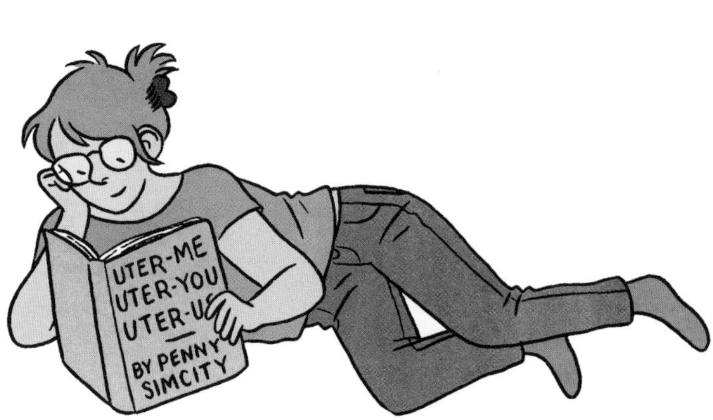
UTER-ME
UTER-YOU
UTER-US
BY PENNY SIMCITY

A WOMAN'S HEALTH IS NEVER DONE

For a large part of human history, people didn't really know how a woman's body worked.

This is mainly because for much of human history, a woman's body was either too sacred or too sexual to study.

Early books on reproduction were written by monks.

I know a thing or two about how babies are made!

After all, I met a woman once.

Even our boy, da Vinci, sketched female anatomy like that of an animal's.

It's impossible to find a female corpse to dissect, so I guess I'll make her pelvis and womb like a squirrel's.

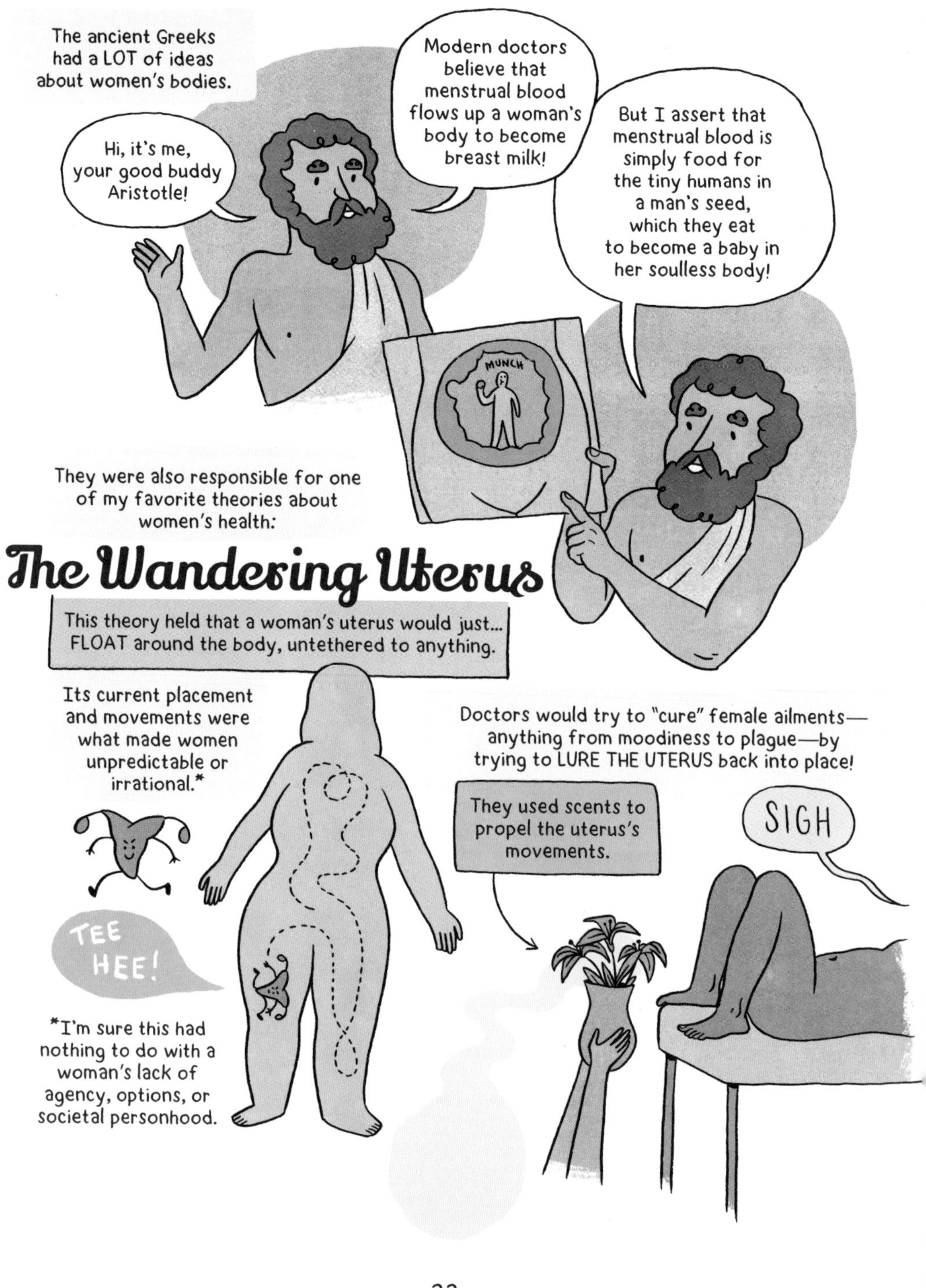
The ancient Greeks had a LOT of ideas about women's bodies.
Hi, it's me, your good buddy Aristotle!
Modern doctors believe that menstrual blood flows up a woman's body to become breast milk!
But I assert that menstrual blood is simply food for the tiny humans in a man's seed, which they eat to become a baby in her soulless body!
MUNCH
They were also responsible for one of my favorite theories about women's health:
The Wandering Uterus
This theory held that a woman's uterus would just... FLOAT around the body, untethered to anything.
Its current placement and movements were what made women unpredictable or irrational.*
TEE HEE!
*I'm sure this had nothing to do with a woman's lack of agency, options, or societal personhood.
Doctors would try to "cure" female ailments—anything from moodiness to plague—by trying to LURE THE UTERUS back into place!
They used scents to propel the uterus's movements.
SIGH

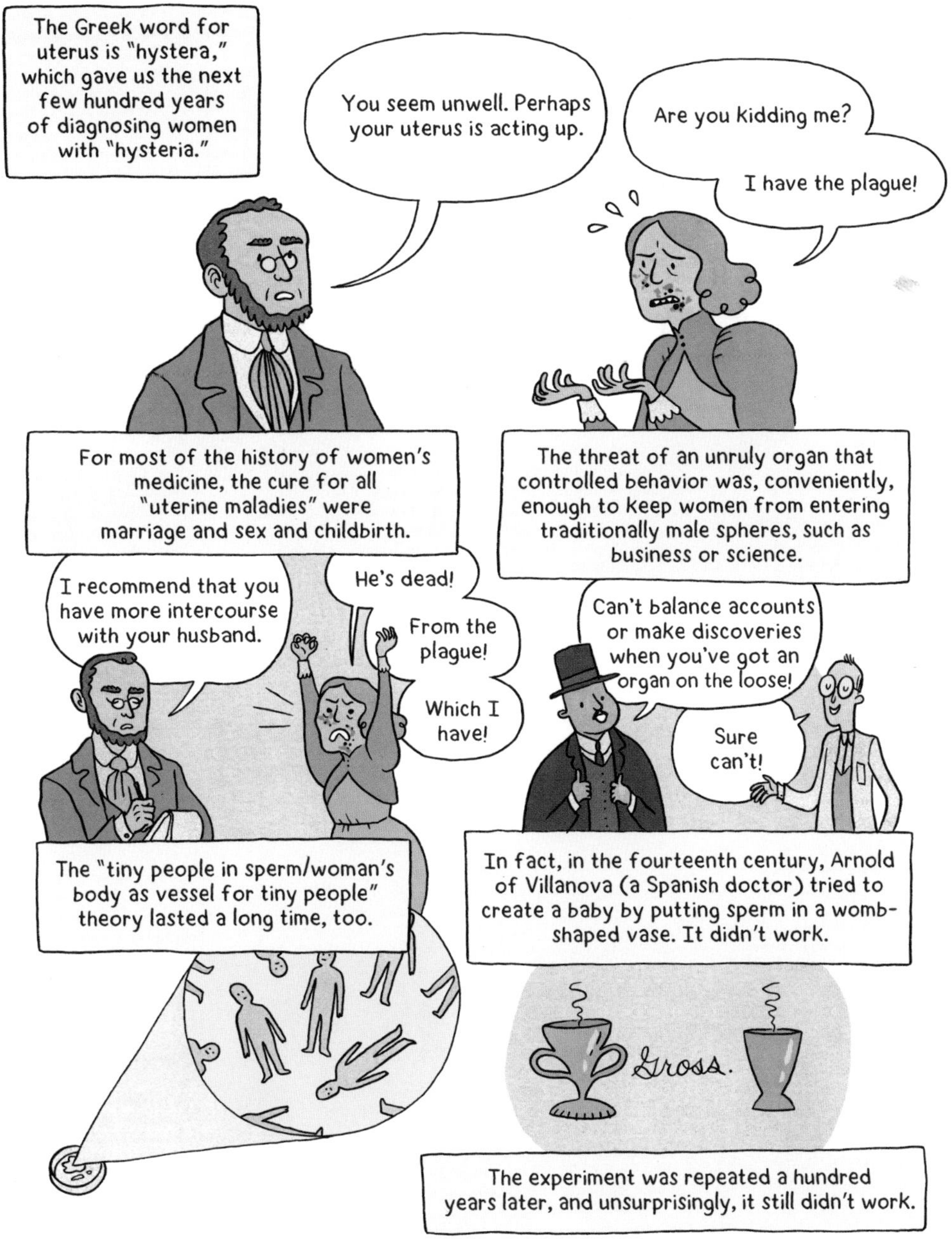
The Greek word for uterus is "hystera," which gave us the next few hundred years of diagnosing women with "hysteria."
You seem unwell. Perhaps your uterus is acting up.
Are you kidding me?
I have the plague!
For most of the history of women's medicine, the cure for all "uterine maladies" were marriage and sex and childbirth.
The threat of an unruly organ that controlled behavior was, conveniently, enough to keep women from entering traditionally male spheres, such as business or science.
I recommend that you have more intercourse with your husband.
He's dead!
From the plague!
Which I have!
Can't balance accounts or make discoveries when you've got an organ on the loose!
Sure can't!
The "tiny people in sperm/woman's body as vessel for tiny people" theory lasted a long time, too.
In fact, in the fourteenth century, Arnold of Villanova (a Spanish doctor) tried to create a baby by putting sperm in a womb-shaped vase. It didn't work.
Gross.
The experiment was repeated a hundred years later, and unsurprisingly, it still didn't work.

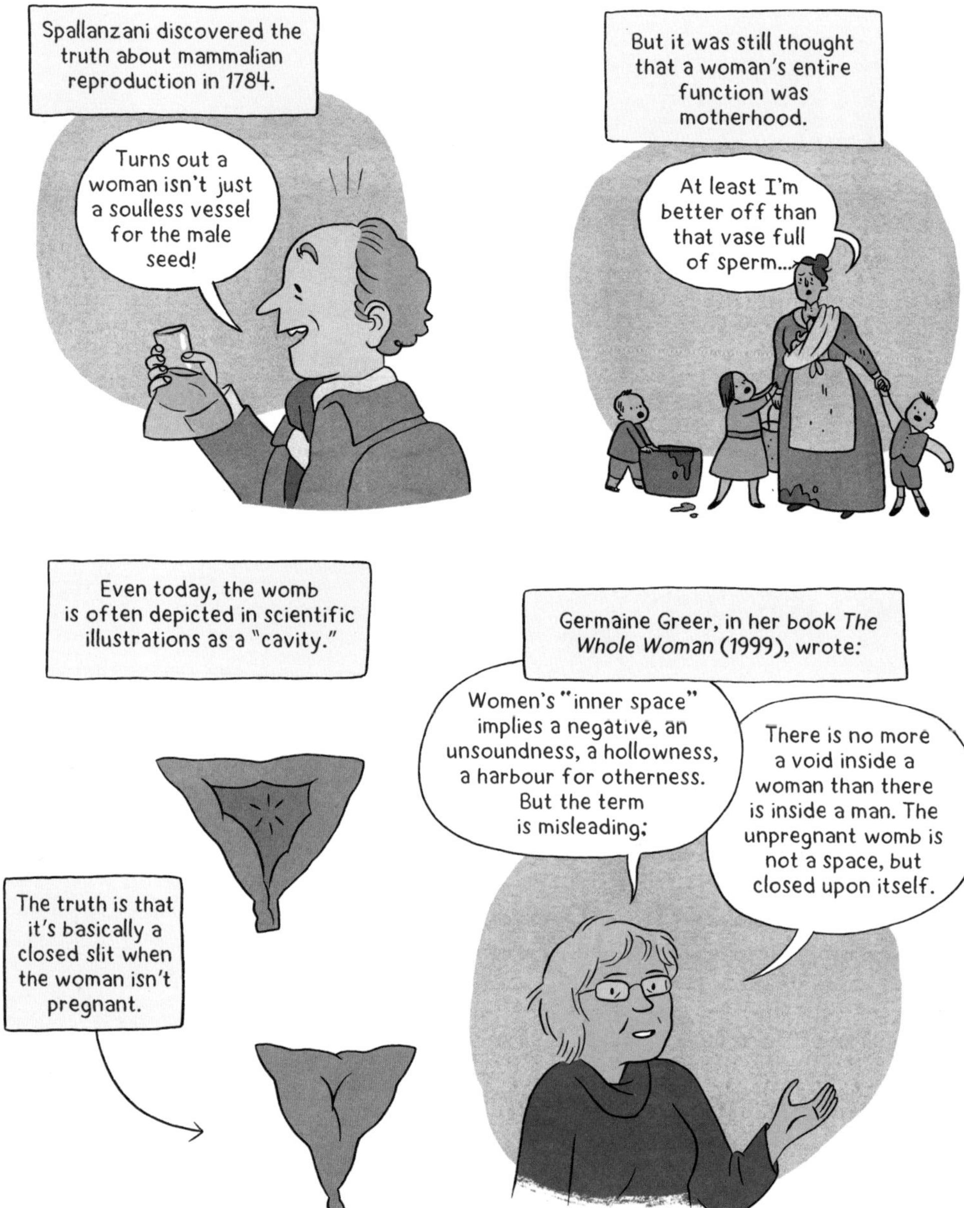
Spallanzani discovered the truth about mammalian reproduction in 1784.
Turns out a woman isn't just a soulless vessel for the male seed!
But it was still thought that a woman's entire function was motherhood.
At least I'm better off than that vase full of sperm...
Even today, the womb is often depicted in scientific illustrations as a "cavity."
The truth is that it's basically a closed slit when the woman isn't pregnant.
Germaine Greer, in her book *The Whole Woman* (1999), wrote:
Women's "inner space" implies a negative, an unsoundness, a hollowness, a harbour for otherness. But the term is misleading;
There is no more a void inside a woman than there is inside a man. The unpregnant womb is not a space, but closed upon itself.

Women's bodies have been used against them for centuries. Take the concept of female virginity:

The hymen isn't a barrier to be broken— it's just a ring of tissue around the vaginal opening—it can tear during rough or unlubricated sex, but it can also stretch.

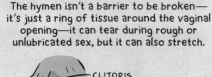

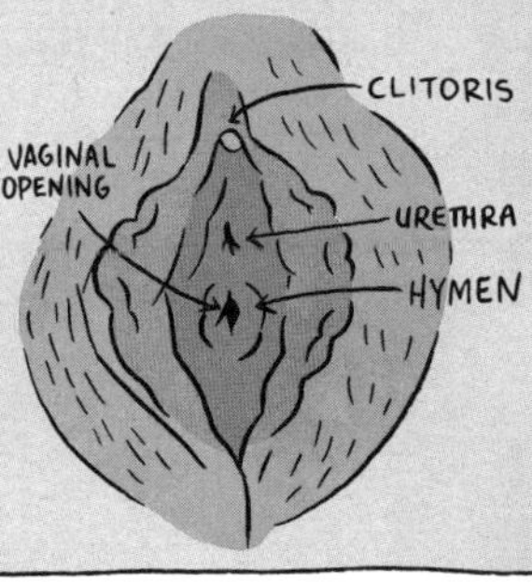

CLITORIS
VAGINAL OPENING
URETHRA
HYMEN

How would menstrual blood pass out of the vagina if there was an obstruction?

HYMEN →

"BROKEN" HYMEN →

The concept of "medical" virginity is misunderstood. But many women have faced censure, ostracization, even death, due to the misunderstanding of female reproductive biology.

Even when science got it RIGHT, there were awful stumbles along the way.

Take J. Marion Sims:

The "Father of Gynecology"

(Named so for his invention of the speculum.)

He was also a straight-up MONSTER.

NOT GONNA DRAW THIS

HORRIBLE

NOPE

He tortured hundreds of slave women, publicly operating on their reproductive organs in order to make his discoveries.

He often recommended removing women's ovaries and slitting their cervix to "cure" them of hysteria or neurosis.

NO WAY

UGH

He had no medical degree, killed and maimed hundreds of women and babies, and the speculum he invented was made from spoons he found.

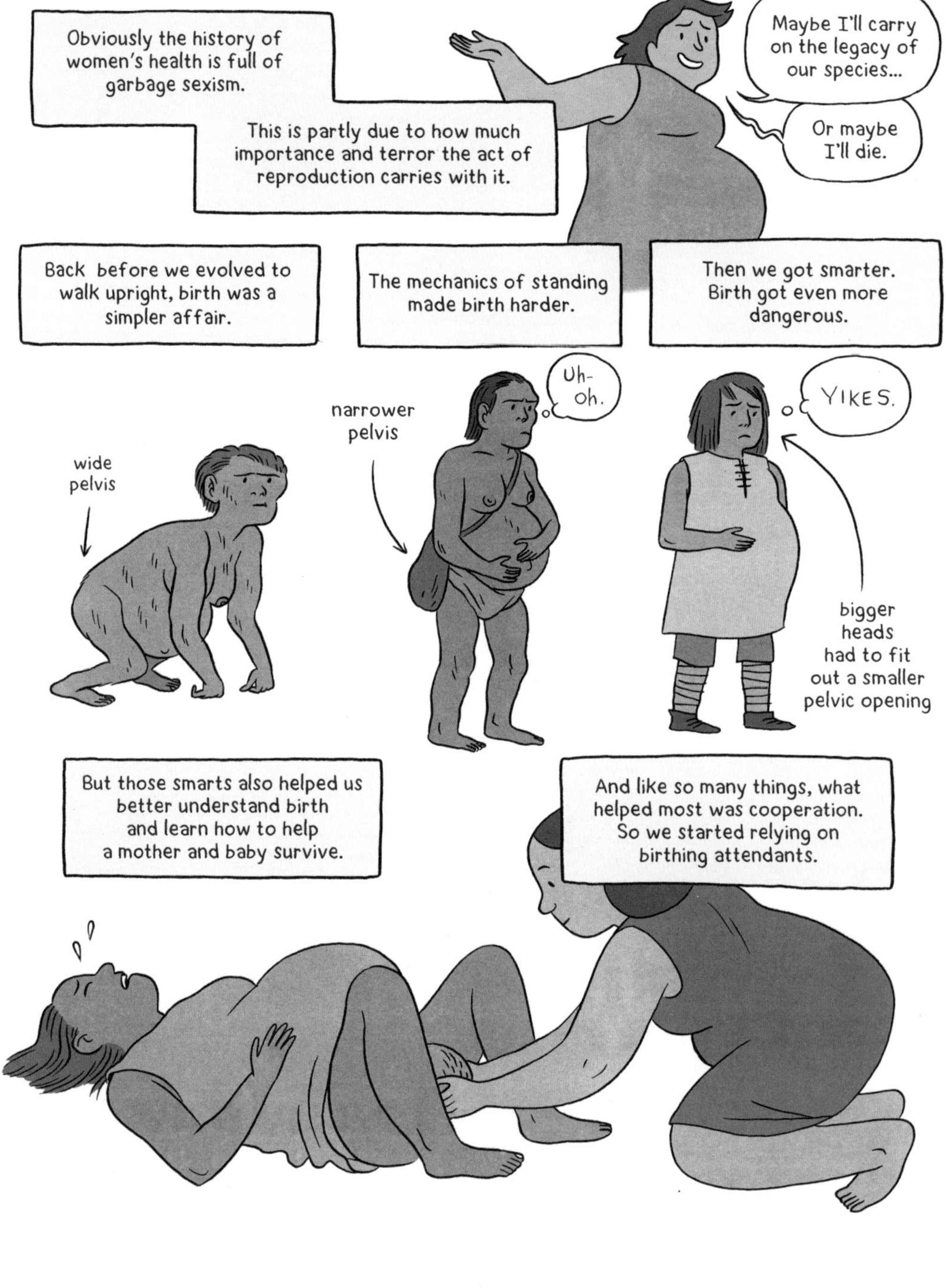

Obviously the history of women's health is full of garbage sexism.
This is partly due to how much importance and terror the act of reproduction carries with it.
Maybe I'll carry on the legacy of our species...
Or maybe I'll die.
Back before we evolved to walk upright, birth was a simpler affair.
The mechanics of standing made birth harder.
Then we got smarter. Birth got even more dangerous.
wide pelvis
narrower pelvis
Uh-oh.
YIKES.
bigger heads had to fit out a smaller pelvic opening
But those smarts also helped us better understand birth and learn how to help a mother and baby survive.
And like so many things, what helped most was cooperation. So we started relying on birthing attendants.

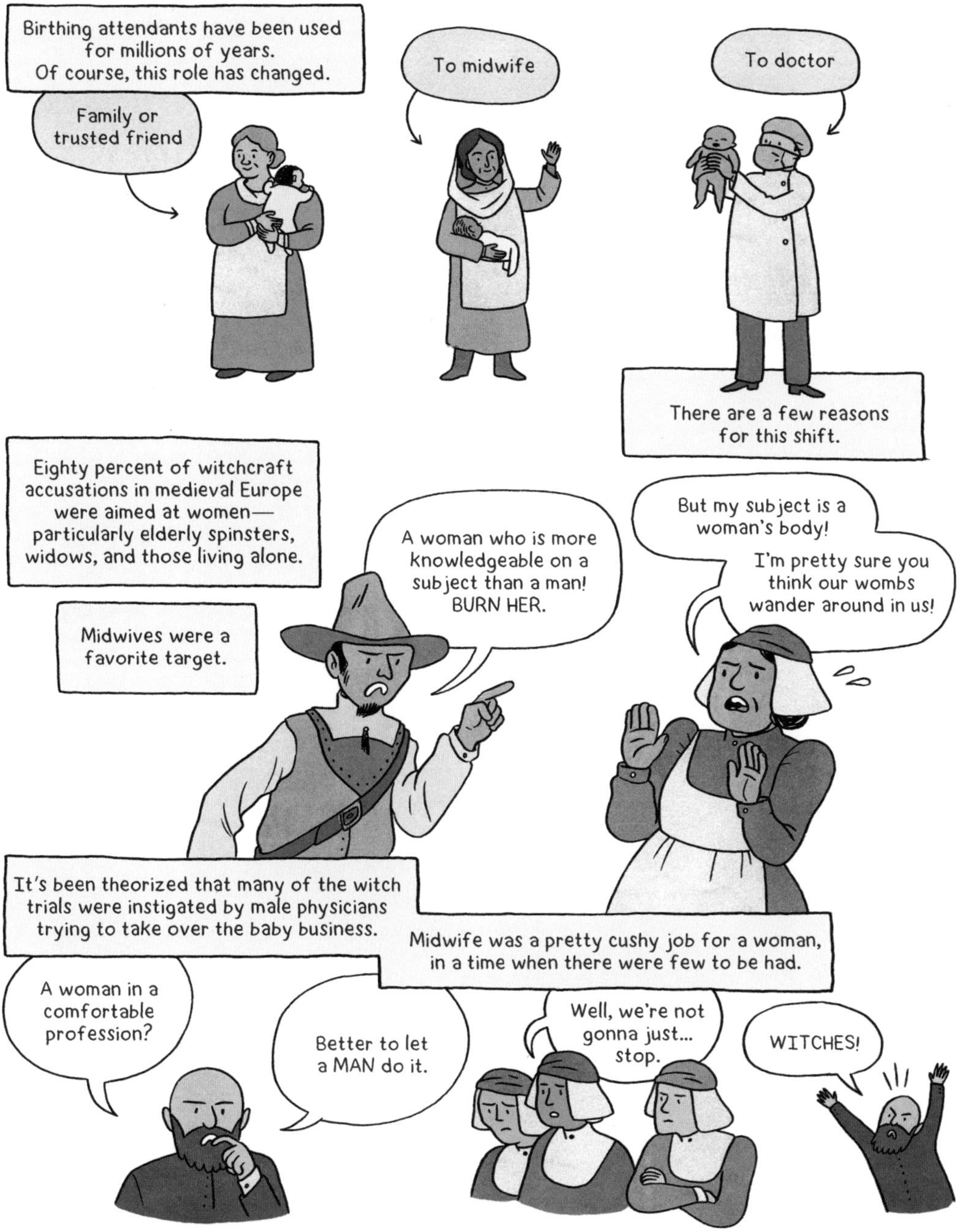

Birthing attendants have been used for millions of years.
Of course, this role has changed.
Family or trusted friend
To midwife
To doctor
There are a few reasons for this shift.
Eighty percent of witchcraft accusations in medieval Europe were aimed at women—particularly elderly spinsters, widows, and those living alone.
Midwives were a favorite target.
A woman who is more knowledgeable on a subject than a man! BURN HER.
But my subject is a woman's body!
I'm pretty sure you think our wombs wander around in us!
It's been theorized that many of the witch trials were instigated by male physicians trying to take over the baby business.
Midwife was a pretty cushy job for a woman, in a time when there were few to be had.
A woman in a comfortable profession?
Better to let a MAN do it.
Well, we're not gonna just... stop.
WITCHES!

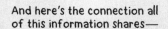
And here's the connection all of this information shares—

NONE OF IT WAS COVERED IN MY SEXUAL EDUCATION, HISTORY, OR SCIENCE CLASSES.

I was taught how to condom a banana, and to memorize the dates of amnesties, and the life-cycle stages of a pill bug...

But I was never taught about the intertwined history and science of taking care of my own body.

Politics

History

Evolution

Abuse

Biology

Mistakes

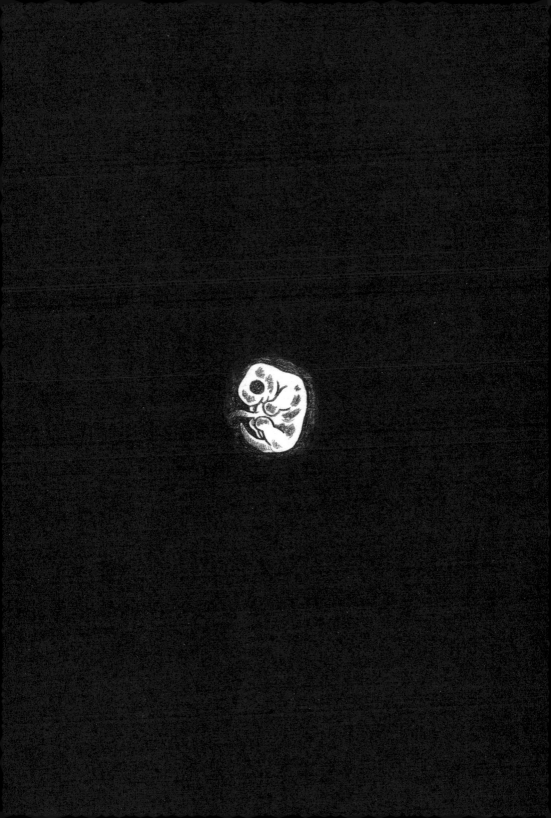

THE FIRST TRY

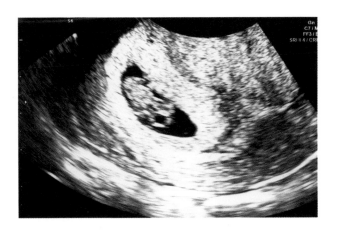

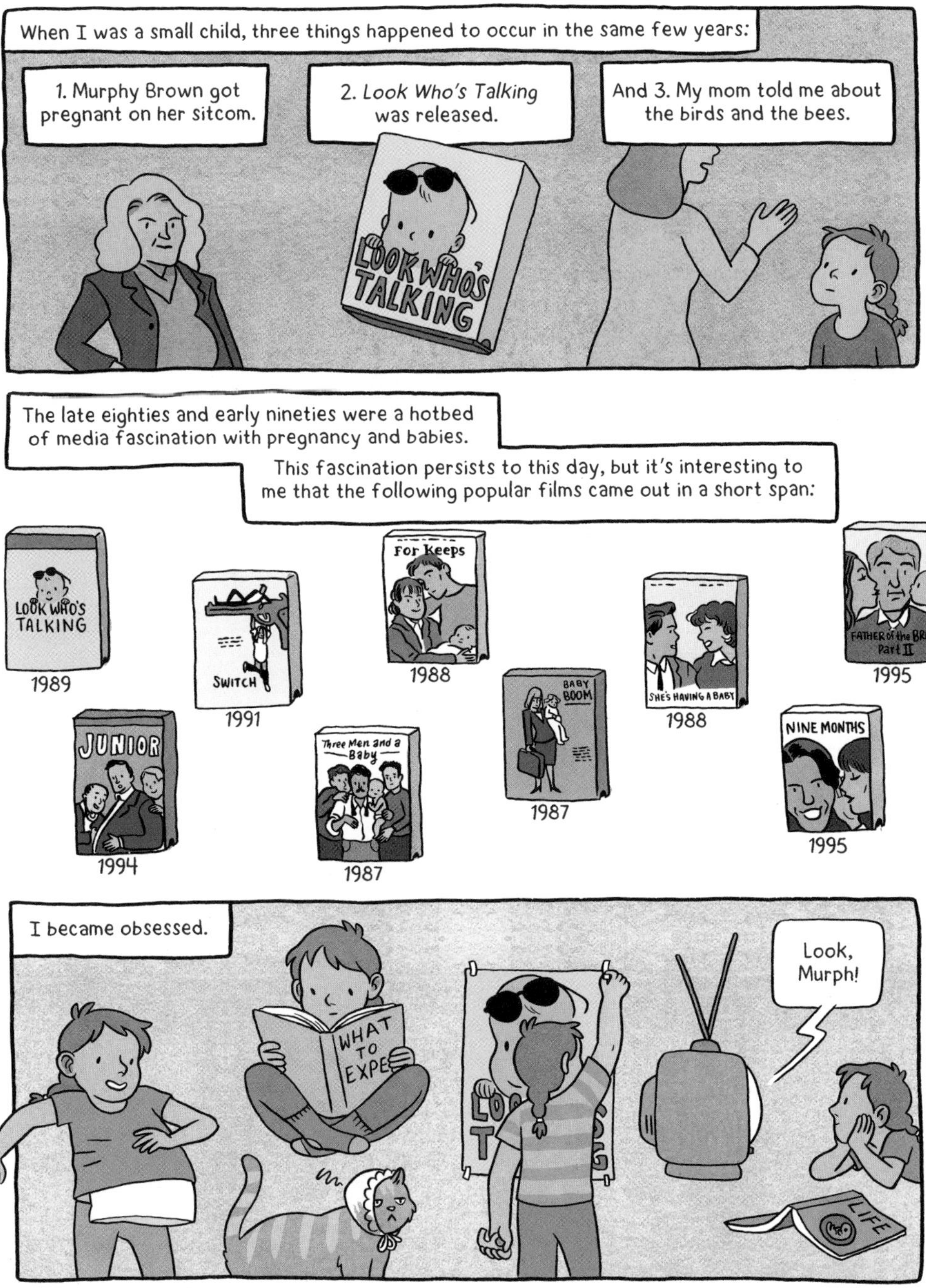
When I was a small child, three things happened to occur in the same few years:
1. Murphy Brown got pregnant on her sitcom.
2. *Look Who's Talking* was released.
LOOK WHO'S TALKING
And 3. My mom told me about the birds and the bees.
The late eighties and early nineties were a hotbed of media fascination with pregnancy and babies.
This fascination persists to this day, but it's interesting to me that the following popular films came out in a short span:
LOOK WHO'S TALKING
1989
JUNIOR
1994
SWITCH
1991
For Keeps
1988
Three Men and a Baby
1987
BABY BOOM
1987
SHE'S HAVING A BABY
1988
FATHER of the BRIDE Part II
1995
NINE MONTHS
1995
I became obsessed.
WHAT TO EXPE
Look, Murph!
LIFE

Equally intriguing to me were pregnant bodies and the actual babies they produced.

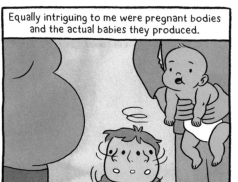

I struggled to understand that I, too, could someday produce a baby with my body.

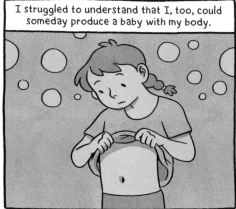

It seemed to me then, and continues to seem, TOTALLY SCI-FI.

So when John and I decided to "not try but not try not to" get pregnant (as we eloquently put it)...

...it was like somewhere, Houston was beginning a countdown.

10 9 8 7

First, I had my birth control implant removed.

The rod was stuck in my arm, and it took two nurses helping my doctor to remove it.

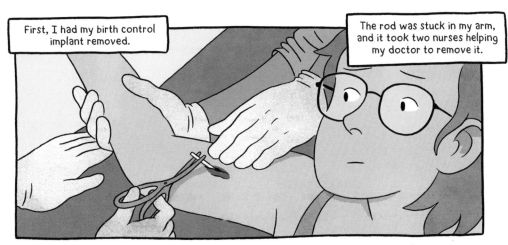

My flesh kept hold of that line of defense.

Are you SURE you're ready?

Of course not, but please take it out anyway.

The doctor told me it wasn't trapped in my muscle or fat, but instead:

Most of what we're made up of is the stuff holding us together.

It struck me as profound that the fibers that wove me together were letting loose this foreign body to make way for another one.

I left the clinic with a bandage, feeling like I had achieved liftoff from Earth.

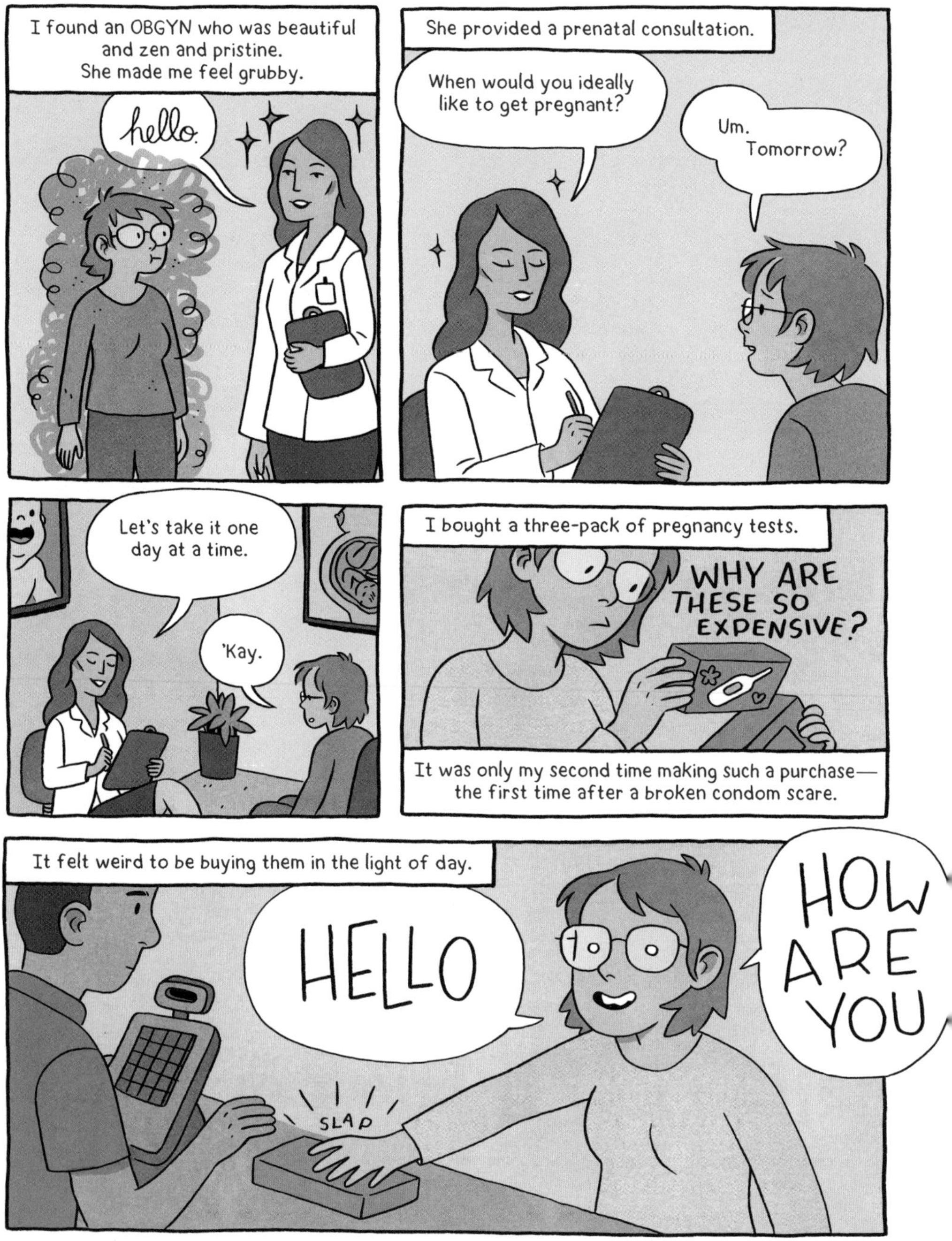
I found an OBGYN who was beautiful and zen and pristine. She made me feel grubby.
hello.
She provided a prenatal consultation.
When would you ideally like to get pregnant?
Um. Tomorrow?
Let's take it one day at a time.
'Kay.
I bought a three-pack of pregnancy tests.
WHY ARE THESE SO EXPENSIVE?
It was only my second time making such a purchase— the first time after a broken condom scare.
It felt weird to be buying them in the light of day.
HELLO
HOW ARE YOU
SLAP

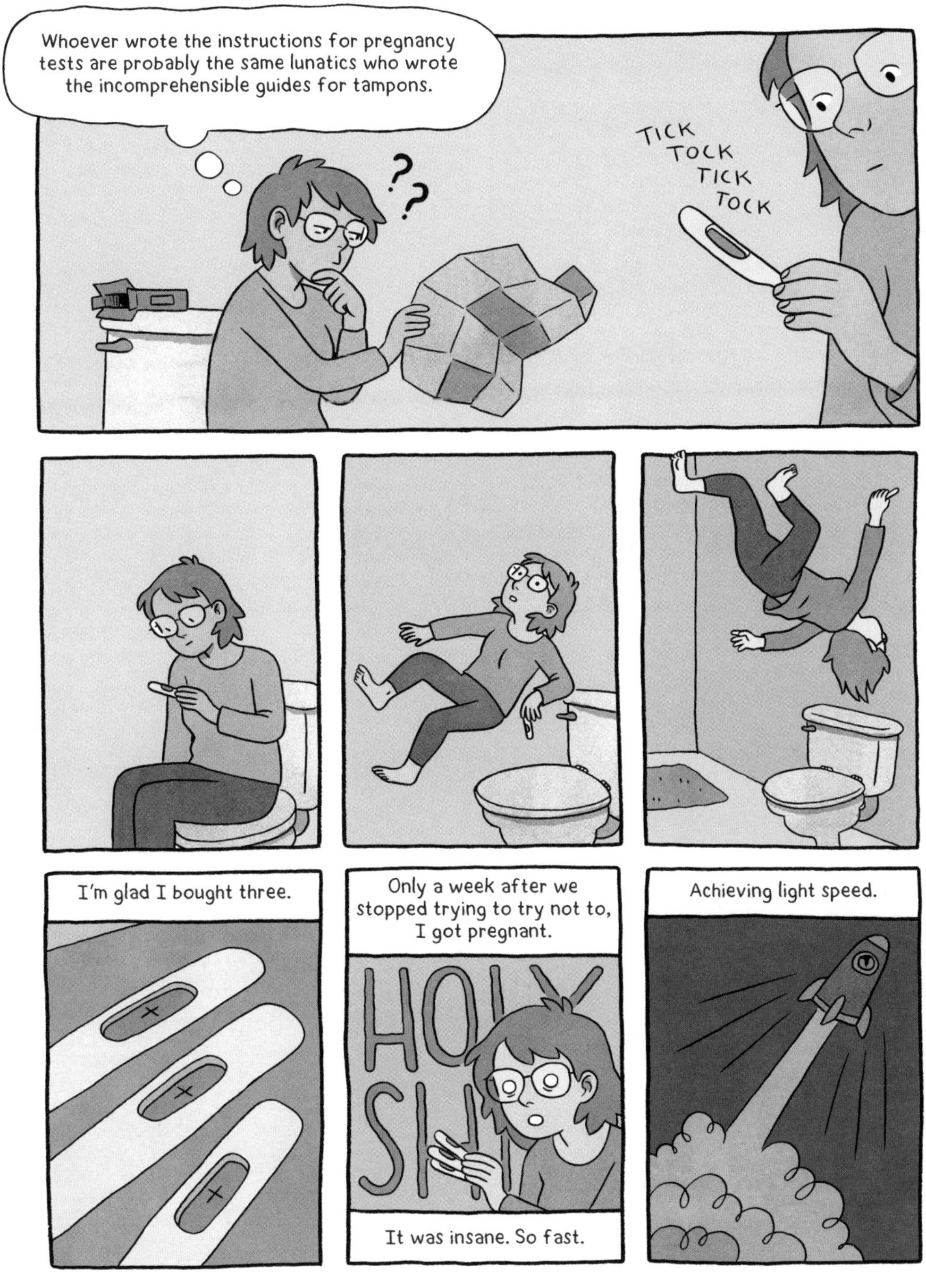

Whoever wrote the instructions for pregnancy tests are probably the same lunatics who wrote the incomprehensible guides for tampons.
TICK TOCK TICK TOCK
I'm glad I bought three.
Only a week after we stopped trying to try not to, I got pregnant.
HOLY SH
It was insane. So fast.
Achieving light speed.

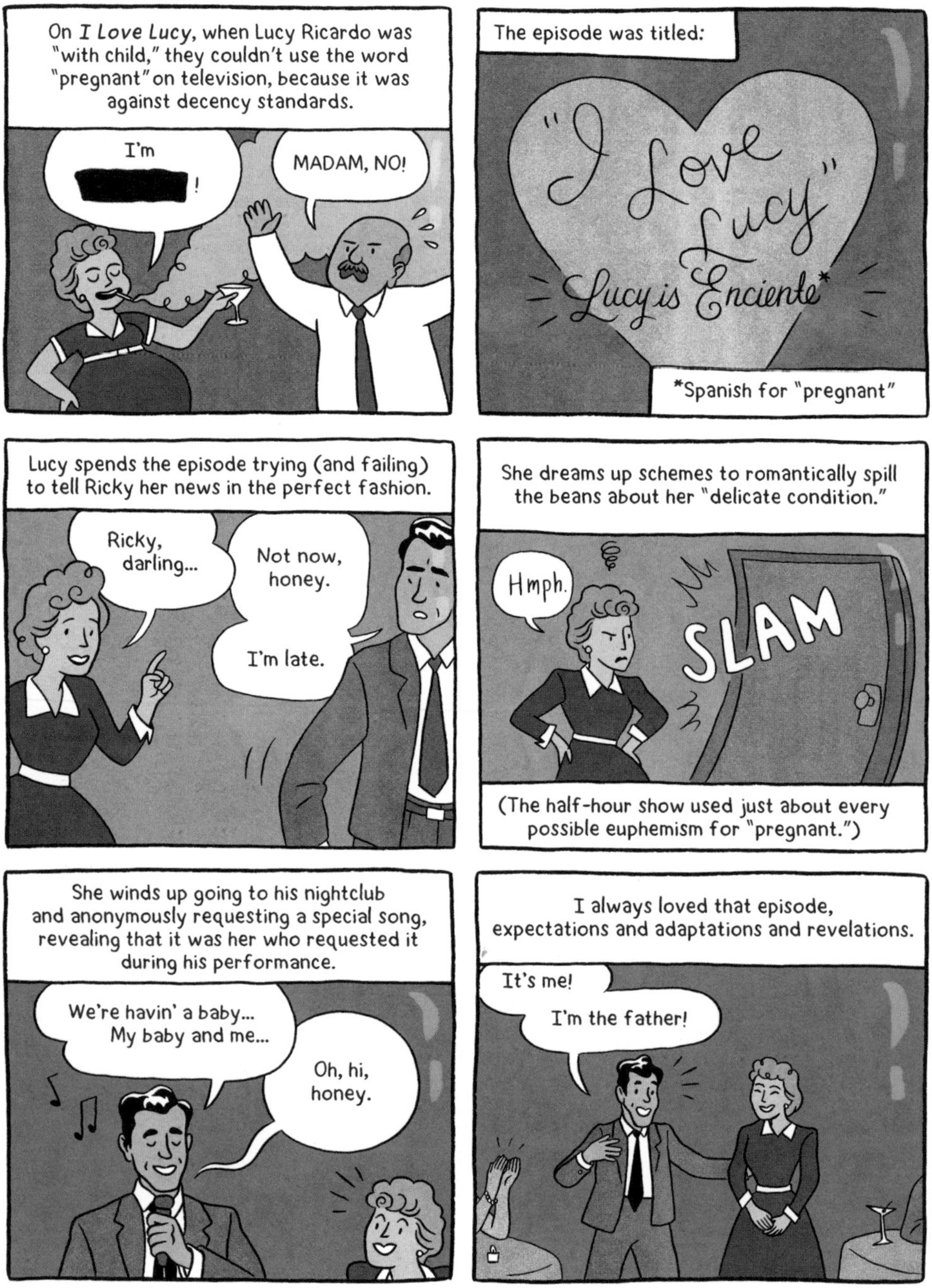
On *I Love Lucy*, when Lucy Ricardo was "with child," they couldn't use the word "pregnant" on television, because it was against decency standards.
I'm [redacted]!
MADAM, NO!
The episode was titled:
"I Love Lucy"
Lucy is Enciente*
*Spanish for "pregnant"
Lucy spends the episode trying (and failing) to tell Ricky her news in the perfect fashion.
Ricky, darling...
Not now, honey.
I'm late.
She dreams up schemes to romantically spill the beans about her "delicate condition."
Hmph.
SLAM
(The half-hour show used just about every possible euphemism for "pregnant.")
She winds up going to his nightclub and anonymously requesting a special song, revealing that it was her who requested it during his performance.
We're havin' a baby... My baby and me...
Oh, hi, honey.
I always loved that episode, expectations and adaptations and revelations.
It's me!
I'm the father!

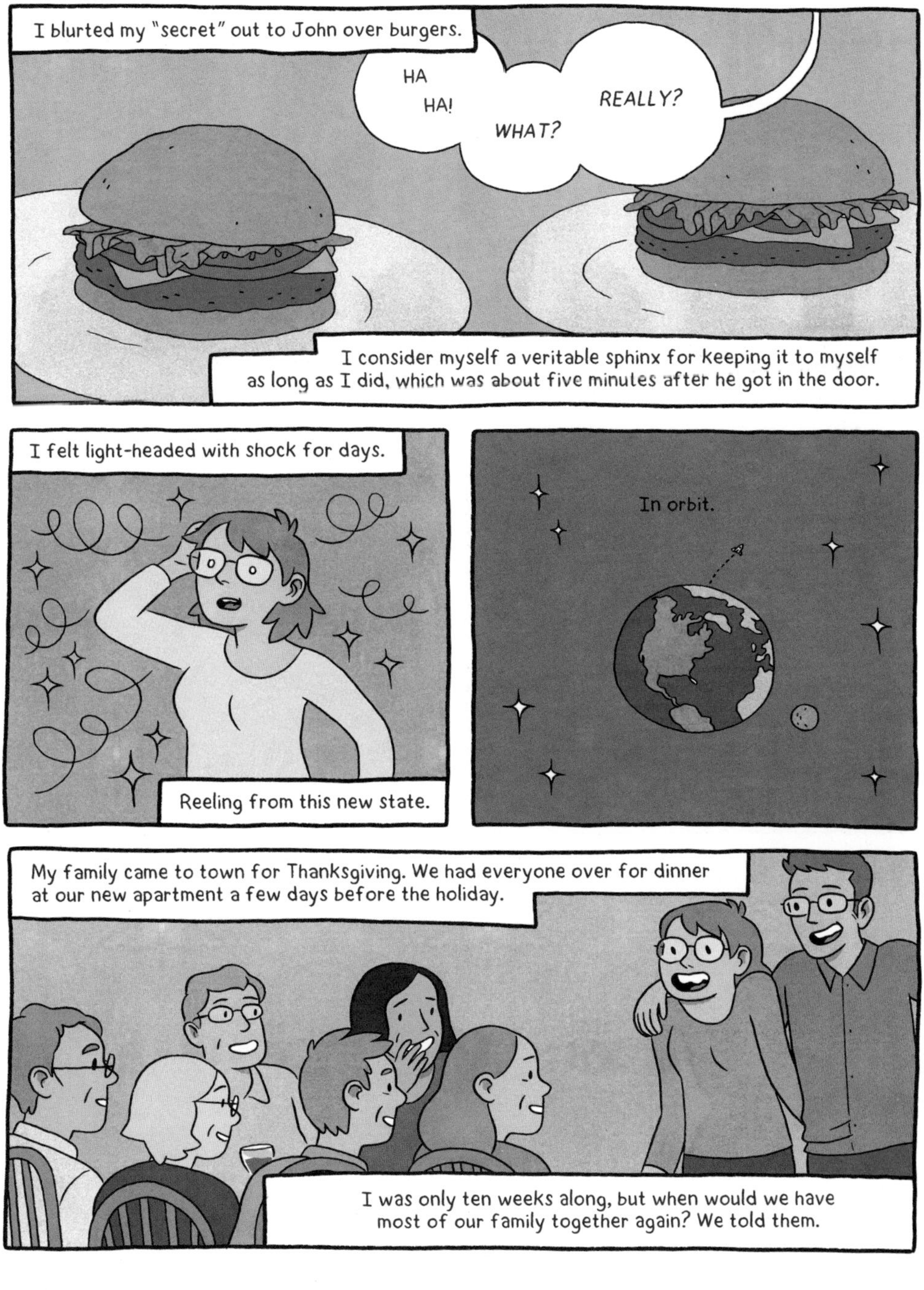
I blurted my "secret" out to John over burgers.
HA HA!
WHAT?
REALLY?
I consider myself a veritable sphinx for keeping it to myself as long as I did, which was about five minutes after he got in the door.
I felt light-headed with shock for days.
Reeling from this new state.
In orbit.
My family came to town for Thanksgiving. We had everyone over for dinner at our new apartment a few days before the holiday.
I was only ten weeks along, but when would we have most of our family together again? We told them.

It felt like my lifetime of yearning had manifested as potential energy.

Not yet.

DO NOT ENTER

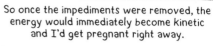

So once the impediments were removed, the energy would immediately become kinetic and I'd get pregnant right away.

Okay, NOW!

DO NOT ENTER

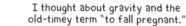

I thought about gravity and the old-timey term "to fall pregnant."

Oh no!

WHOOP!

I'll catch you, even though I have no pants!

After years of painful, difficult contraception, it seemed right that conception should come with ease.

Like a long, difficult climb...

...and then a slide.

But it turns out that the science of reproduction doesn't follow a concrete set of rules, like physics.

NATURE IS CHAOS!

Except the adage:

What goes up must come down.

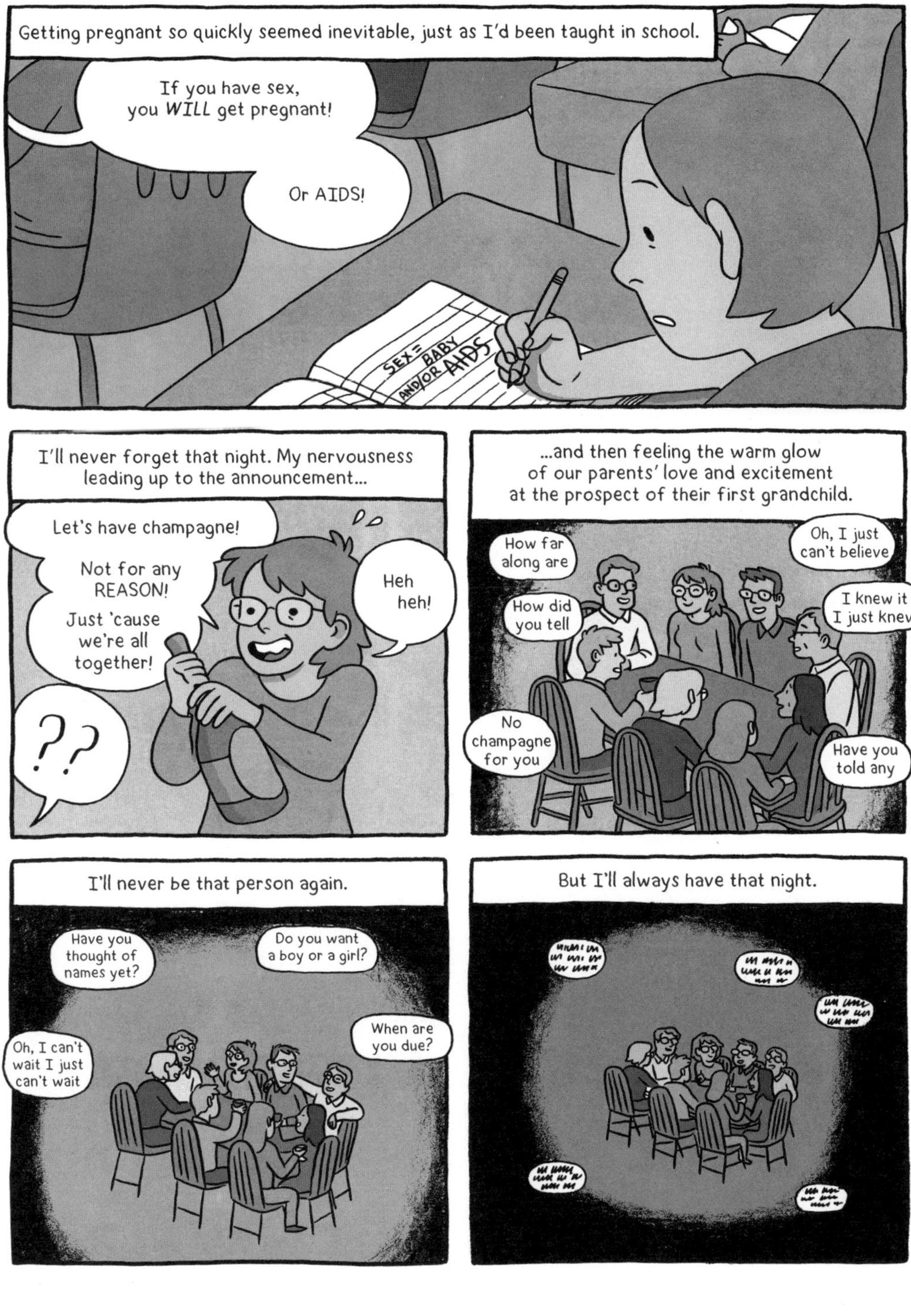
Getting pregnant so quickly seemed inevitable, just as I'd been taught in school.
If you have sex, you WILL get pregnant!
Or AIDS!
SEX = BABY AND/OR AIDS
I'll never forget that night. My nervousness leading up to the announcement...
Let's have champagne!
Not for any REASON!
Just 'cause we're all together!
??
Heh heh!
...and then feeling the warm glow of our parents' love and excitement at the prospect of their first grandchild.
How far along are
Oh, I just can't believe
How did you tell
I knew it I just knew
No champagne for you
Have you told any
I'll never be that person again.
Have you thought of names yet?
Do you want a boy or a girl?
When are you due?
Oh, I can't wait I just can't wait
But I'll always have that night.

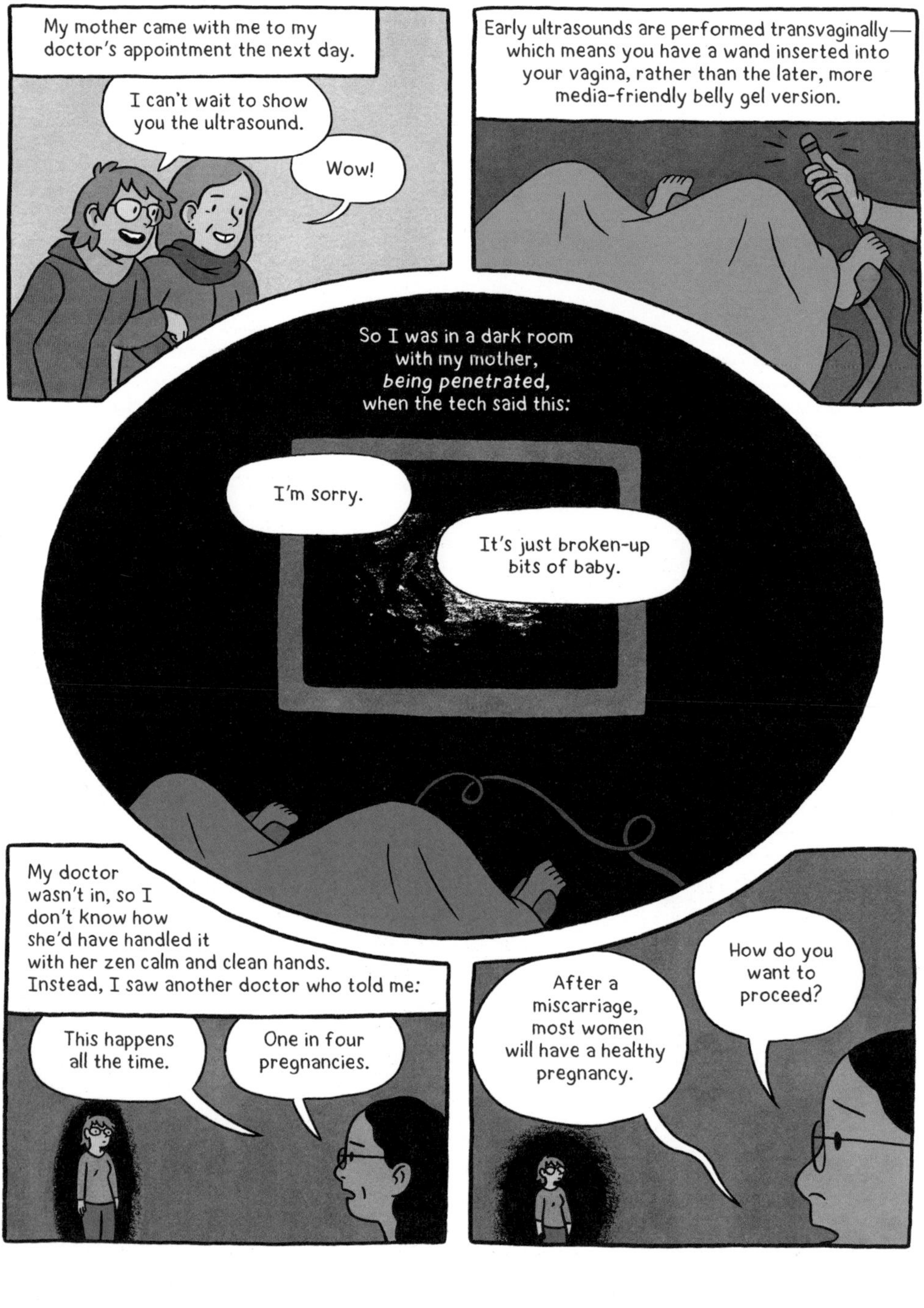
My mother came with me to my doctor's appointment the next day.
I can't wait to show you the ultrasound.
Wow!
Early ultrasounds are performed transvaginally— which means you have a wand inserted into your vagina, rather than the later, more media-friendly belly gel version.
So I was in a dark room with my mother, *being penetrated,* when the tech said this:
I'm sorry.
It's just broken-up bits of baby.
My doctor wasn't in, so I don't know how she'd have handled it with her zen calm and clean hands. Instead, I saw another doctor who told me:
This happens all the time.
One in four pregnancies.
After a miscarriage, most women will have a healthy pregnancy.
How do you want to proceed?

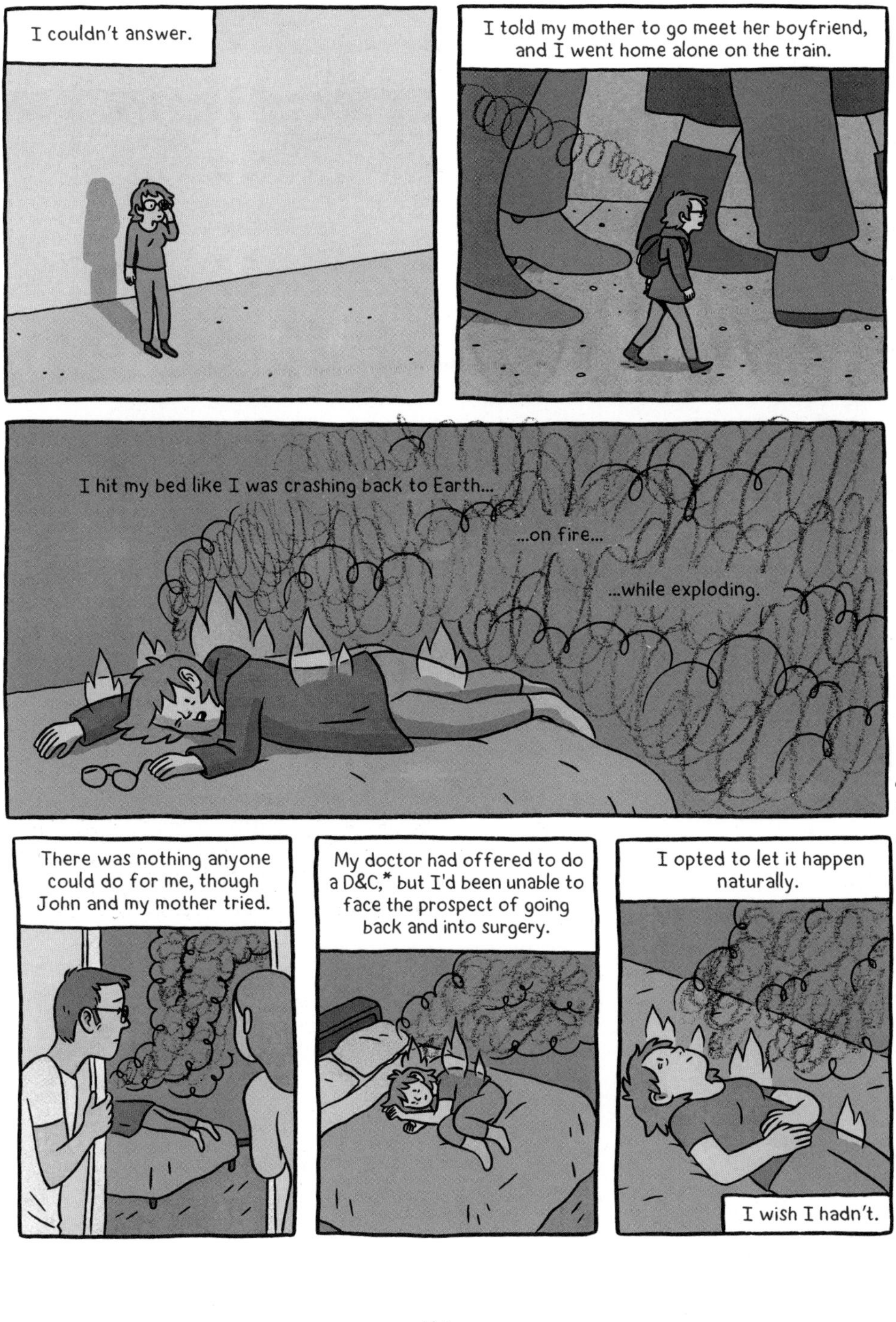
I couldn't answer.
I told my mother to go meet her boyfriend, and I went home alone on the train.
I hit my bed like I was crashing back to Earth...
...on fire...
...while exploding.
There was nothing anyone could do for me, though John and my mother tried.
My doctor had offered to do a D&C,* but I'd been unable to face the prospect of going back and into surgery.
I opted to let it happen naturally.
I wish I hadn't.

*A Dilation and Curettage (D&C) is a procedure to remove tissue from inside your uterus.

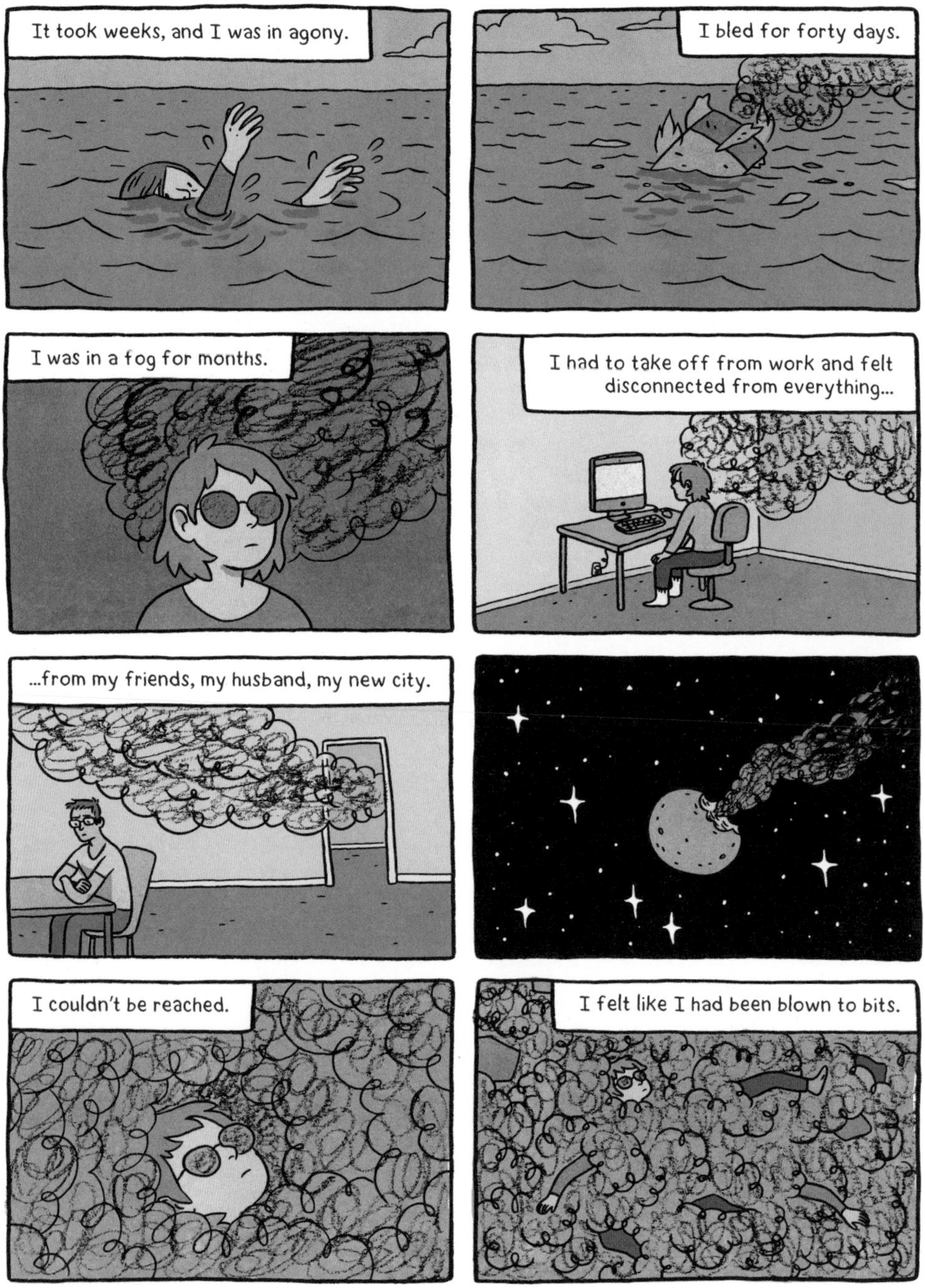
It took weeks, and I was in agony.
I bled for forty days.
I was in a fog for months.
I had to take off from work and felt disconnected from everything...
...from my friends, my husband, my new city.
I couldn't be reached.
I felt like I had been blown to bits.

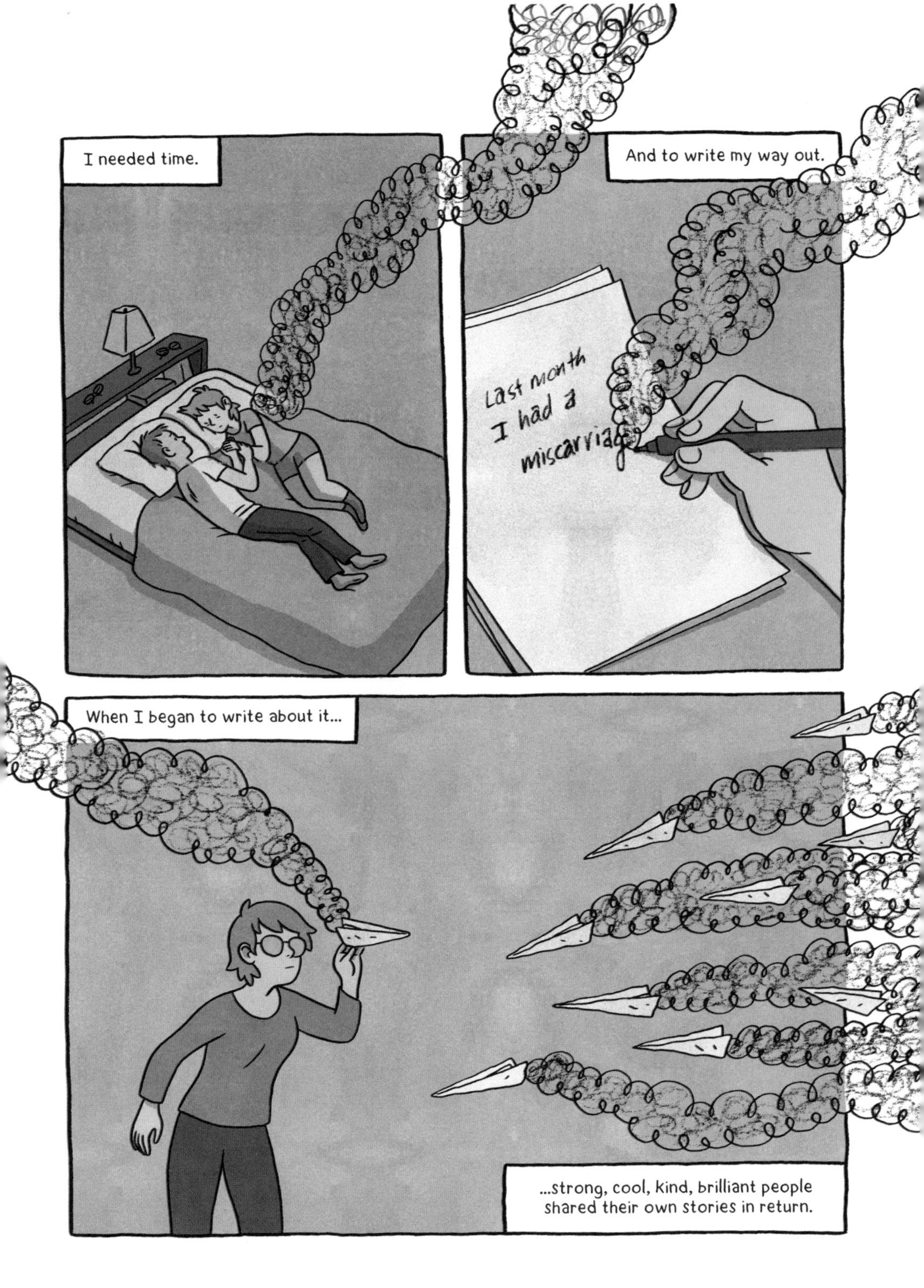
I needed time.
And to write my way out.
Last month I had a miscarriag
When I began to write about it...
...strong, cool, kind, brilliant people shared their own stories in return.

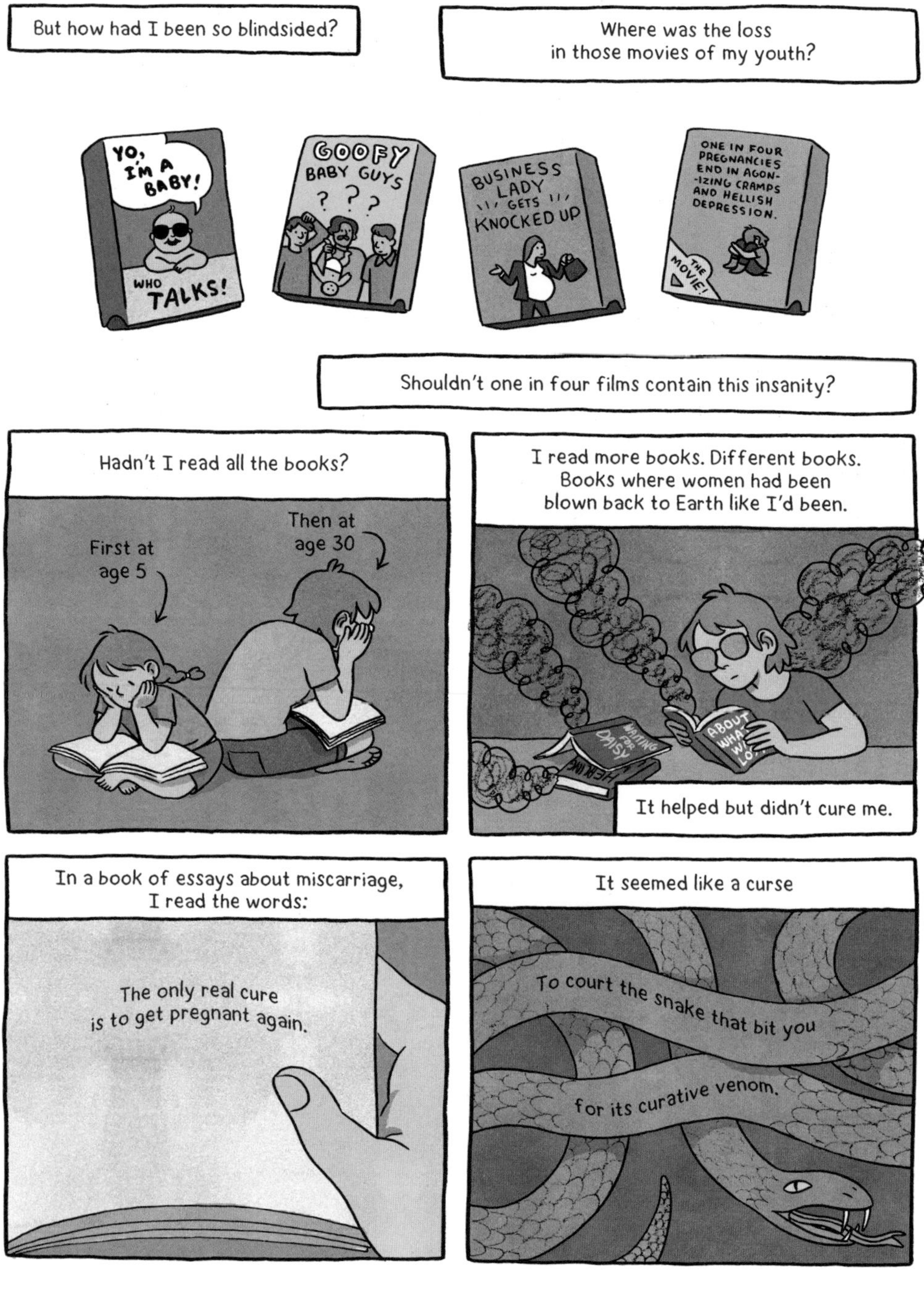

But how had I been so blindsided?
Where was the loss in those movies of my youth?
YO, I'M A BABY!
WHO TALKS!
GOOFY BABY GUYS
? ? ?
BUSINESS LADY GETS KNOCKED UP
ONE IN FOUR PREGNANCIES END IN AGON-IZING CRAMPS AND HELLISH DEPRESSION.
THE MOVIE!
Shouldn't one in four films contain this insanity?
Hadn't I read all the books?
First at age 5
Then at age 30
I read more books. Different books. Books where women had been blown back to Earth like I'd been.
WAITING FOR DAISY
It helped but didn't cure me.
In a book of essays about miscarriage, I read the words:
The only real cure is to get pregnant again.
It seemed like a curse
To court the snake that bit you
for its curative venom.

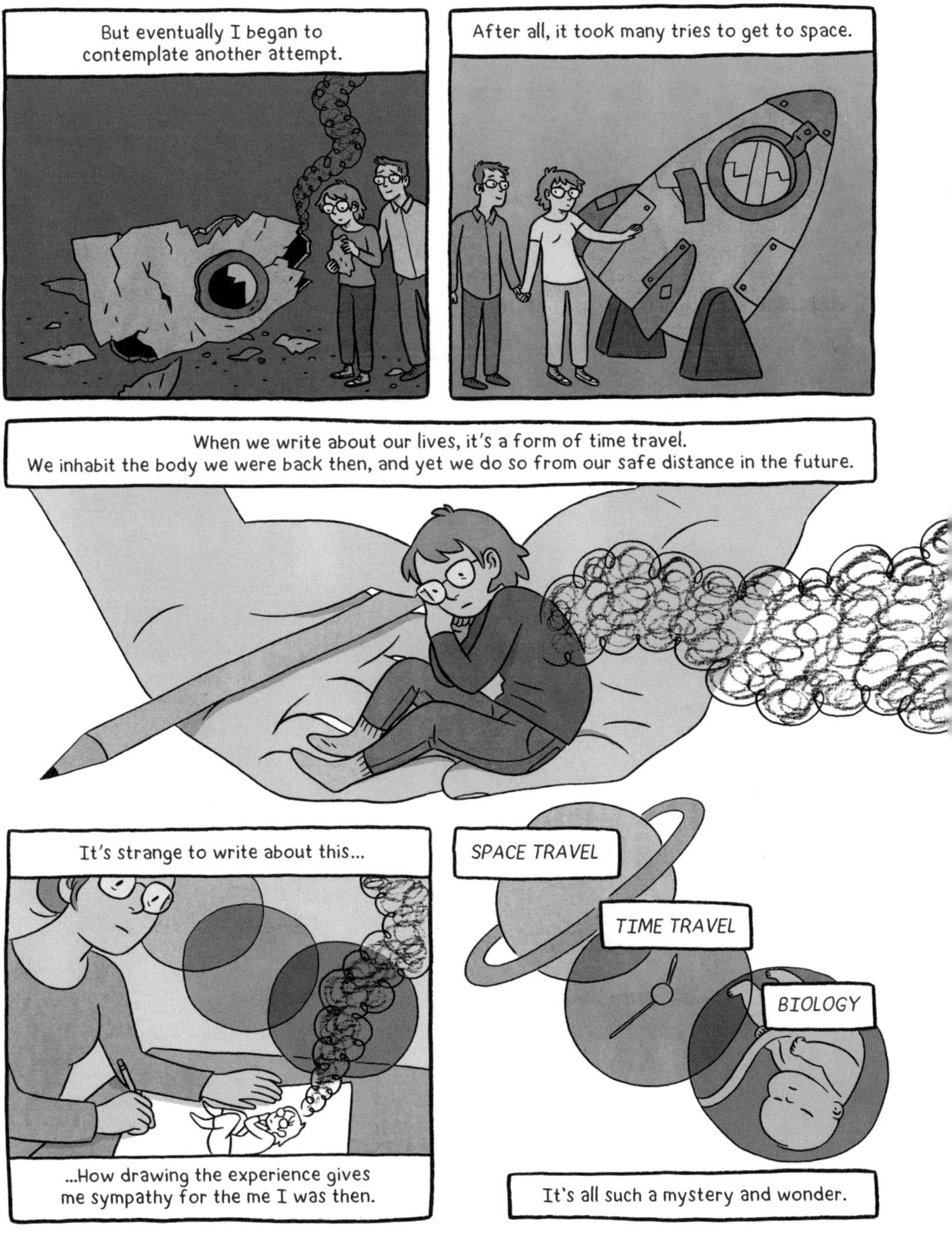

But eventually I began to contemplate another attempt.
After all, it took many tries to get to space.
When we write about our lives, it's a form of time travel.
We inhabit the body we were back then, and yet we do so from our safe distance in the future.
It's strange to write about this...
...How drawing the experience gives me sympathy for the me I was then.
SPACE TRAVEL
TIME TRAVEL
BIOLOGY
It's all such a mystery and wonder.

TIME FOR MORE PREGNANCY RESEARCH

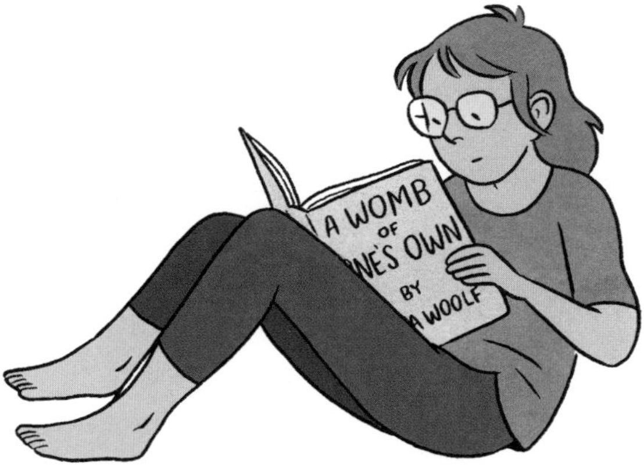
A WOMB
OF
NE'S OWN
BY
A WOOLF

MISCARRIAGE MYTHS

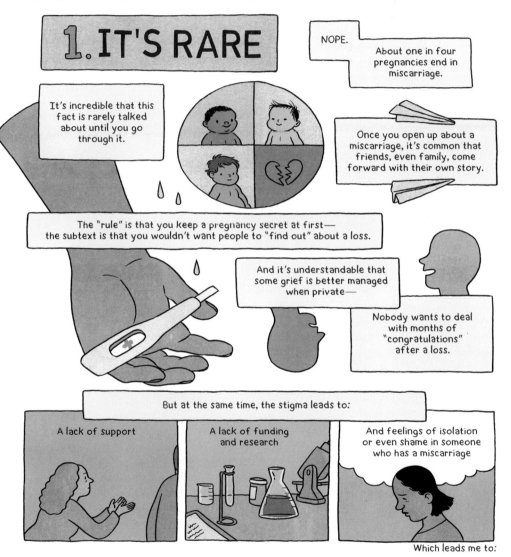

1. IT'S RARE

NOPE.

About one in four pregnancies end in miscarriage.

It's incredible that this fact is rarely talked about until you go through it.

Once you open up about a miscarriage, it's common that friends, even family, come forward with their own story.

The "rule" is that you keep a pregnancy secret at first— the subtext is that you wouldn't want people to "find out" about a loss.

And it's understandable that some grief is better managed when private—

Nobody wants to deal with months of "congratulations" after a loss.

But at the same time, the stigma leads to:

A lack of support

A lack of funding and research

And feelings of isolation or even shame in someone who has a miscarriage

Which leads me to:

2. IT'S YOUR FAULT

This is one of the most common reactions to a miscarriage. There's so much superstition and hearsay around pregnancy, it's no wonder people blame themselves.

But let's break it down:

I HAD THAT SIP OF WINE

A 2013 Harvard study showed that about half of pregnant women drank some alcohol (usually a small amount, early on in pregnancy)...

...and there was no higher correlation of miscarriage, premature birth, low birthrate, or pre-eclampsia between those who drank and those who did not.

Booze is still not recommended for pregnant people or growing fetuses, but it's almost certainly not the cause of a miscarriage.

IT WAS ALL THOSE YEARS ON BIRTH CONTROL

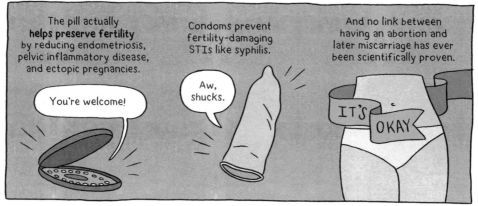

The pill actually **helps preserve fertility** by reducing endometriosis, pelvic inflammatory disease, and ectopic pregnancies.

You're welcome!

Condoms prevent fertility-damaging STIs like syphilis.

Aw, shucks.

And no link between having an abortion and later miscarriage has ever been scientifically proven.

IT'S OKAY

I DIDN'T WANT IT ENOUGH

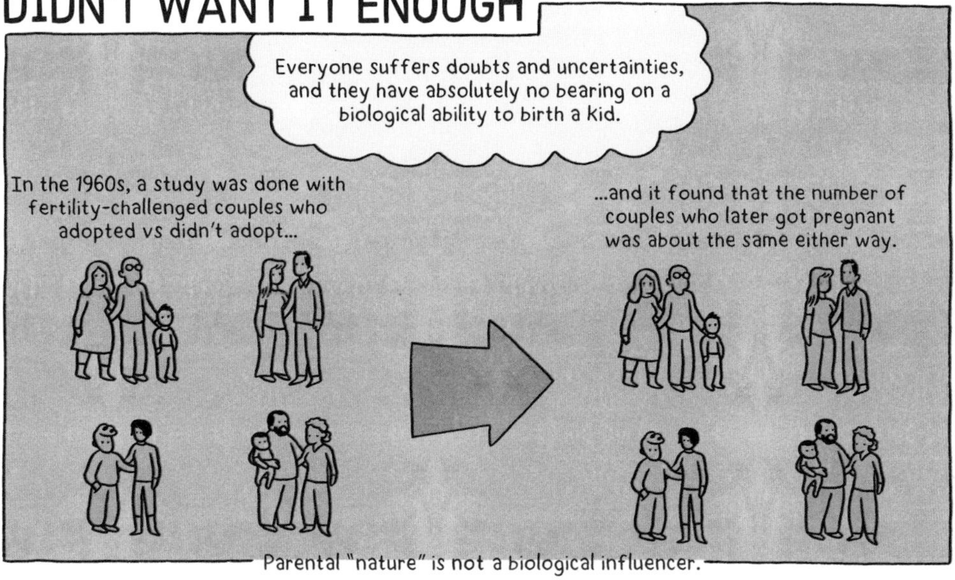
Everyone suffers doubts and uncertainties, and they have absolutely no bearing on a biological ability to birth a kid.
In the 1960s, a study was done with fertility-challenged couples who adopted vs didn't adopt...
...and it found that the number of couples who later got pregnant was about the same either way.

Parental "nature" is not a biological influencer.

I PUSHED MYSELF TOO HARD

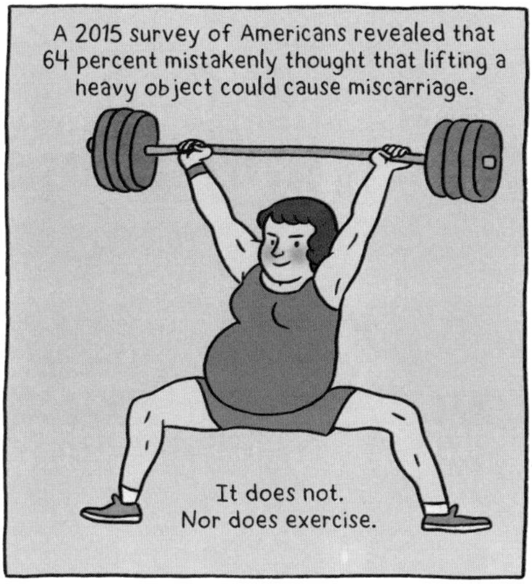
A 2015 survey of Americans revealed that 64 percent mistakenly thought that lifting a heavy object could cause miscarriage.
It does not.
Nor does exercise.

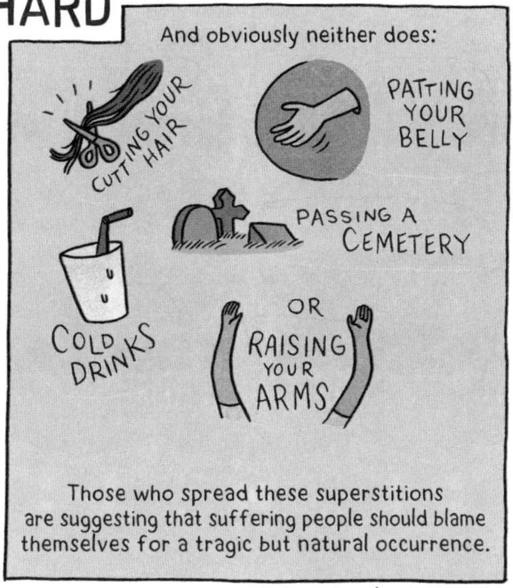
And obviously neither does:
CUTTING YOUR HAIR
PATTING YOUR BELLY
PASSING A CEMETERY
COLD DRINKS
OR
RAISING YOUR ARMS
Those who spread these superstitions are suggesting that suffering people should blame themselves for a tragic but natural occurrence.

Which leads me to...

3. IT'S STRESS

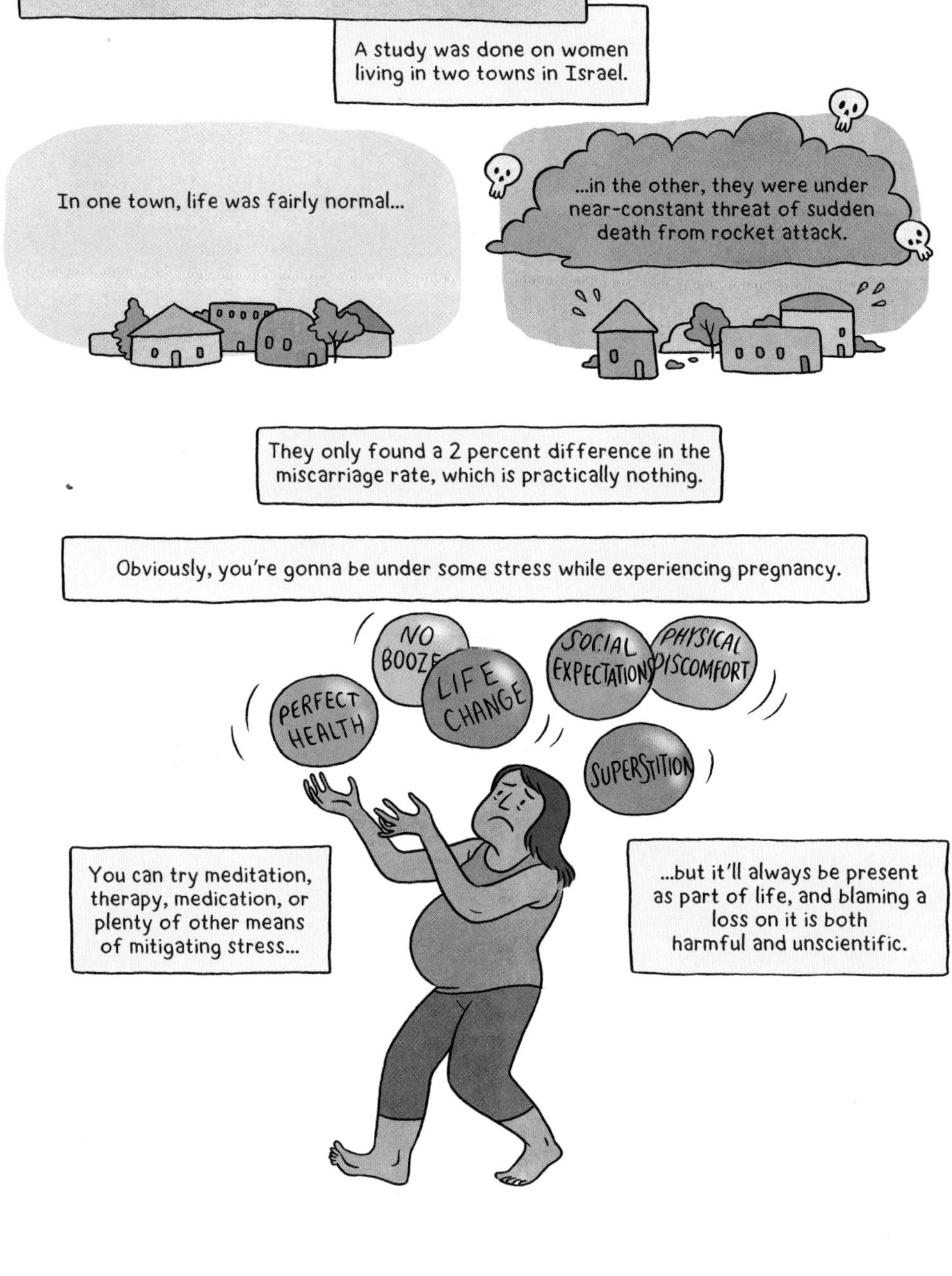
A study was done on women living in two towns in Israel.
In one town, life was fairly normal...
...in the other, they were under near-constant threat of sudden death from rocket attack.
They only found a 2 percent difference in the miscarriage rate, which is practically nothing.
Obviously, you're gonna be under some stress while experiencing pregnancy.
PERFECT HEALTH
LIFE CHANGE
SOCIAL EXPECTATIONS
PHYSICAL DISCOMFORT
SUPERSTITION
You can try meditation, therapy, medication, or plenty of other means of mitigating stress...
...but it'll always be present as part of life, and blaming a loss on it is both harmful and unscientific.

4. IT'S NOT *REAL* GRIEF

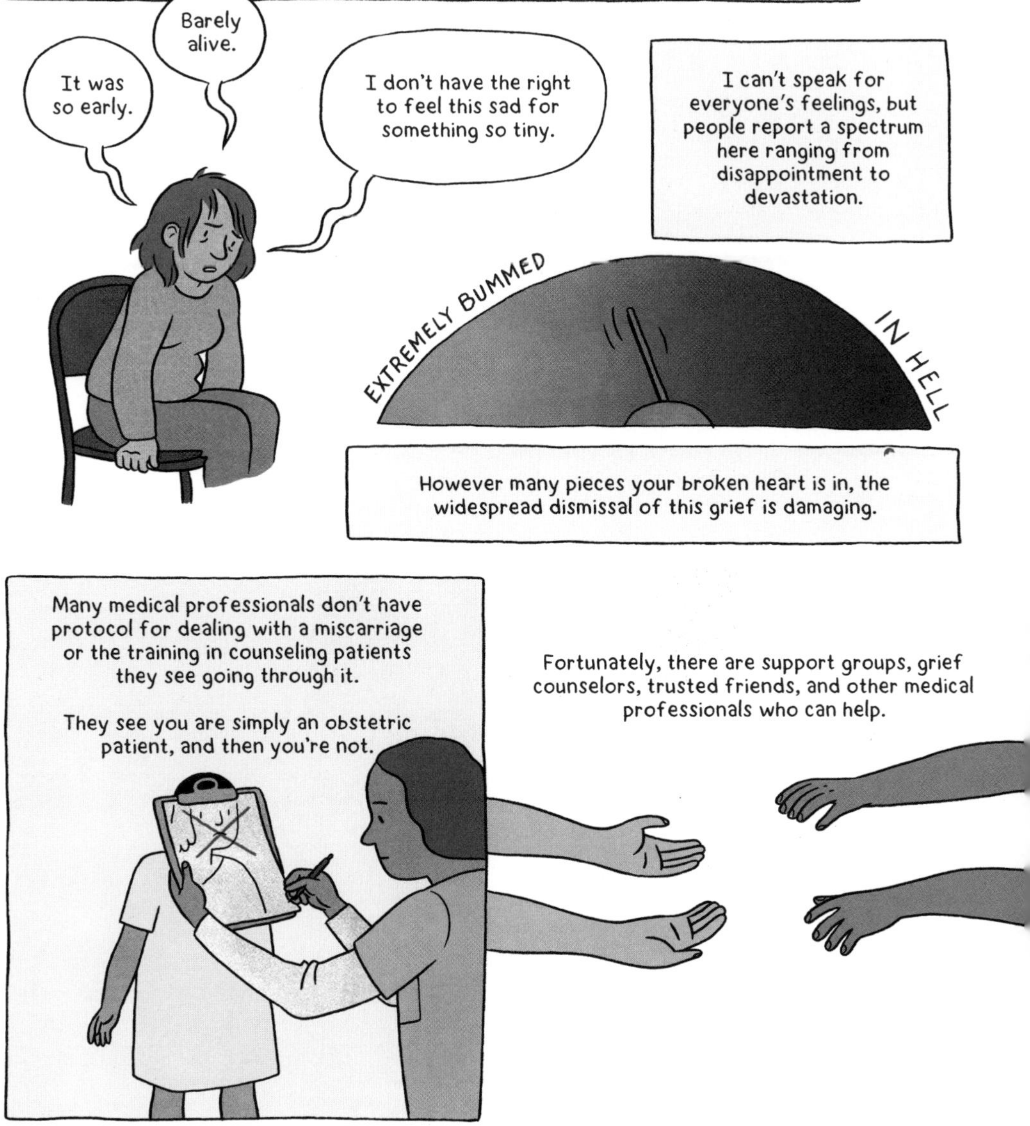
It was so early.
Barely alive.
I don't have the right to feel this sad for something so tiny.
I can't speak for everyone's feelings, but people report a spectrum here ranging from disappointment to devastation.
EXTREMELY BUMMED
IN HELL
However many pieces your broken heart is in, the widespread dismissal of this grief is damaging.
Many medical professionals don't have protocol for dealing with a miscarriage or the training in counseling patients they see going through it.
They see you are simply an obstetric patient, and then you're not.
Fortunately, there are support groups, grief counselors, trusted friends, and other medical professionals who can help.

5. NOTHING CAN BE DONE

Sixty percent of miscarriages occur due to a chromosomal abnormality in the embryo.

Unavoidable.

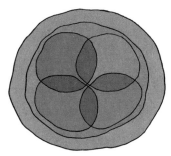

And natural.

But many other underlying diagnoses can be treated:

| Thyroid issues and other hormonal disorders can usually be resolved with medication... | ...likewise, blood clotting can be managed through medication... | ...And uterine growths such as septums and fibroids can be removed. |

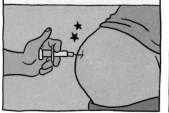
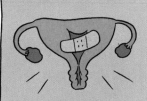

Please Remember

THE VAST MAJORITY OF PEOPLE WHO SUFFER A MISCARRIAGE GO ON TO HAVE A HEALTHY PREGNANCY.

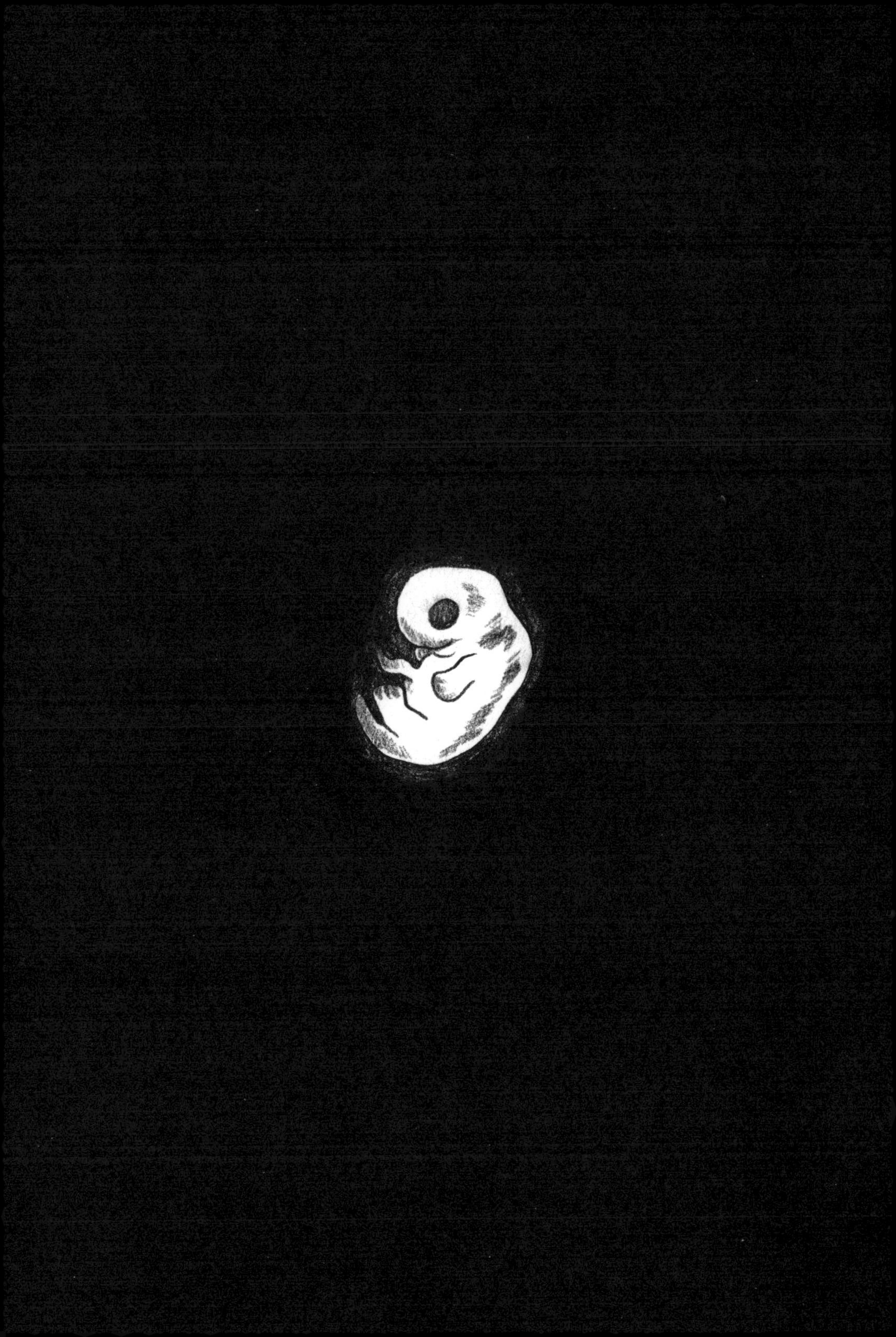

KID GLOVES

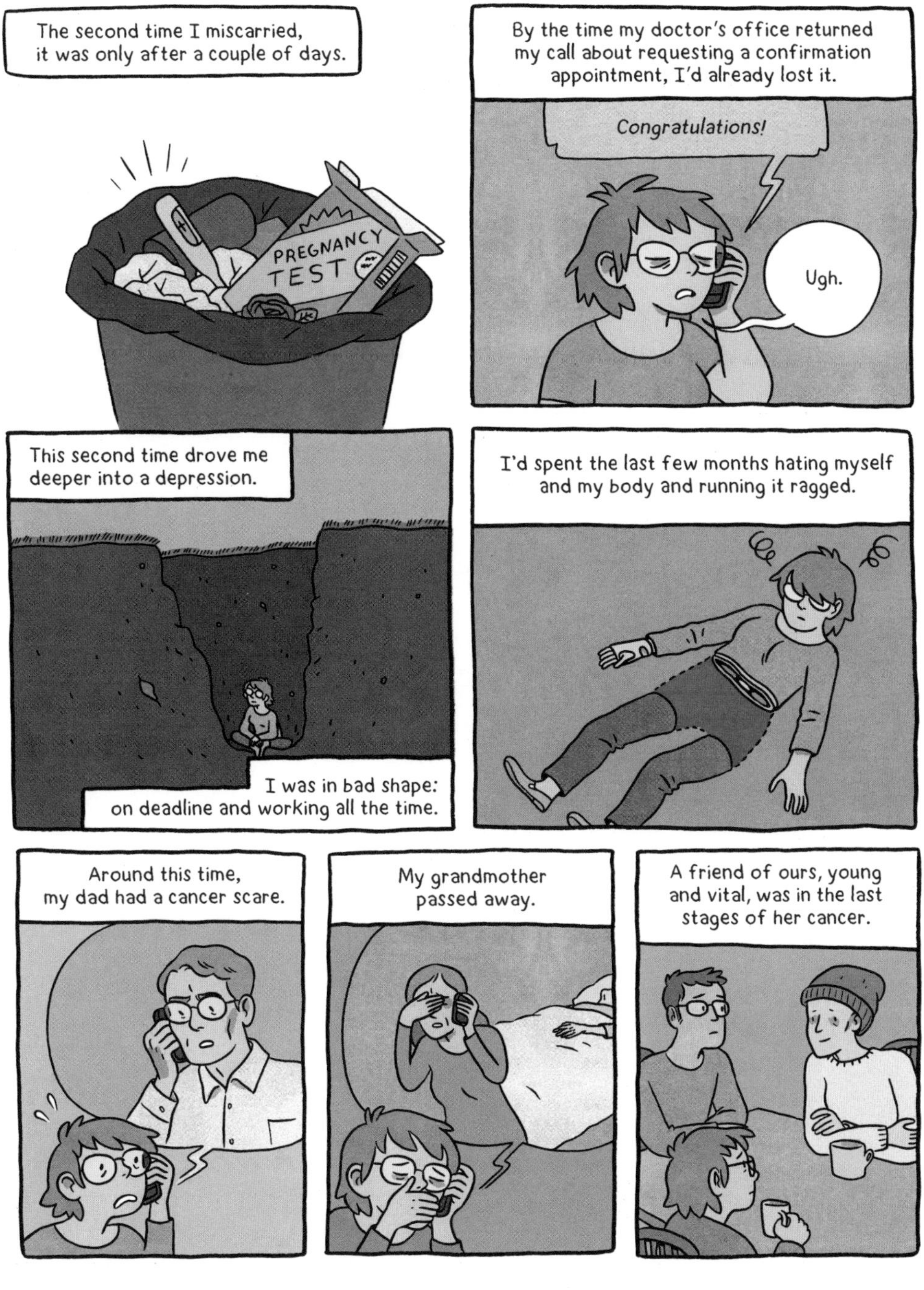
The second time I miscarried, it was only after a couple of days.
PREGNANCY TEST
By the time my doctor's office returned my call about requesting a confirmation appointment, I'd already lost it.
Congratulations!
Ugh.
This second time drove me deeper into a depression.
I was in bad shape: on deadline and working all the time.
I'd spent the last few months hating myself and my body and running it ragged.
Around this time, my dad had a cancer scare.
My grandmother passed away.
A friend of ours, young and vital, was in the last stages of her cancer.

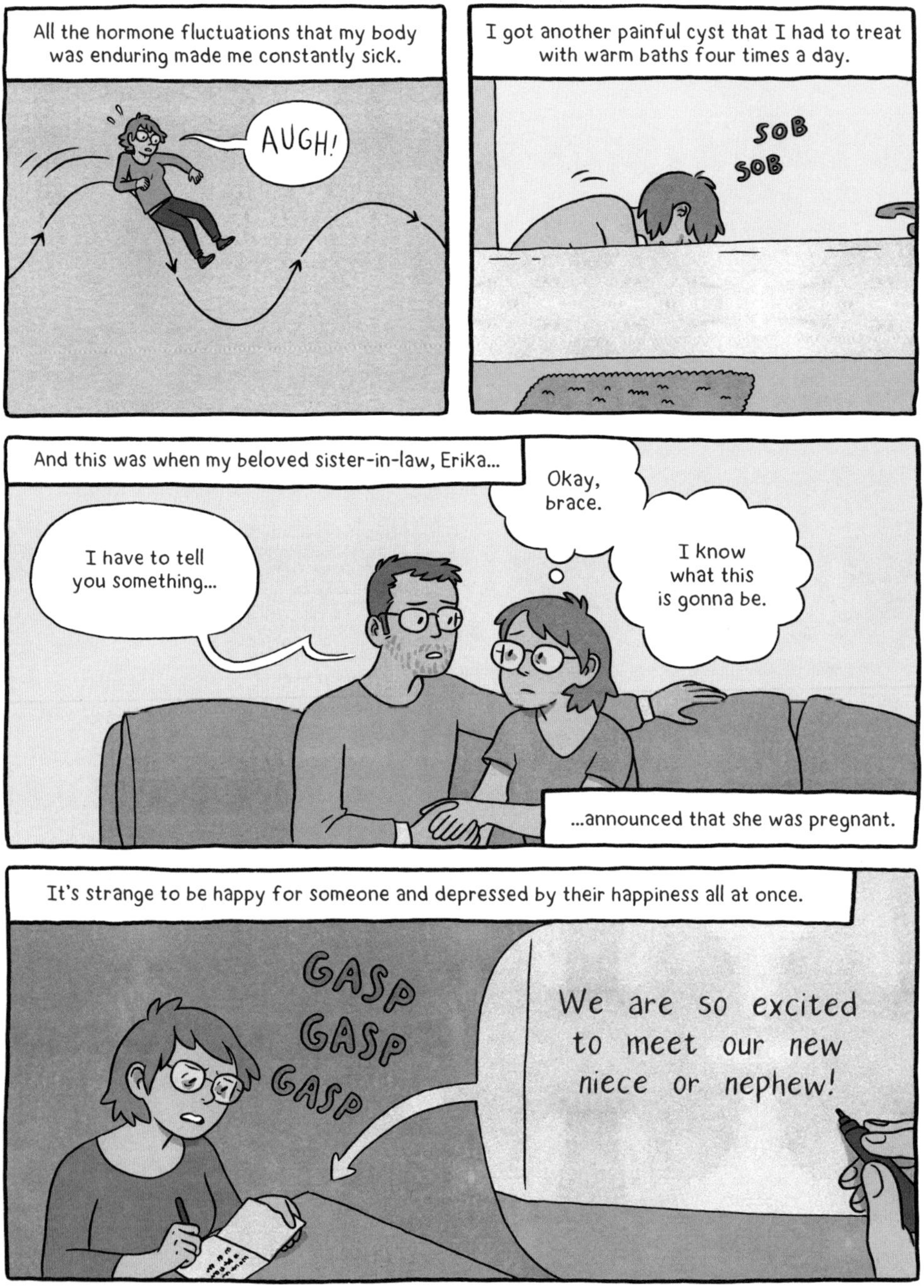
All the hormone fluctuations that my body was enduring made me constantly sick.
AUGH!
I got another painful cyst that I had to treat with warm baths four times a day.
SOB
SOB
And this was when my beloved sister-in-law, Erika...
I have to tell you something...
Okay, brace.
I know what this is gonna be.
...announced that she was pregnant.
It's strange to be happy for someone and depressed by their happiness all at once.
GASP
GASP
GASP
We are so excited to meet our new niece or nephew!

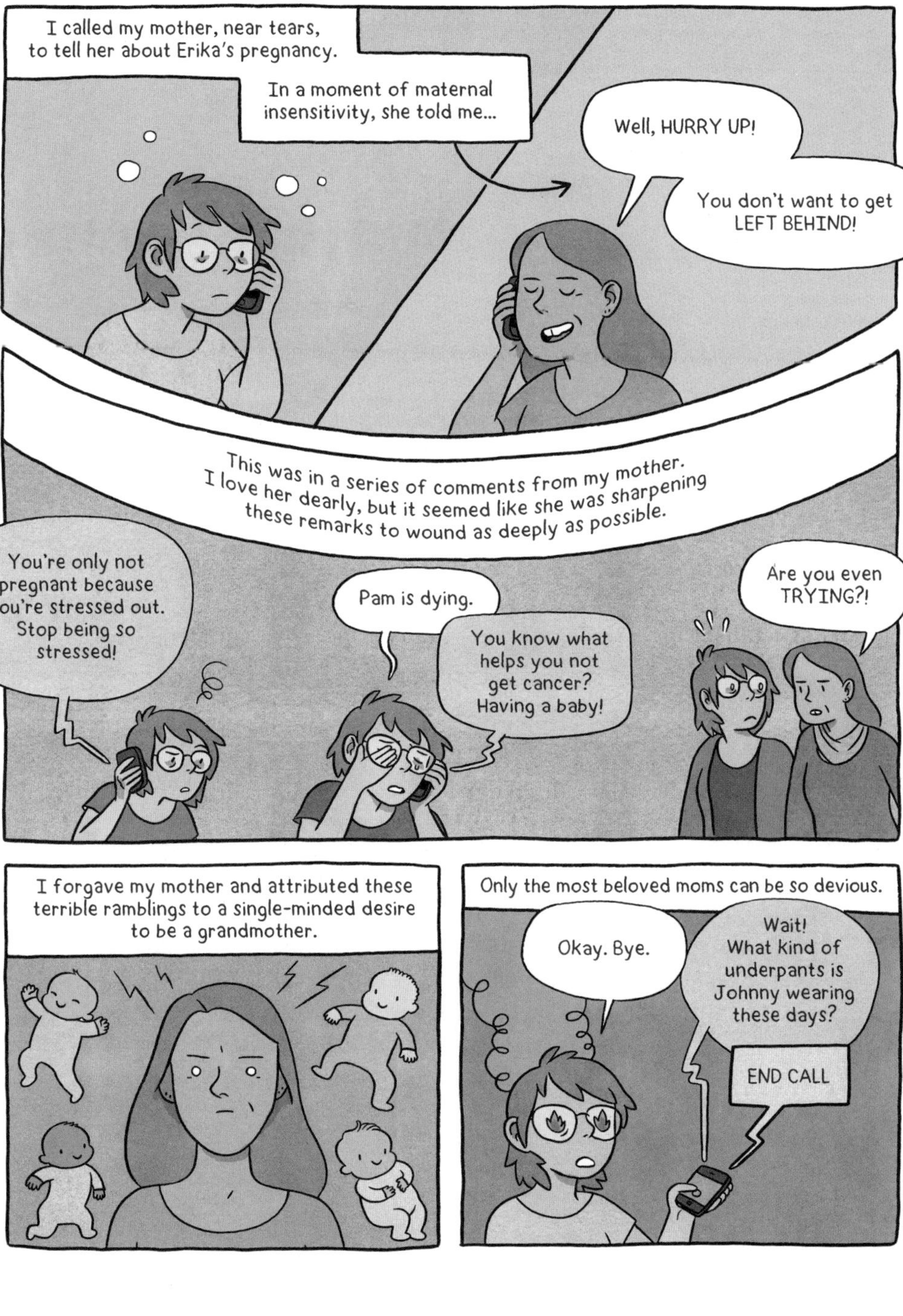

I called my mother, near tears, to tell her about Erika's pregnancy.
In a moment of maternal insensitivity, she told me...
Well, HURRY UP!
You don't want to get LEFT BEHIND!
This was in a series of comments from my mother. I love her dearly, but it seemed like she was sharpening these remarks to wound as deeply as possible.
You're only not pregnant because you're stressed out. Stop being so stressed!
Pam is dying.
You know what helps you not get cancer? Having a baby!
Are you even TRYING?!
I forgave my mother and attributed these terrible ramblings to a single-minded desire to be a grandmother.
Only the most beloved moms can be so devious.
Okay. Bye.
Wait! What kind of underpants is Johnny wearing these days?
END CALL

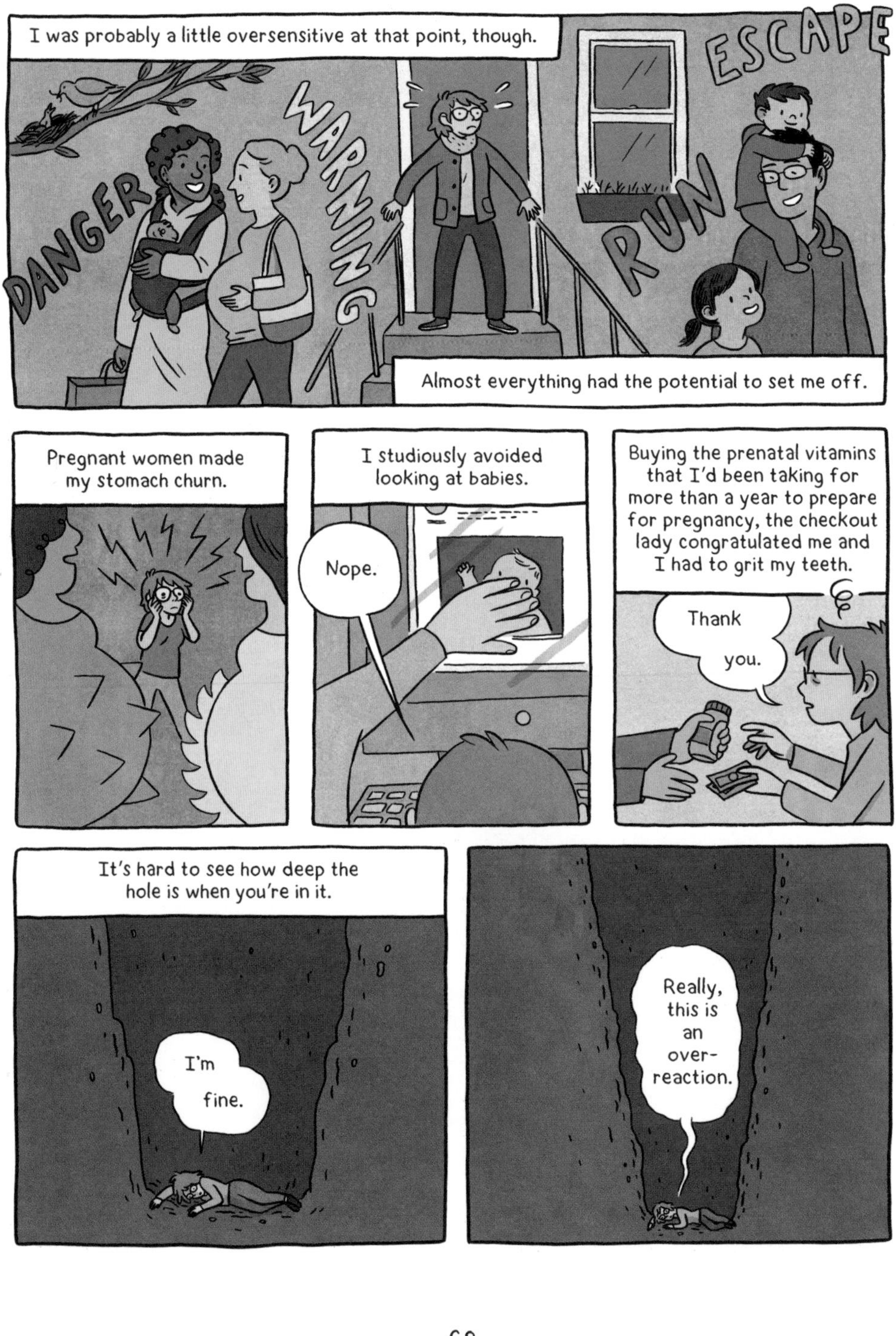
I was probably a little oversensitive at that point, though.
DANGER
WARNING
RUN
ESCAPE
Almost everything had the potential to set me off.
Pregnant women made my stomach churn.
I studiously avoided looking at babies.
Nope.
Buying the prenatal vitamins that I'd been taking for more than a year to prepare for pregnancy, the checkout lady congratulated me and I had to grit my teeth.
Thank you.
It's hard to see how deep the hole is when you're in it.
I'm fine.
Really, this is an over-reaction.

But little by little...

Hey...

...Wait.

...I began to climb my way out.

How did I get so far down here?

I finished my book and handed it in.

TA-DA!

This is... a lot of pages!

WH'I|UMP

After eight months of work and depression, my creative juices were depleted to practically nothing.

Can *enjoy* my job

Has ideas

Can do my job

Zombie mode

Can basically function

DANGER LEVEL: CRITICAL

But there was a world outside my studio and malfunctioning uterus.

Yep!

The sun *is* bright!

AAAUGH!

HISS!

I decided to take time off: from my newly finished book and trying to conceive.

That's one nice day in the sunshine.

DANGER LEVEL CRITICAL

I'd take the summer to get well.

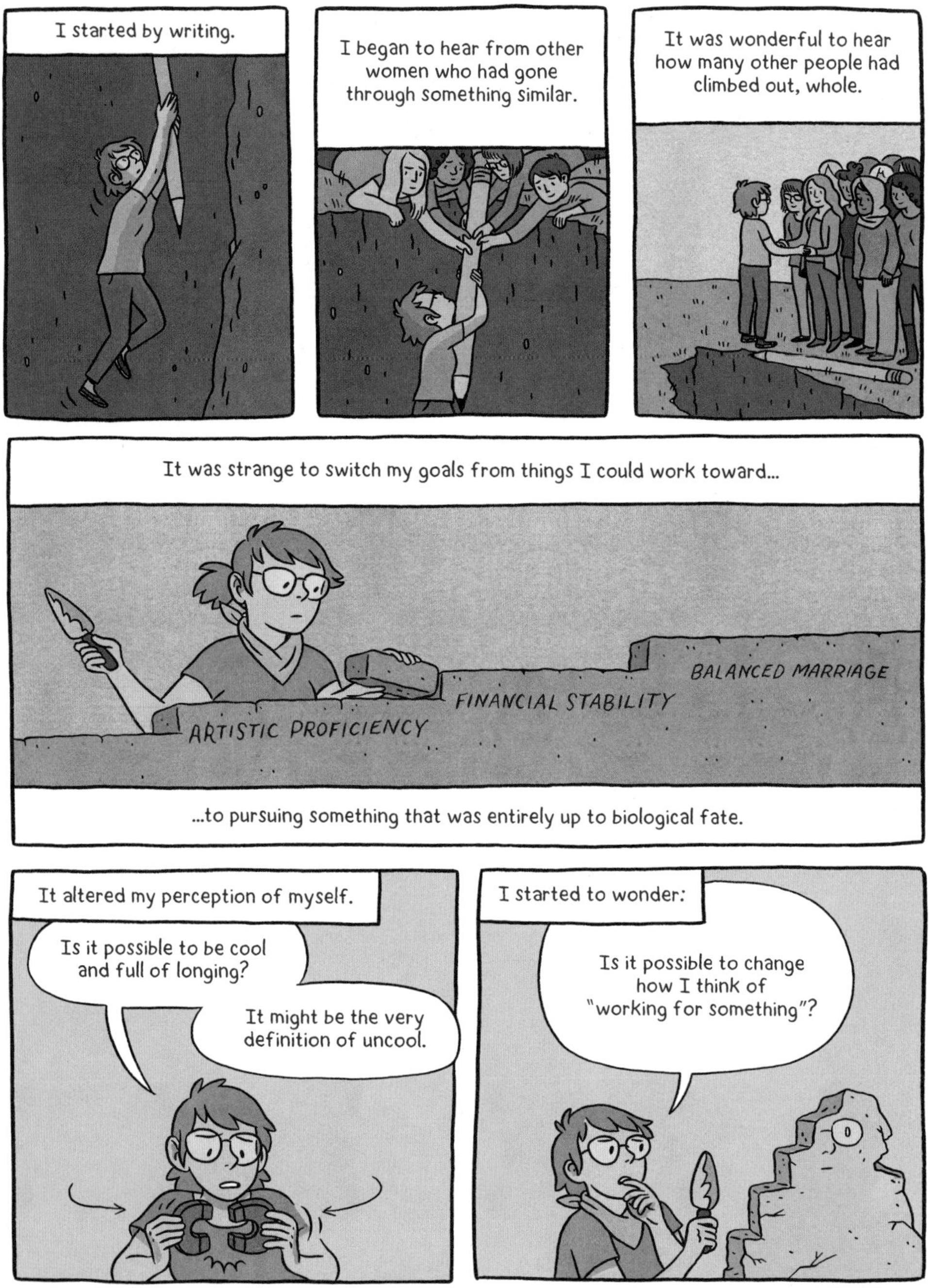

I started by writing.
I began to hear from other women who had gone through something similar.
It was wonderful to hear how many other people had climbed out, whole.
It was strange to switch my goals from things I could work toward...
ARTISTIC PROFICIENCY
FINANCIAL STABILITY
BALANCED MARRIAGE
...to pursuing something that was entirely up to biological fate.
It altered my perception of myself.
Is it possible to be cool and full of longing?
It might be the very definition of uncool.
I started to wonder:
Is it possible to change how I think of "working for something"?

Around this time, I went to sell and sign my books at a comic arts festival.

After the long weekend of working the show, I dined out with a group and was seated beside the cool wife of a brilliant artist.

She began to talk to a person seated across from her about her kids and about how they'd struggled to get pregnant.

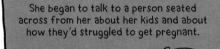

How the renowned Neil Gaiman had comforted her after her miscarriage, saying:

I bet the next time I see you, you'll be pregnant!

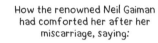

And how his prediction had come true.

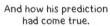

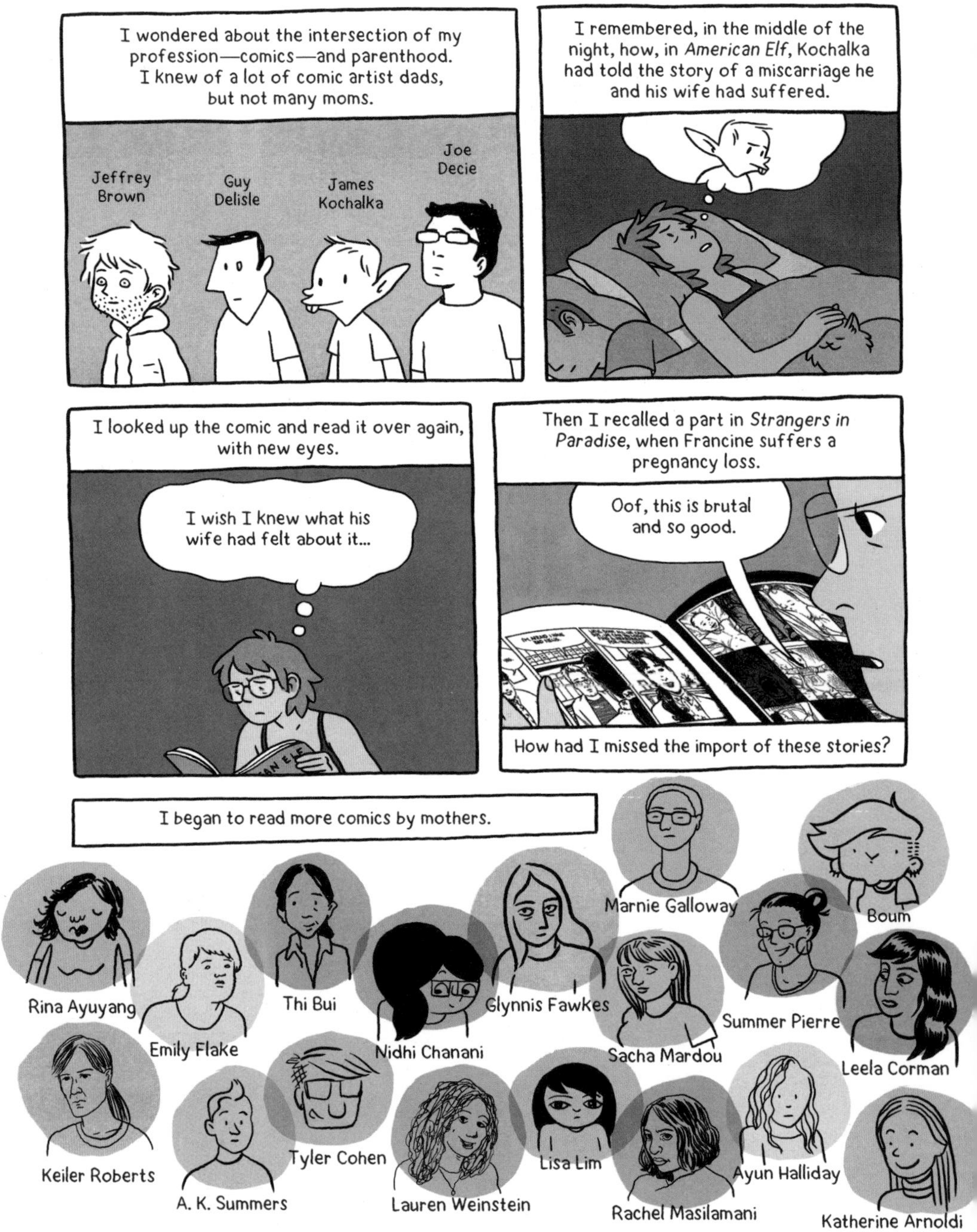
I wondered about the intersection of my profession—comics—and parenthood. I knew of a lot of comic artist dads, but not many moms.
Jeffrey Brown
Guy Delisle
James Kochalka
Joe Decie
I remembered, in the middle of the night, how, in *American Elf*, Kochalka had told the story of a miscarriage he and his wife had suffered.
I looked up the comic and read it over again, with new eyes.
I wish I knew what his wife had felt about it...
Then I recalled a part in *Strangers in Paradise*, when Francine suffers a pregnancy loss.
Oof, this is brutal and so good.
How had I missed the import of these stories?
I began to read more comics by mothers.
Marnie Galloway
Boum
Rina Ayuyang
Thi Bui
Glynnis Fawkes
Summer Pierre
Emily Flake
Nidhi Chanani
Sacha Mardou
Leela Corman
Keiler Roberts
Tyler Cohen
Lisa Lim
Ayun Halliday
A. K. Summers
Lauren Weinstein
Rachel Masilamani
Katherine Arnoldi

I started seeing my therapist again.

I thought I hated my body as a teenager—this is a whole new level!

Here's an idea:

Be gentle with yourself. Coddle yourself.

Handle yourself as you would your own baby...

...with kid gloves.

I gave acupuncture a try.

Is it supposed to hurt?

This hurts.

Shut up, Lucy, your own negativity is ruining this!

I didn't like it.

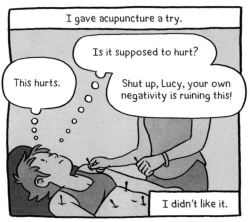

I began swimming every day, again.

I started meditating.

BREATHE   BREATHE

My dad's cancer treatment was working!

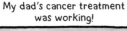

(Though he couldn't hug me because the radioactive seeds with which he'd been implanted threatened fertility.)

Instead of seeing babies and pregnant women everywhere, I started seeing warrior women.

Everyone's been through serious loss.

I ran into my favorite writing professor from college, who then sent me an article she wrote about her own miscarriage.

I thought about my grandmothers—both of whom had experienced pregnancy loss, but were gone before they could share their stories with me.

My maternal grandmother had actually adopted, after being told she couldn't have children, before going on to birth three babies.

My paternal grandmother still spoke, after four children and many years, of their miscarried child by name.

This stuff went deep and was lodged in my family history.

It seemed genetic, like I had inherited this burden of sadness over our uncertain biology.

My therapist urged me to see a reproductive endocrinologist.

Usually this isn't done until a year of trying produces no results, and it's only been seven months.

The thought of continuing to miscarry was too much to contemplate.

But...

They wouldn't tell me to keep trying if I kept falling off a cliff with every attempt.

I need help.

NOD NOD

Everyone at my RE's office had a beautiful accent.

The RE was a soft-spoken Israeli man who told us:

What we do here is make people happy.

He gave me a hysteroscopy,* to see the terrain inside my uterus.

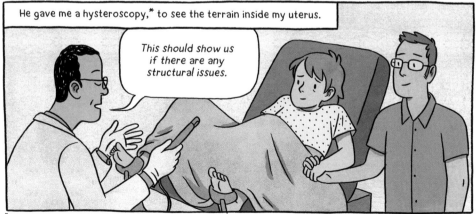

This should show us if there are any structural issues.

*A hysteroscopy is when a doctor fills your uterus with dye so that they can examine any problems therein, using a small camera.

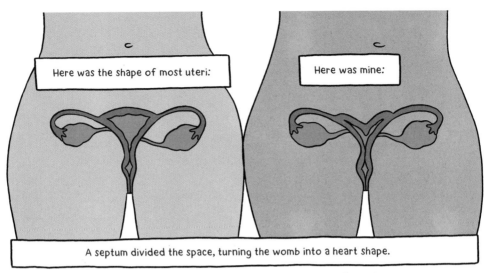

Here was the shape of most uteri:

Here was mine:

A septum divided the space, turning the womb into a heart shape.

Did I want a baby so much that my body had contorted itself to this cartoon shape?

Like a Care Bear...

...or a troll!

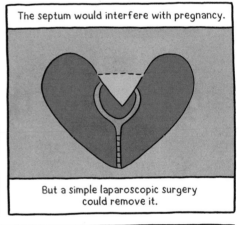

The septum would interfere with pregnancy.

But a simple laparoscopic surgery could remove it.

I wonder, still, if this was something I inherited from my mother (who tried and failed to have more children after I was born) or from either grandmother...

...but it's impossible to know.

It was such a relief to have something, anything, to blame.

Did I do something wrong to deserve this?

NO, PAST ME!

And something so fixable—when for many people I knew, infertility arose from irreversible causes.

YOU JUST HAVE A WEIRDO UTERUS!

I felt, after a year of feeling cursed...

Thank you.

Thank you.

Thank you.

...suddenly lucky.

I told my acupuncturist the diagnosis at our last appointment.

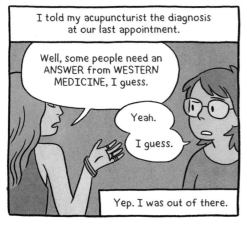

Well, some people need an ANSWER from WESTERN MEDICINE, I guess.

Yeah.

I guess.

Yep. I was out of there.

My operation was the following week.

Afterward, John bought me a big cookie and let me wear his comfy sweatshirt.

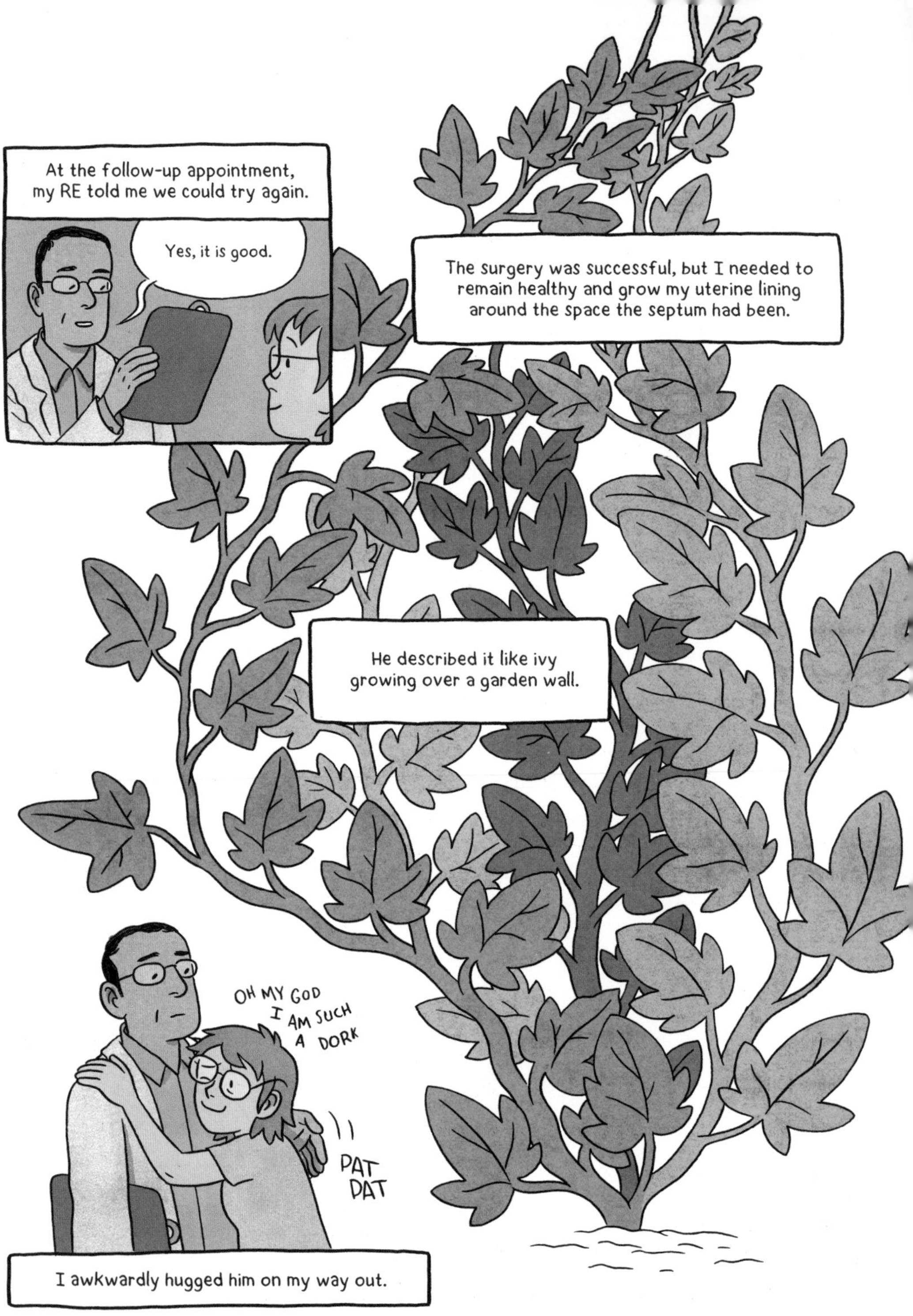
At the follow-up appointment, my RE told me we could try again.
Yes, it is good.
The surgery was successful, but I needed to remain healthy and grow my uterine lining around the space the septum had been.
He described it like ivy growing over a garden wall.
OH MY GOD I AM SUCH A DORK
PAT PAT
I awkwardly hugged him on my way out.

A few weeks of waiting...

Can I drink that?

I'd better not, just in case.

BEER

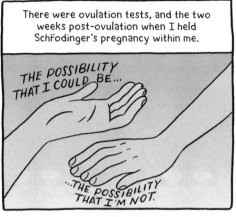

There were ovulation tests, and the two weeks post-ovulation when I held Schrödinger's pregnancy within me.

THE POSSIBILITY THAT I COULD BE...

...THE POSSIBILITY THAT I'M NOT.

I tried to let go, be human, relax, handle myself with kid gloves.

I did girlie meditations.

Imagine a rose garden.

I sat out on the porch and looked at the Chicago skyline.

I treated myself like I would treat a child.

Are you in bed? It's eight PM!

Yep! Bedtime!

I grew the ivy over the garden wall.

It only took a couple months.

HEY LOOK, MORE PREGNANCY RESEARCH

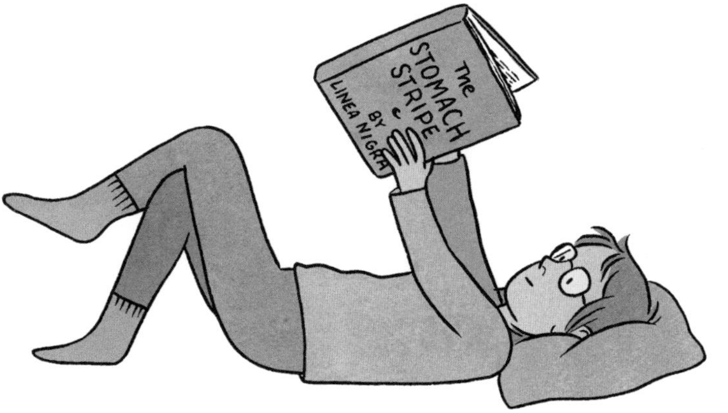
THE STOMACH STRIPE
BY LINEA NIGRA

CONCEPTION MISCONCEPTIONS

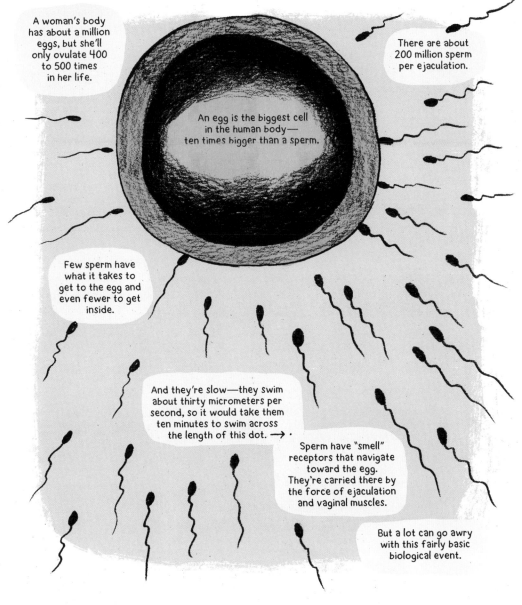

A woman's body has about a million eggs, but she'll only ovulate 400 to 500 times in her life.

An egg is the biggest cell in the human body— ten times bigger than a sperm.

There are about 200 million sperm per ejaculation.

Few sperm have what it takes to get to the egg and even fewer to get inside.

And they're slow—they swim about thirty micrometers per second, so it would take them ten minutes to swim across the length of this dot. →·

Sperm have "smell" receptors that navigate toward the egg. They're carried there by the force of ejaculation and vaginal muscles.

But a lot can go awry with this fairly basic biological event.

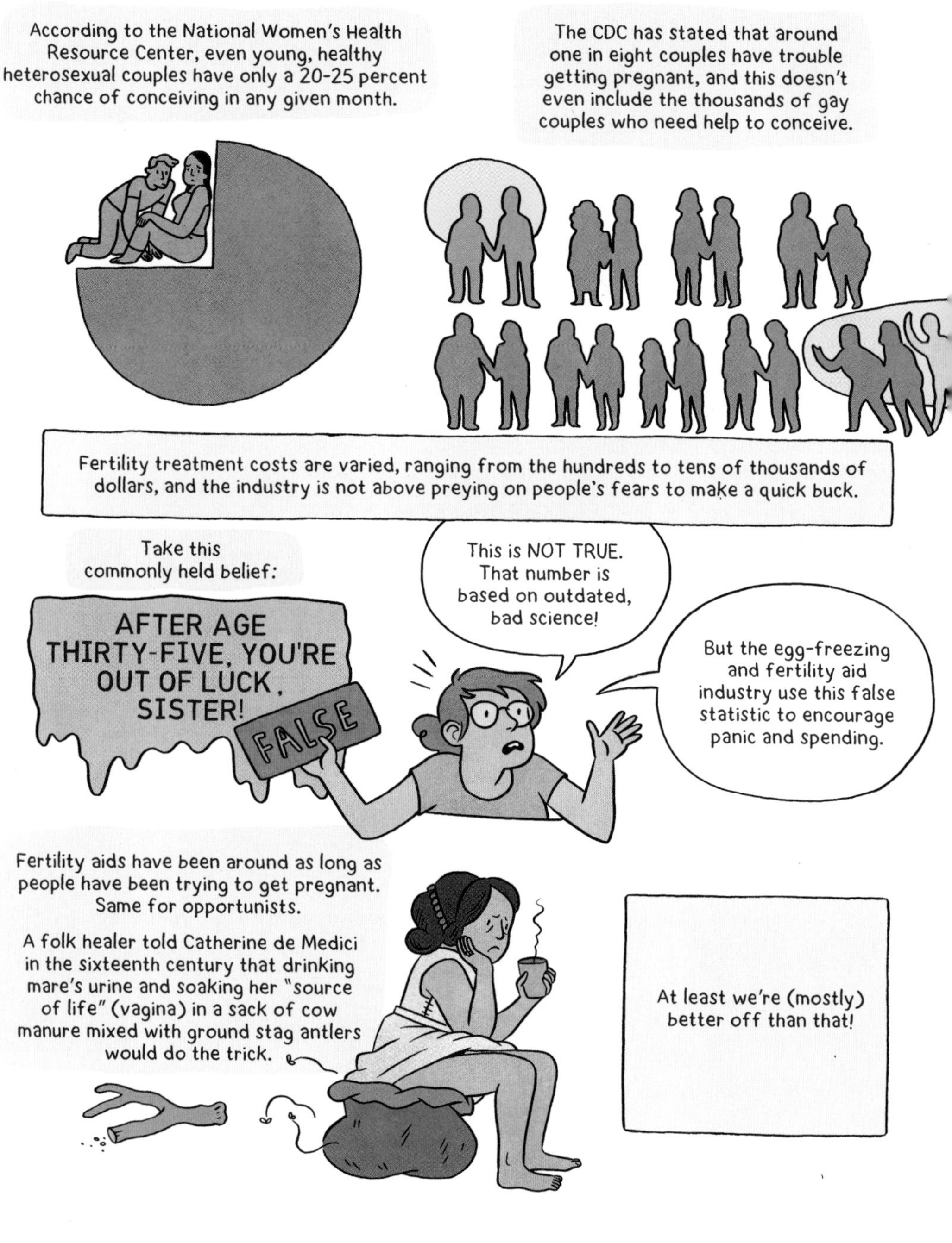
According to the National Women's Health Resource Center, even young, healthy heterosexual couples have only a 20-25 percent chance of conceiving in any given month.
The CDC has stated that around one in eight couples have trouble getting pregnant, and this doesn't even include the thousands of gay couples who need help to conceive.
Fertility treatment costs are varied, ranging from the hundreds to tens of thousands of dollars, and the industry is not above preying on people's fears to make a quick buck.
Take this commonly held belief:
AFTER AGE THIRTY-FIVE, YOU'RE OUT OF LUCK, SISTER!
FALSE
This is NOT TRUE. That number is based on outdated, bad science!
But the egg-freezing and fertility aid industry use this false statistic to encourage panic and spending.
Fertility aids have been around as long as people have been trying to get pregnant. Same for opportunists.
A folk healer told Catherine de Medici in the sixteenth century that drinking mare's urine and soaking her "source of life" (vagina) in a sack of cow manure mixed with ground stag antlers would do the trick.
At least we're (mostly) better off than that!

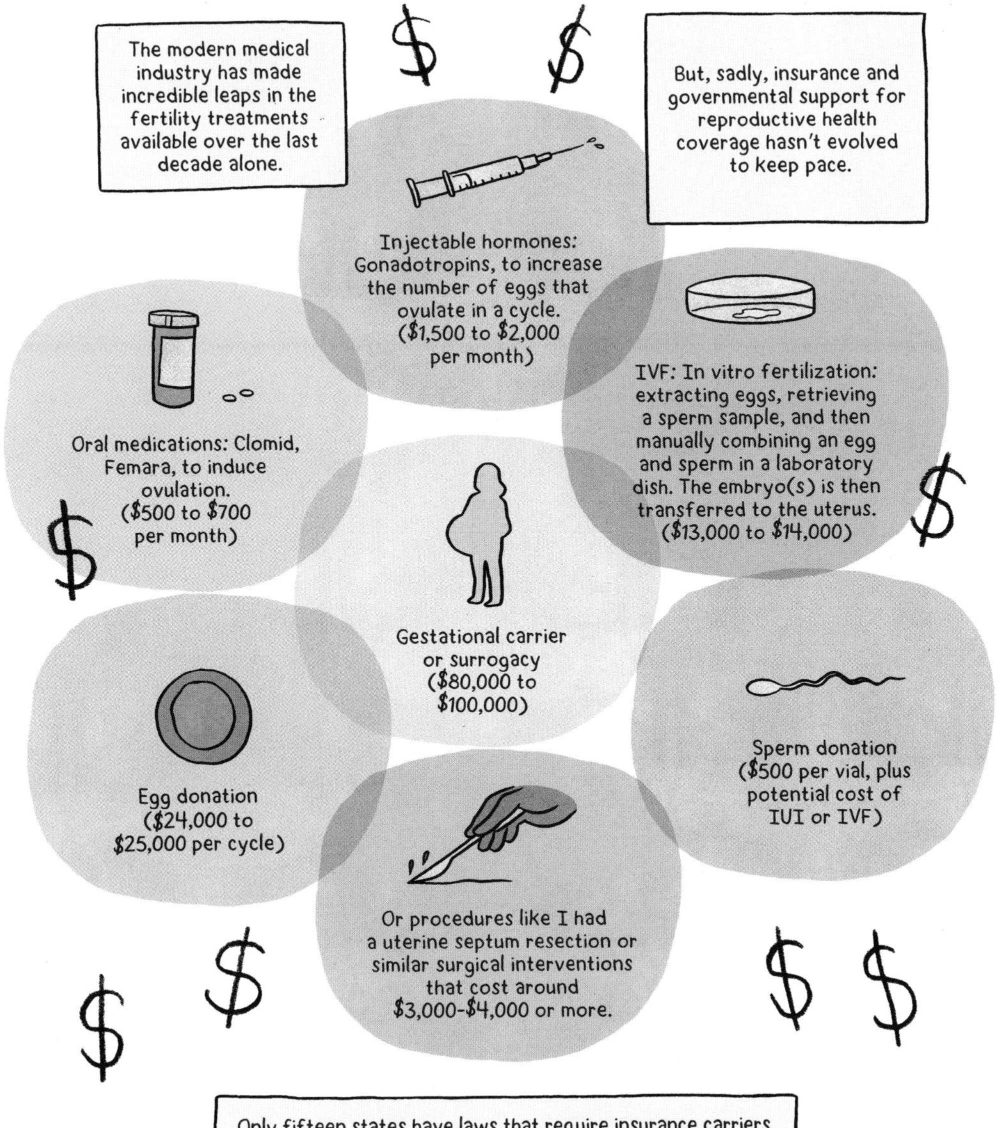

The modern medical industry has made incredible leaps in the fertility treatments available over the last decade alone.

But, sadly, insurance and governmental support for reproductive health coverage hasn't evolved to keep pace.

Injectable hormones: Gonadotropins, to increase the number of eggs that ovulate in a cycle. ($1,500 to $2,000 per month)

IVF: In vitro fertilization: extracting eggs, retrieving a sperm sample, and then manually combining an egg and sperm in a laboratory dish. The embryo(s) is then transferred to the uterus. ($13,000 to $14,000)

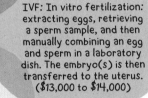

Oral medications: Clomid, Femara, to induce ovulation. ($500 to $700 per month)

Gestational carrier or surrogacy ($80,000 to $100,000)

Sperm donation ($500 per vial, plus potential cost of IUI or IVF)

Egg donation ($24,000 to $25,000 per cycle)

Or procedures like I had a uterine septum resection or similar surgical interventions that cost around $3,000-$4,000 or more.

Only fifteen states have laws that require insurance carriers to offer plans that include fertility treatment coverage, which limits access to those who can afford the hefty bills.

Once you manage to conceive, then the trouble truly starts:

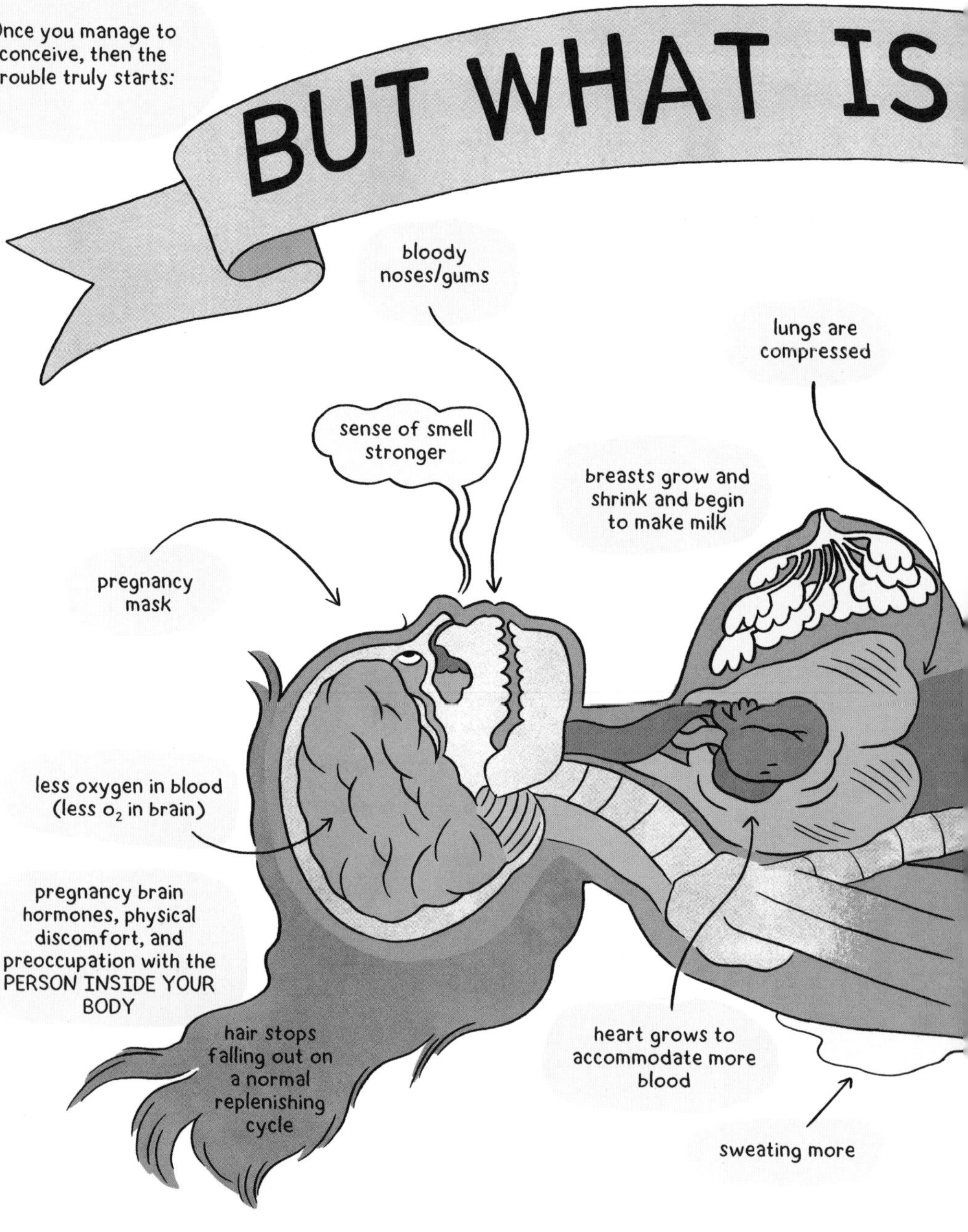

BUT WHAT IS
bloody noses/gums
lungs are compressed
sense of smell stronger
breasts grow and shrink and begin to make milk
pregnancy mask
less oxygen in blood (less o_2 in brain)
pregnancy brain hormones, physical discomfort, and preoccupation with the PERSON INSIDE YOUR BODY
hair stops falling out on a normal replenishing cycle
heart grows to accommodate more blood
sweating more

HAPPENING?

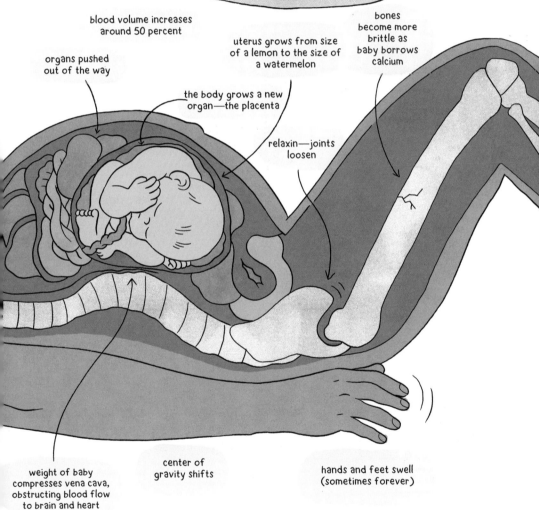

blood volume increases around 50 percent

organs pushed out of the way

the body grows a new organ—the placenta

uterus grows from size of a lemon to the size of a watermelon

bones become more brittle as baby borrows calcium

relaxin—joints loosen

weight of baby compresses vena cava, obstructing blood flow to brain and heart

center of gravity shifts

hands and feet swell (sometimes forever)

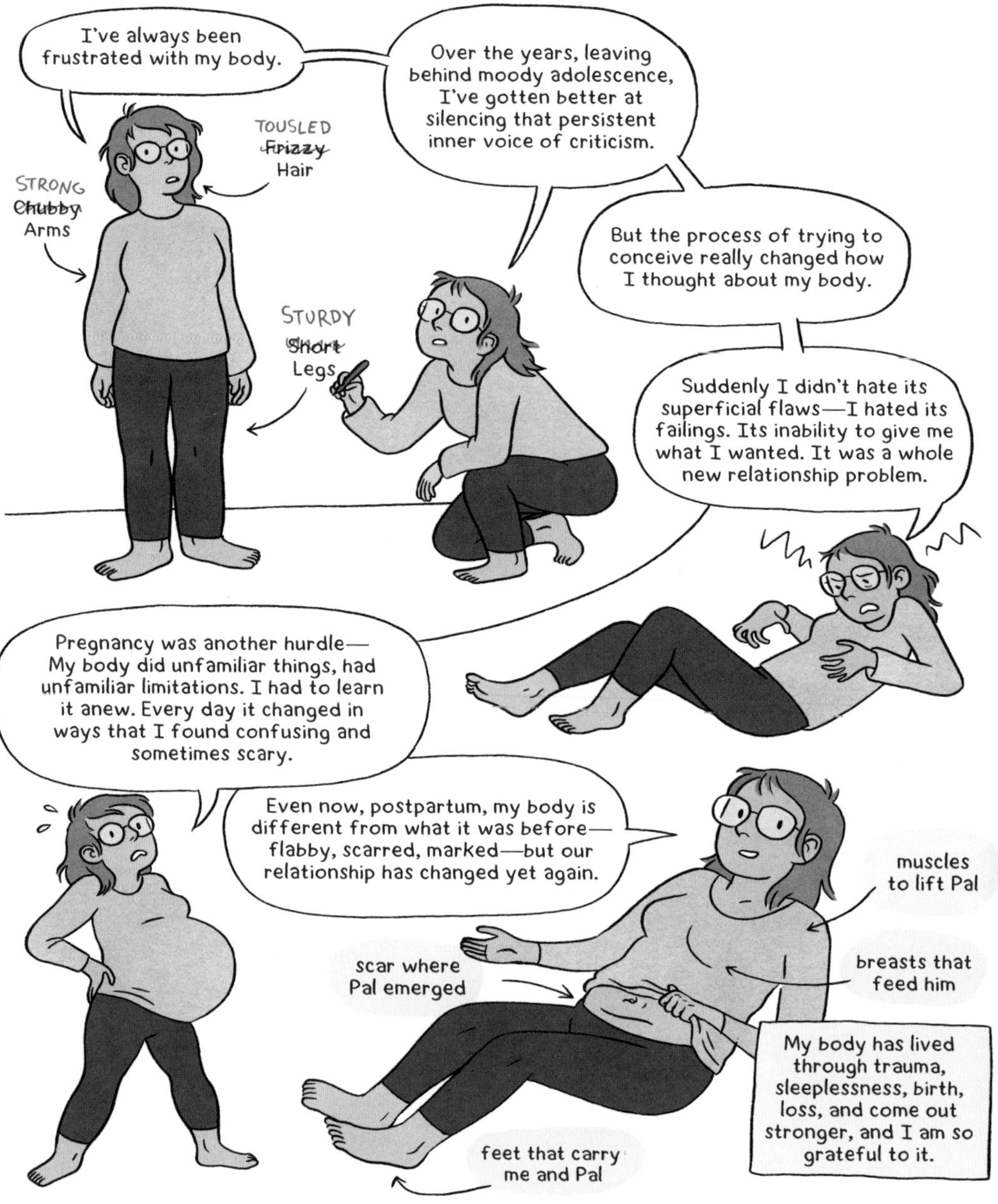
I've always been frustrated with my body.
TOUSLED
~~Frizzy~~
Hair
STRONG
~~Chubby~~
Arms
Over the years, leaving behind moody adolescence, I've gotten better at silencing that persistent inner voice of criticism.
STURDY
~~Short~~
Legs
But the process of trying to conceive really changed how I thought about my body.
Suddenly I didn't hate its superficial flaws—I hated its failings. Its inability to give me what I wanted. It was a whole new relationship problem.
Pregnancy was another hurdle—My body did unfamiliar things, had unfamiliar limitations. I had to learn it anew. Every day it changed in ways that I found confusing and sometimes scary.
Even now, postpartum, my body is different from what it was before—flabby, scarred, marked—but our relationship has changed yet again.
muscles to lift Pal
scar where Pal emerged
breasts that feed him
My body has lived through trauma, sleeplessness, birth, loss, and come out stronger, and I am so grateful to it.
feet that carry me and Pal

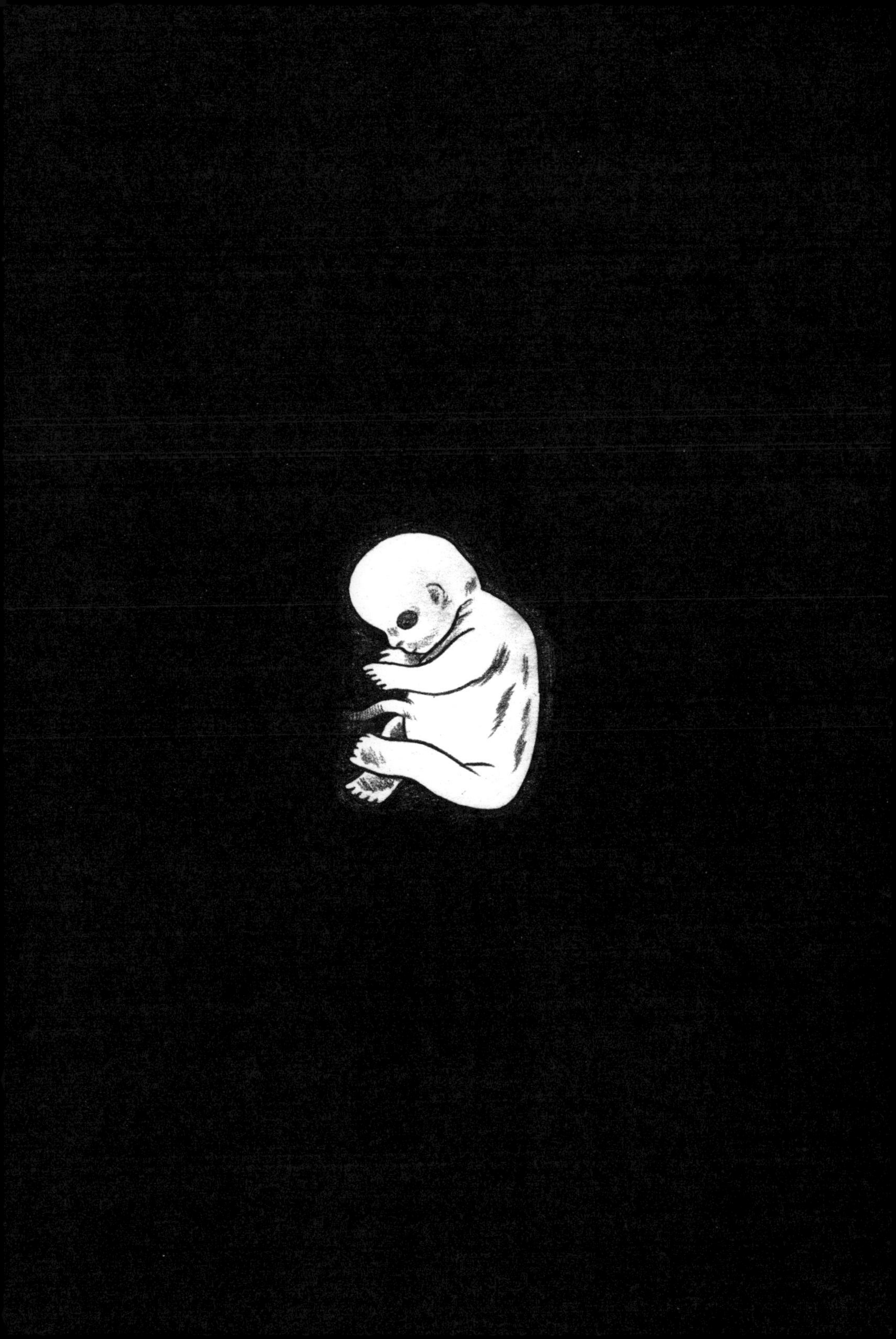

THE FOUL FIRST

There is a superstition that your mind-set during the first trimester of pregnancy will affect your child.

If that was the case, I was likely to give birth to an actual fear demon.

I spent weeks two through six in a haze of terror.

Can I withstand another miscarriage?

What if I GO CRAZY?

It wasn't helped much by the hormonal supplements prescribed by my RE to boost my pregnancy staying power.

Pregnancy hormones times four!

I had recurring nightmares that I had to nurse a sick snake.

I'm absolutely phobic of snakes and have been my entire life.

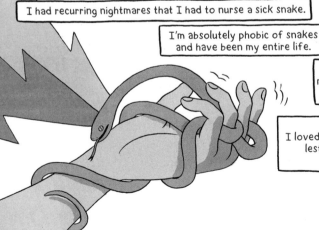

The creature perched listlessly on my drawing hand, flicking its tongue against the pads of my fingers.

I loved the snake, so I had to care for it, lest it startle and bite and kill me.

The meaning was pretty clear.

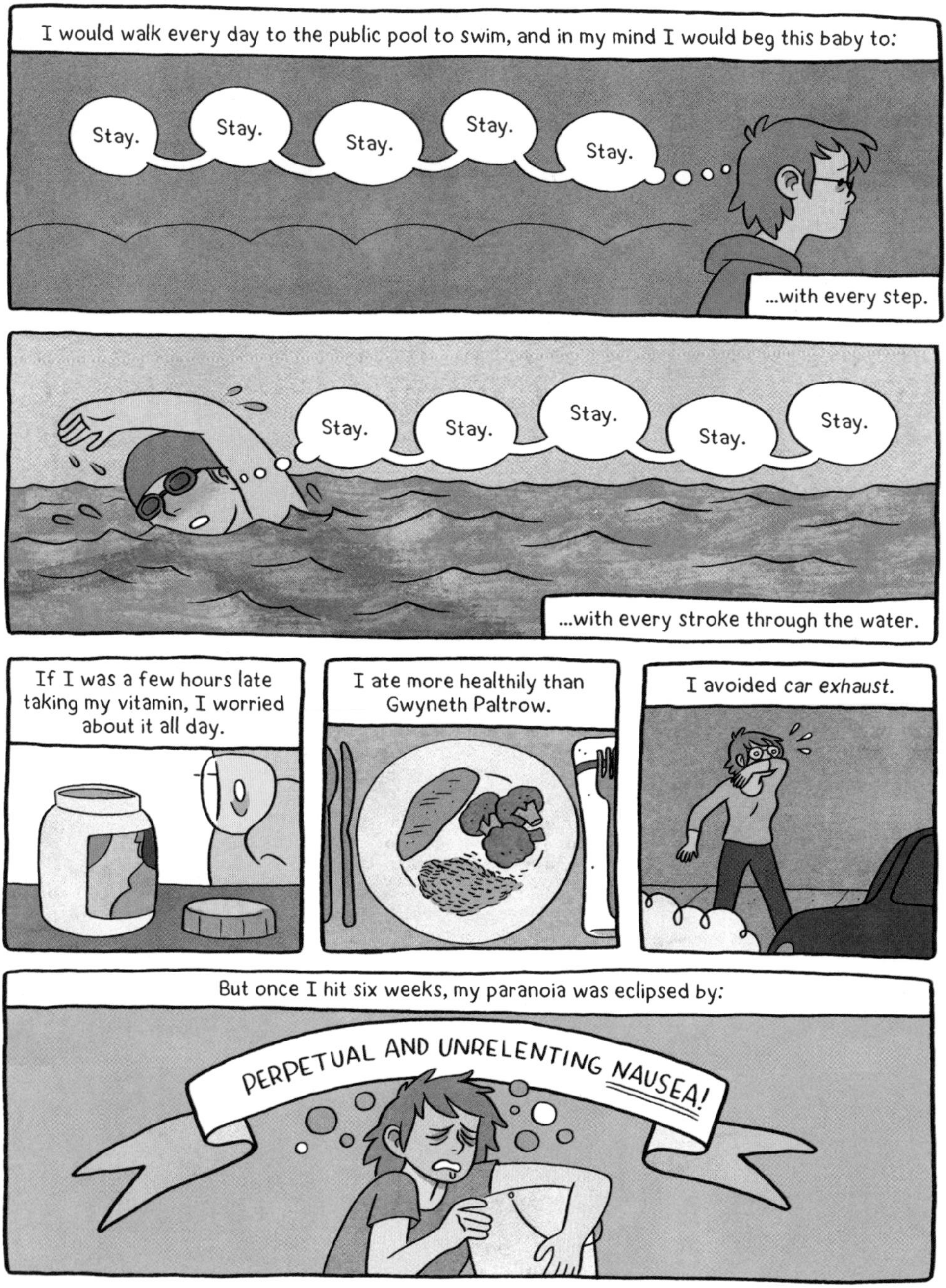

I would walk every day to the public pool to swim, and in my mind I would beg this baby to:
Stay.
Stay.
Stay.
Stay.
Stay.
...with every step.
Stay.
Stay.
Stay.
Stay.
Stay.
...with every stroke through the water.
If I was a few hours late taking my vitamin, I worried about it all day.
I ate more healthily than Gwyneth Paltrow.
I avoided *car exhaust.*
But once I hit six weeks, my paranoia was eclipsed by:
PERPETUAL AND UNRELENTING NAUSEA!

On a sitcom, when a woman is pregnant, she's sitting with friends and behaving normally...

HA HA HA HA HA

Until the morning, when she suddenly prances to the bathroom, to indicate to the audience that *something is up.*

OOoooooOOOoooooHH!

I did not find this to be the case, for me.

Recall, if you are able to bring yourself to do so, the worst hangover of your life.

Frozen in bed, lest the slightest muscle movement bring forth the meager contents of your stomach...

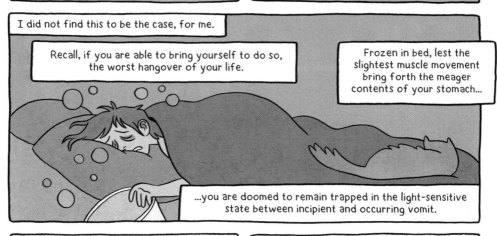

...you are doomed to remain trapped in the light-sensitive state between incipient and occurring vomit.

I think this is why it is so often referred to as "morning sickness," not because it only lasts for the morning (not true at all)...

ALL DAY!

...but because it resembles "the morning after" a night of bad vodka cocktails.

Helllp meeee.

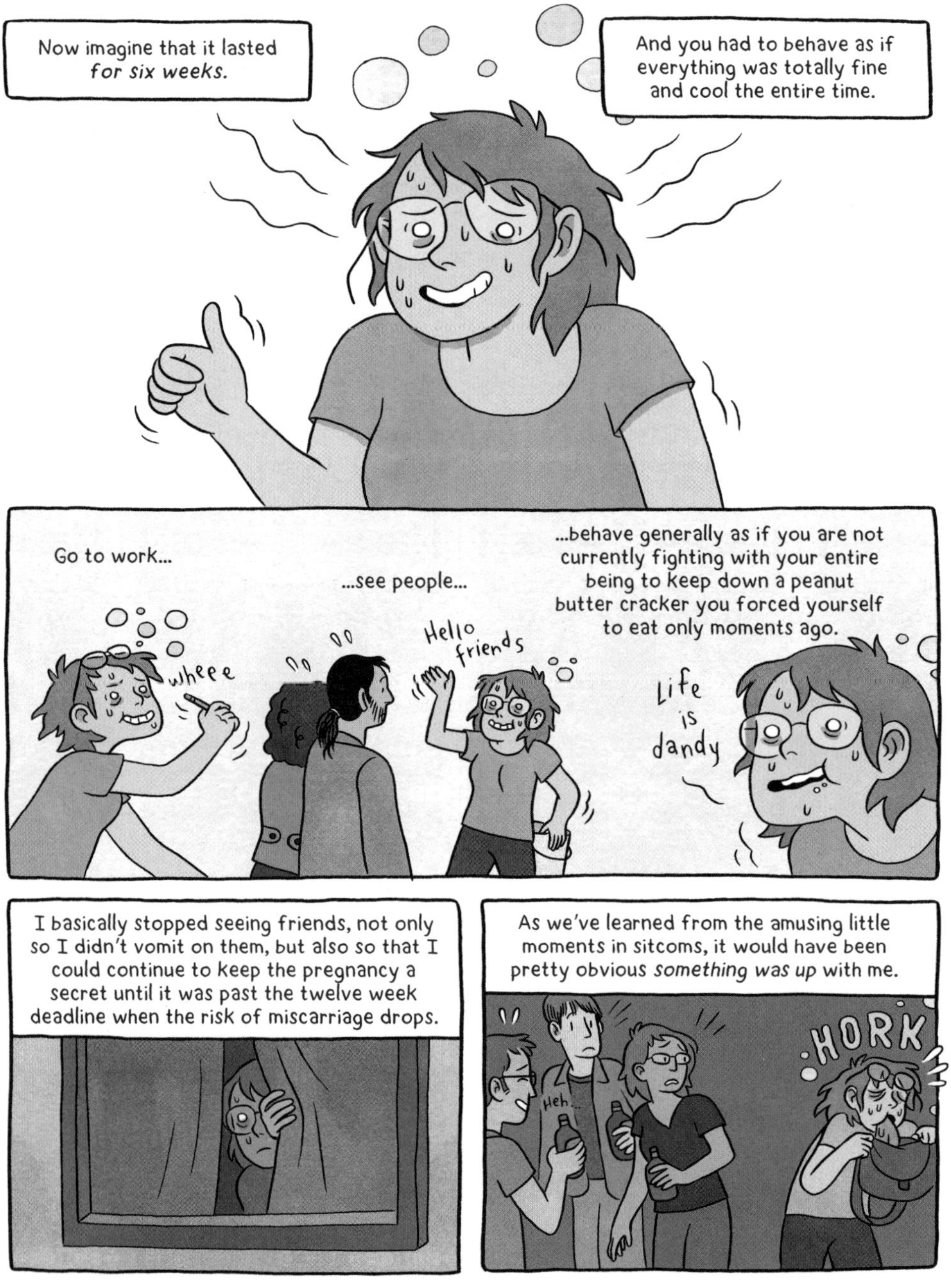

Now imagine that it lasted *for six weeks.*
And you had to behave as if everything was totally fine and cool the entire time.
Go to work...
wheee
...see people...
Hello friends
...behave generally as if you are not currently fighting with your entire being to keep down a peanut butter cracker you forced yourself to eat only moments ago.
Life is dandy
I basically stopped seeing friends, not only so I didn't vomit on them, but also so that I could continue to keep the pregnancy a secret until it was past the twelve week deadline when the risk of miscarriage drops.
As we've learned from the amusing little moments in sitcoms, it would have been pretty obvious *something was up* with me.
Heh...
HORK

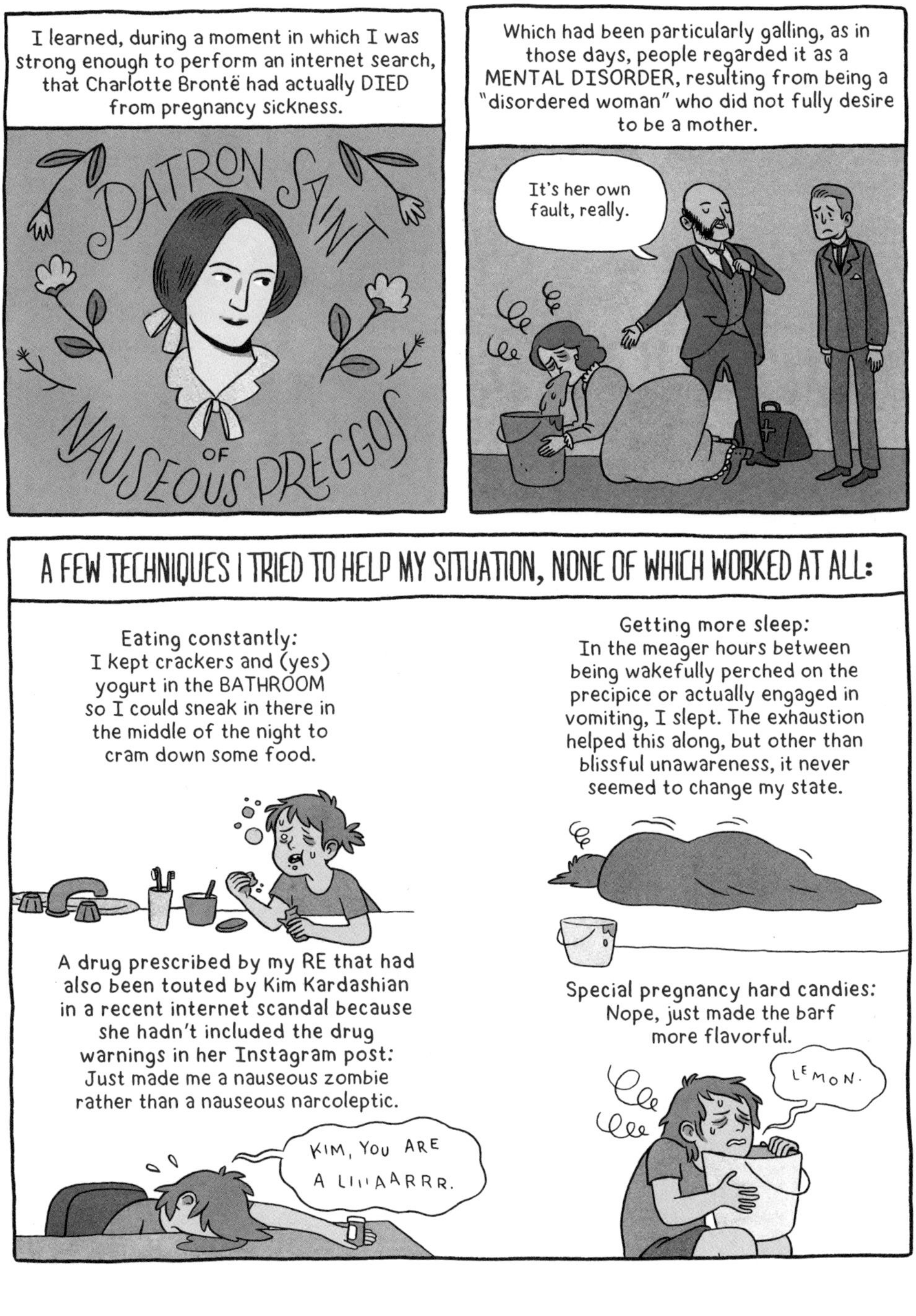
I learned, during a moment in which I was strong enough to perform an internet search, that Charlotte Brontë had actually DIED from pregnancy sickness.
PATRON SAINT OF NAUSEOUS PREGGOS
Which had been particularly galling, as in those days, people regarded it as a MENTAL DISORDER, resulting from being a "disordered woman" who did not fully desire to be a mother.
It's her own fault, really.
A FEW TECHNIQUES I TRIED TO HELP MY SITUATION, NONE OF WHICH WORKED AT ALL:
Eating constantly: I kept crackers and (yes) yogurt in the BATHROOM so I could sneak in there in the middle of the night to cram down some food.
A drug prescribed by my RE that had also been touted by Kim Kardashian in a recent internet scandal because she hadn't included the drug warnings in her Instagram post: Just made me a nauseous zombie rather than a nauseous narcoleptic.
KIM, YOU ARE A LIIIAARRR.
Getting more sleep: In the meager hours between being wakefully perched on the precipice or actually engaged in vomiting, I slept. The exhaustion helped this along, but other than blissful unawareness, it never seemed to change my state.
Special pregnancy hard candies: Nope, just made the barf more flavorful.
LEMON.

I hate to complain about getting "what I wanted," but it was pretty extreme.

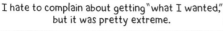

I've never thrown up harder in my life, and I've had food poisoning TWICE.

And this was at least once EVERY DAY. For SIX WEEKS.

That's at least forty-two pukes!

I frequently Googled "do I have hyperemesis gravidarum?"

This is when pregnancy sickness is so extreme that it often lasts all nine months and you have to be hospitalized.

When Lucy was in Egypt's land...

I tried to imagine a world where I could survive the better part of a year like this.

I also Googled "Are suspended animation pods a real thing I can do?"

And "Do animals get morning sickness?" (Answer: No, not really, because the ones who did DIED.)

See you in eight months!

Oh noooooooooo....

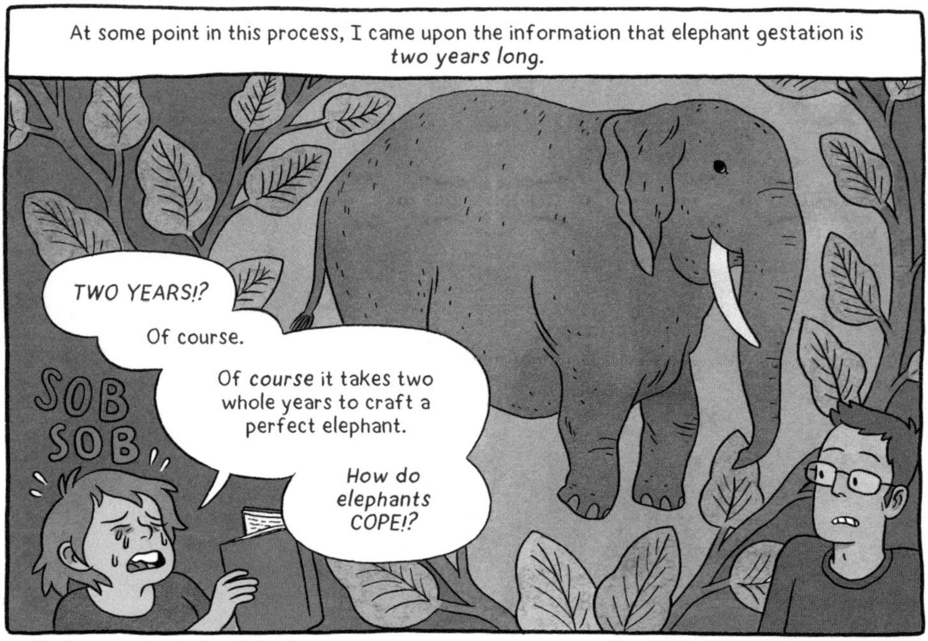
At some point in this process, I came upon the information that elephant gestation is *two years long.*
SOB SOB
TWO YEARS!?
Of course.
Of *course* it takes two whole years to craft a perfect elephant.
How do elephants COPE!?

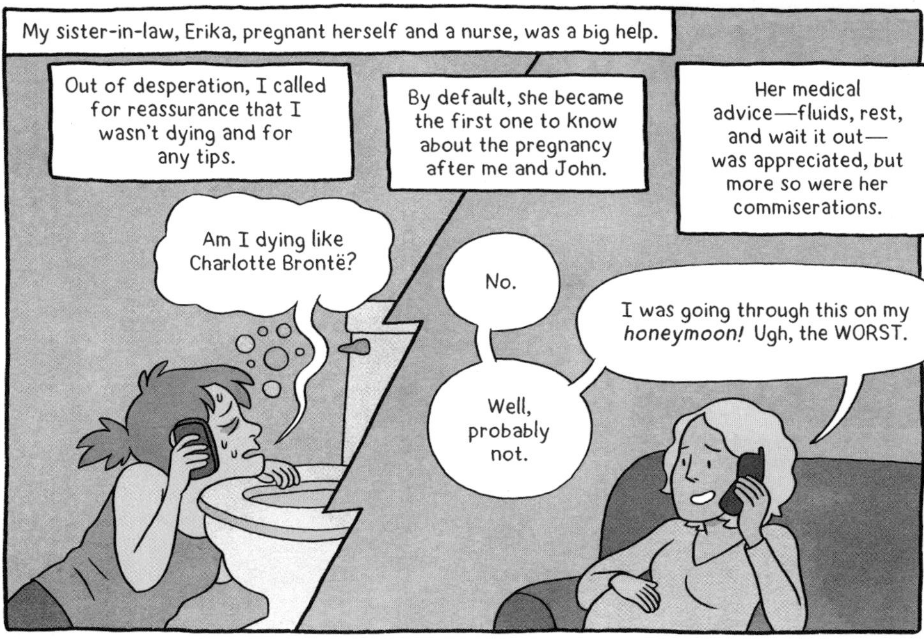
My sister-in-law, Erika, pregnant herself and a nurse, was a big help.
Out of desperation, I called for reassurance that I wasn't dying and for any tips.
By default, she became the first one to know about the pregnancy after me and John.
Her medical advice—fluids, rest, and wait it out—was appreciated, but more so were her commiserations.
Am I dying like Charlotte Brontë?
No.
Well, probably not.
I was going through this on my *honeymoon!* Ugh, the WORST.

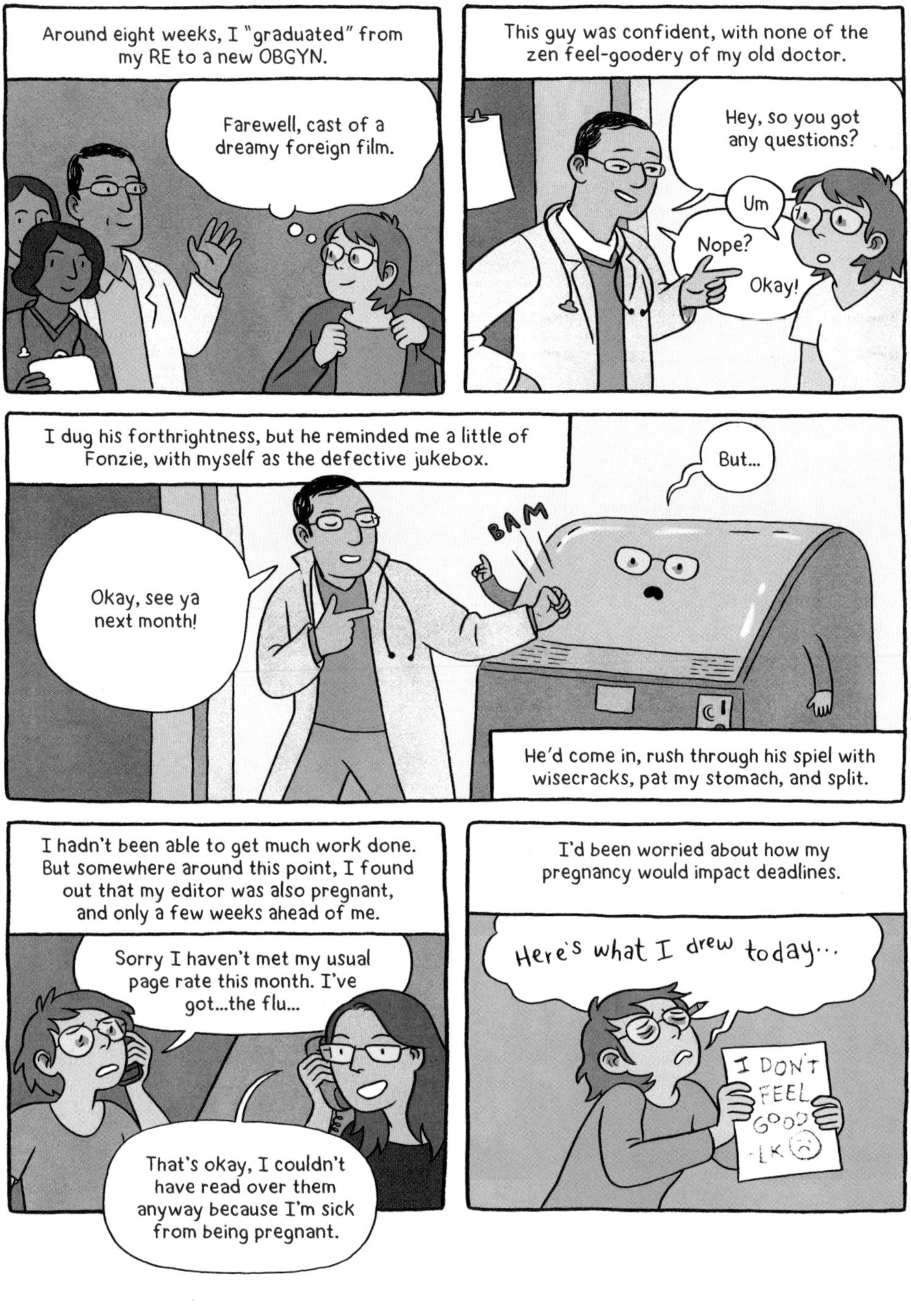
Around eight weeks, I "graduated" from my RE to a new OBGYN.
Farewell, cast of a dreamy foreign film.
This guy was confident, with none of the zen feel-goodery of my old doctor.
Hey, so you got any questions?
Um
Nope?
Okay!
I dug his forthrightness, but he reminded me a little of Fonzie, with myself as the defective jukebox.
Okay, see ya next month!
BAM
But...
He'd come in, rush through his spiel with wisecracks, pat my stomach, and split.
I hadn't been able to get much work done. But somewhere around this point, I found out that my editor was also pregnant, and only a few weeks ahead of me.
Sorry I haven't met my usual page rate this month. I've got...the flu...
That's okay, I couldn't have read over them anyway because I'm sick from being pregnant.
I'd been worried about how my pregnancy would impact deadlines.
Here's what I drew today...
I DON'T FEEL GOOD -LK

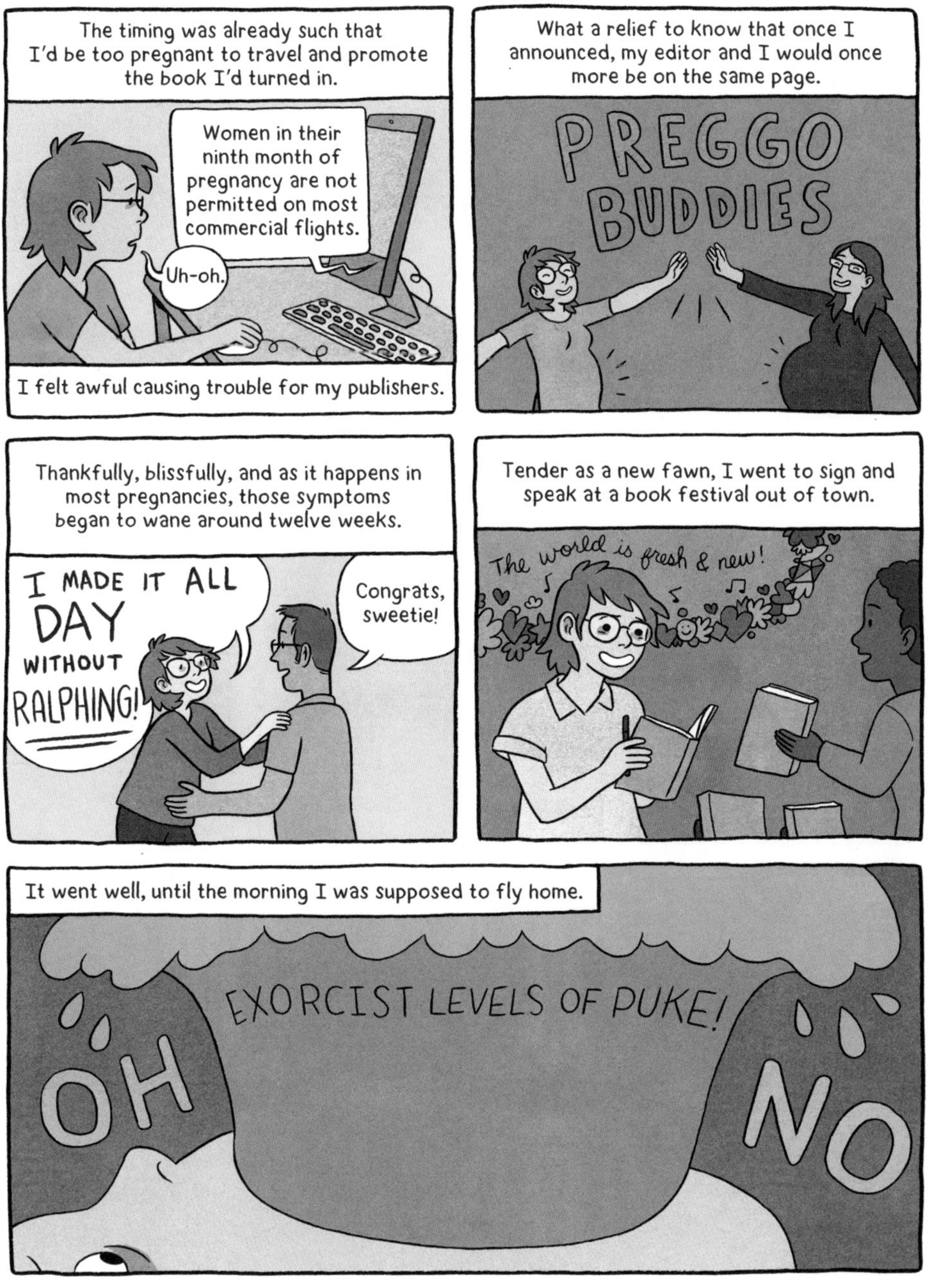
The timing was already such that I'd be too pregnant to travel and promote the book I'd turned in.
Women in their ninth month of pregnancy are not permitted on most commercial flights.
Uh-oh.
I felt awful causing trouble for my publishers.
What a relief to know that once I announced, my editor and I would once more be on the same page.
PREGGO BUDDIES
Thankfully, blissfully, and as it happens in most pregnancies, those symptoms began to wane around twelve weeks.
I MADE IT ALL DAY WITHOUT RALPHING!
Congrats, sweetie!
Tender as a new fawn, I went to sign and speak at a book festival out of town.
The world is fresh & new!
It went well, until the morning I was supposed to fly home.
EXORCIST LEVELS OF PUKE!
OH
NO

There is frequently a hormone surge right around twelve weeks that causes an uptick in nausea, right before it fully dissipates.

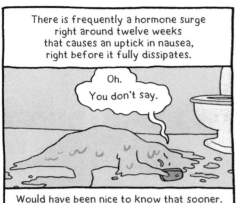

Oh.
You don't say.

Would have been nice to know that sooner.

I called the airline from the bathroom floor.

Oh, not to worry, we can put you on a flight a few hours later.

Otherwise, you'll have to pay the rescheduling fee.

Okay.

I made it to the airport in a cab thanks to sheer dint of will and a plastic bag.

PANT PANT

It's $50 if you vomit in my cab.

I made it through security without being flagged for bird flu.

I became intimately acquainted with the airport bathroom toilets outside my gate.

I have had better days.

Please let me board and don't suspect I am suffering the results of a bioterrorism superbug!

green, sweaty skin

vomit splash on glasses

Hello yes Chicago please thank you bye

Don't yak
Don't yak
Don't yak
Don't yak

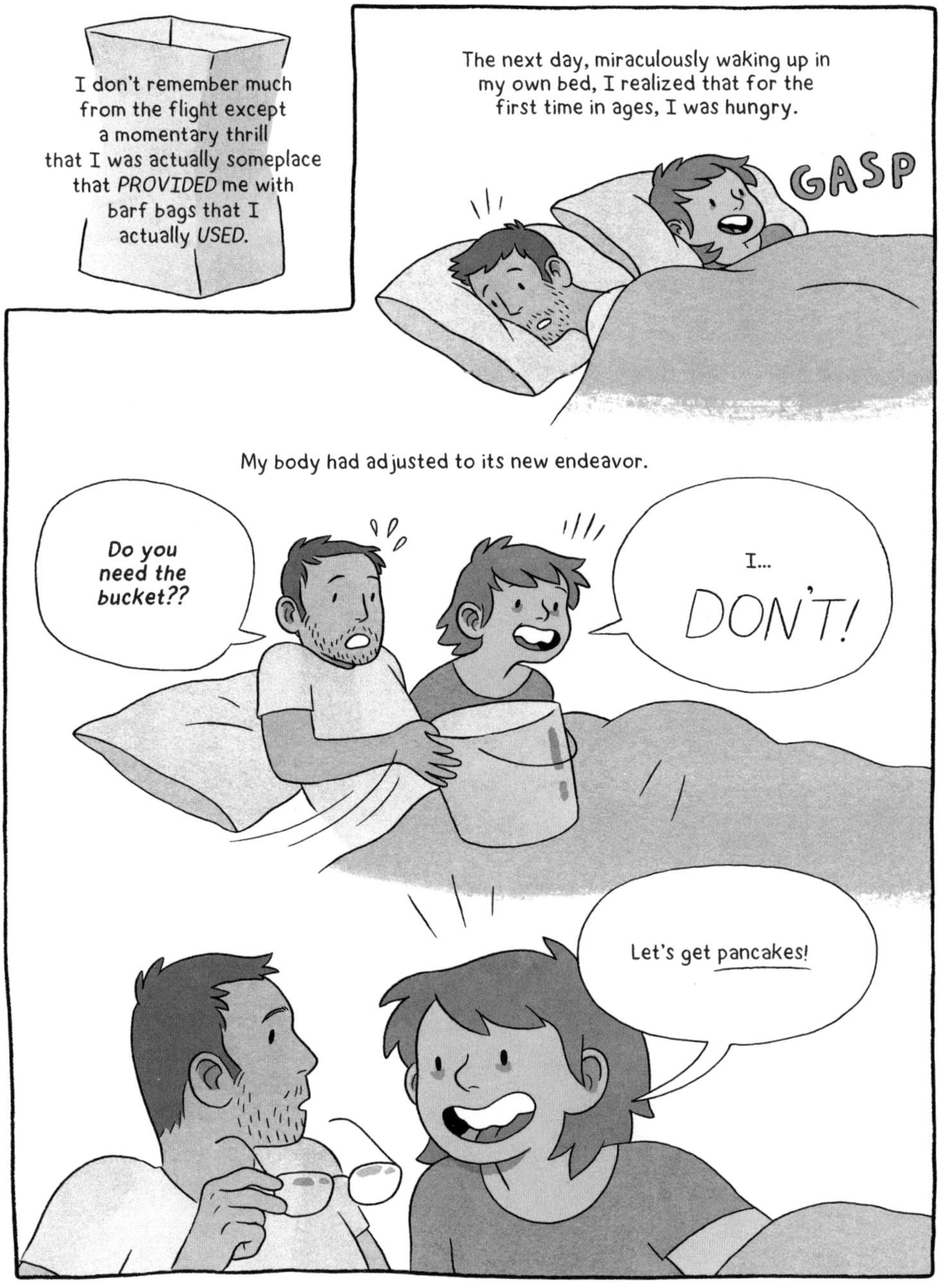
I don't remember much from the flight except a momentary thrill that I was actually someplace that *PROVIDED* me with barf bags that I actually *USED*.
The next day, miraculously waking up in my own bed, I realized that for the first time in ages, I was hungry.
GASP
My body had adjusted to its new endeavor.
Do you need the bucket??
I... DON'T!
Let's get pancakes!

LET'S DO SOME PREGNANCY RESEARCH

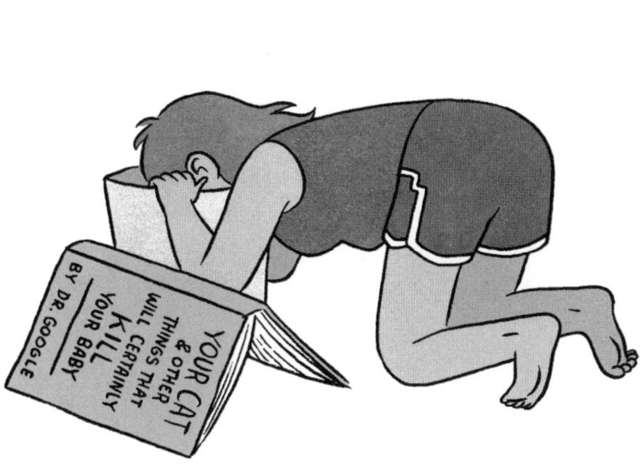
YOUR CAT
& OTHER
THINGS THAT
WILL CERTAINLY
KILL
YOUR BABY
BY DR. GOOGLE

PREGNANCY SUPERSTITIONS

We tend to look for things to believe in during periods of high uncertainty and when the outcome is of huge importance.

Erika Brady, Ph.D., a professor of folk studies at Western Kentucky University

A FEW FAVORITES

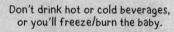

Don't look at the moon, or the baby will be a lunatic or sleepwalker. Carry a key to protect the baby.

Don't drink hot or cold beverages, or you'll freeze/burn the baby.

Brrrrrr!

You should never raise your arms above your head, because it strangles the baby.

GAK!

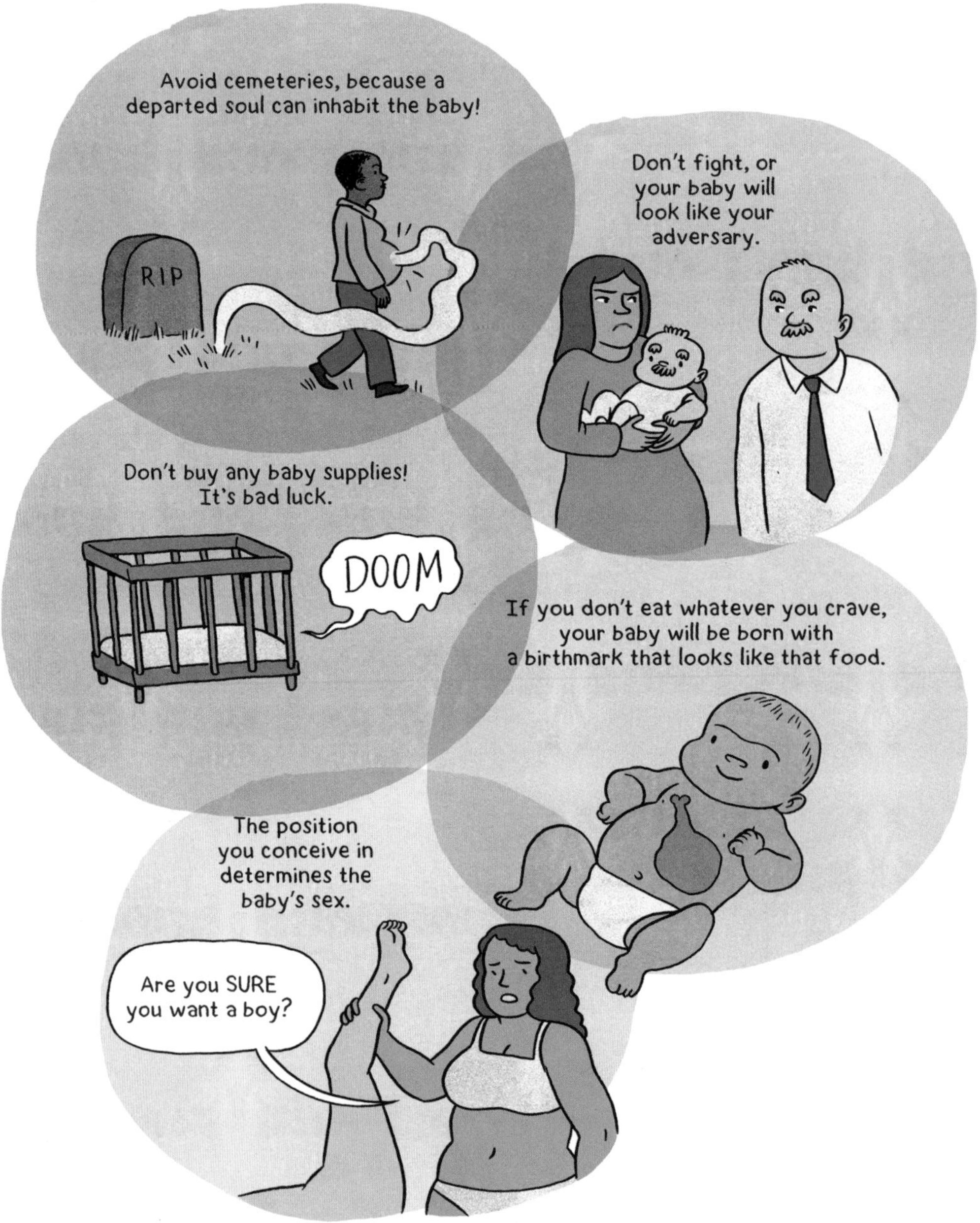
Avoid cemeteries, because a departed soul can inhabit the baby!
RIP
Don't fight, or your baby will look like your adversary.
Don't buy any baby supplies! It's bad luck.
DOOM
If you don't eat whatever you crave, your baby will be born with a birthmark that looks like that food.
The position you conceive in determines the baby's sex.
Are you SURE you want a boy?

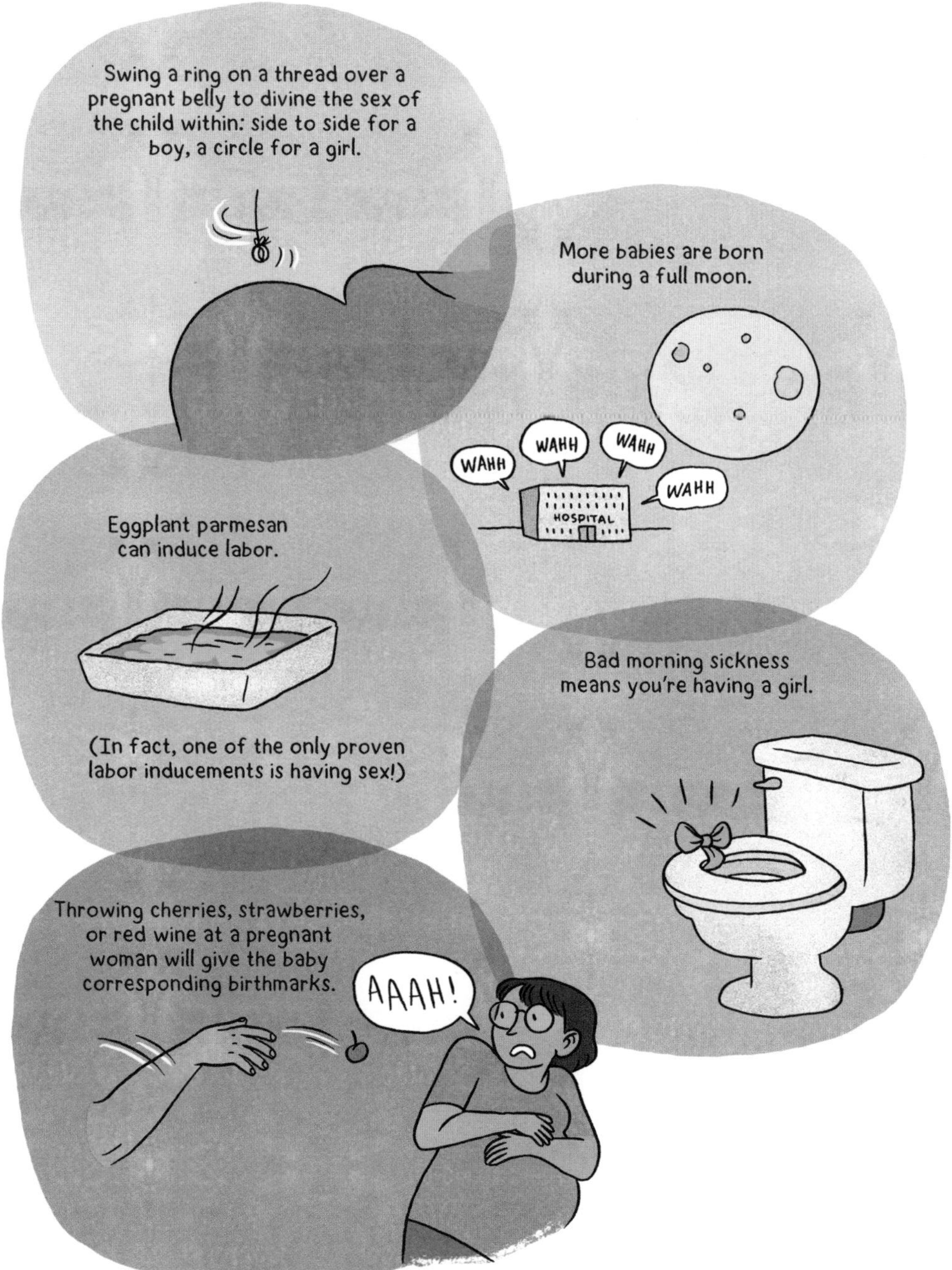
Swing a ring on a thread over a pregnant belly to divine the sex of the child within: side to side for a boy, a circle for a girl.
More babies are born during a full moon.
WAHH
WAHH
WAHH
WAHH
HOSPITAL
Eggplant parmesan can induce labor.
(In fact, one of the only proven labor inducements is having sex!)
Bad morning sickness means you're having a girl.
Throwing cherries, strawberries, or red wine at a pregnant woman will give the baby corresponding birthmarks.
AAAH!

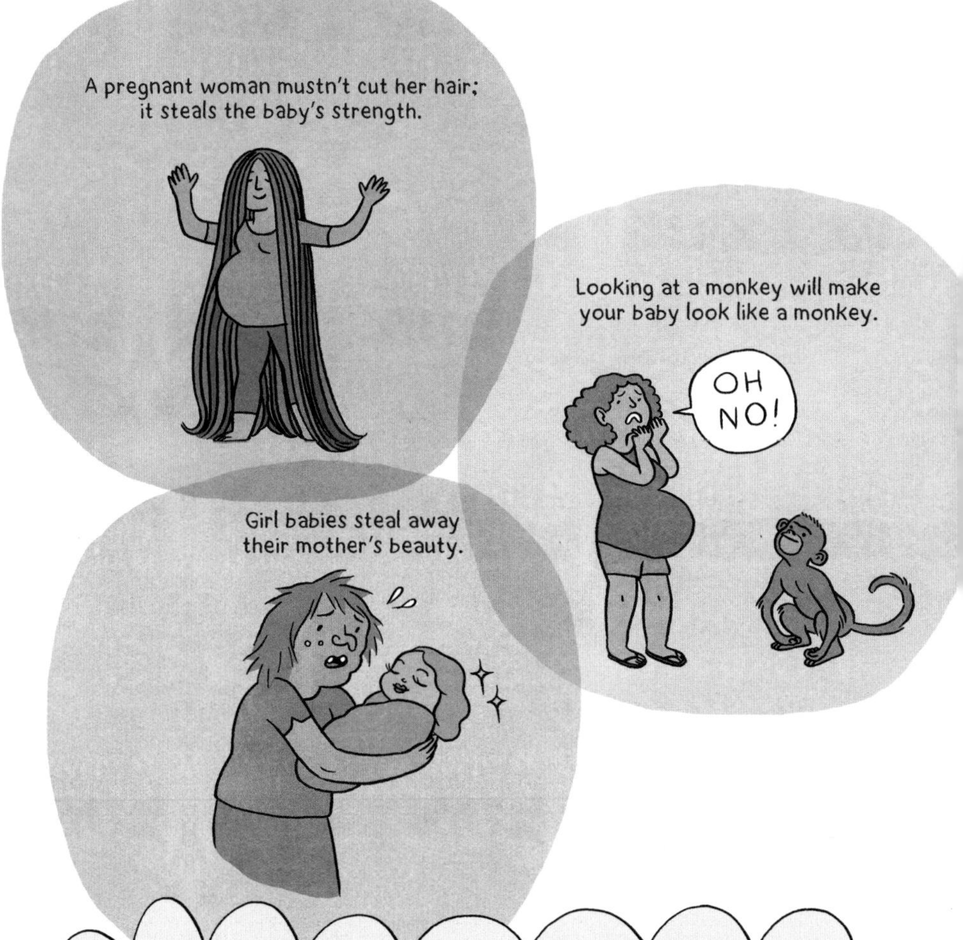
A pregnant woman mustn't cut her hair; it steals the baby's strength.
Looking at a monkey will make your baby look like a monkey.
OH NO!
Girl babies steal away their mother's beauty.

GOOD NEWS, PREGGOS, NONE OF THIS STUFF IS TRUE

But believe whatever you'd like if it helps you get through the slog!

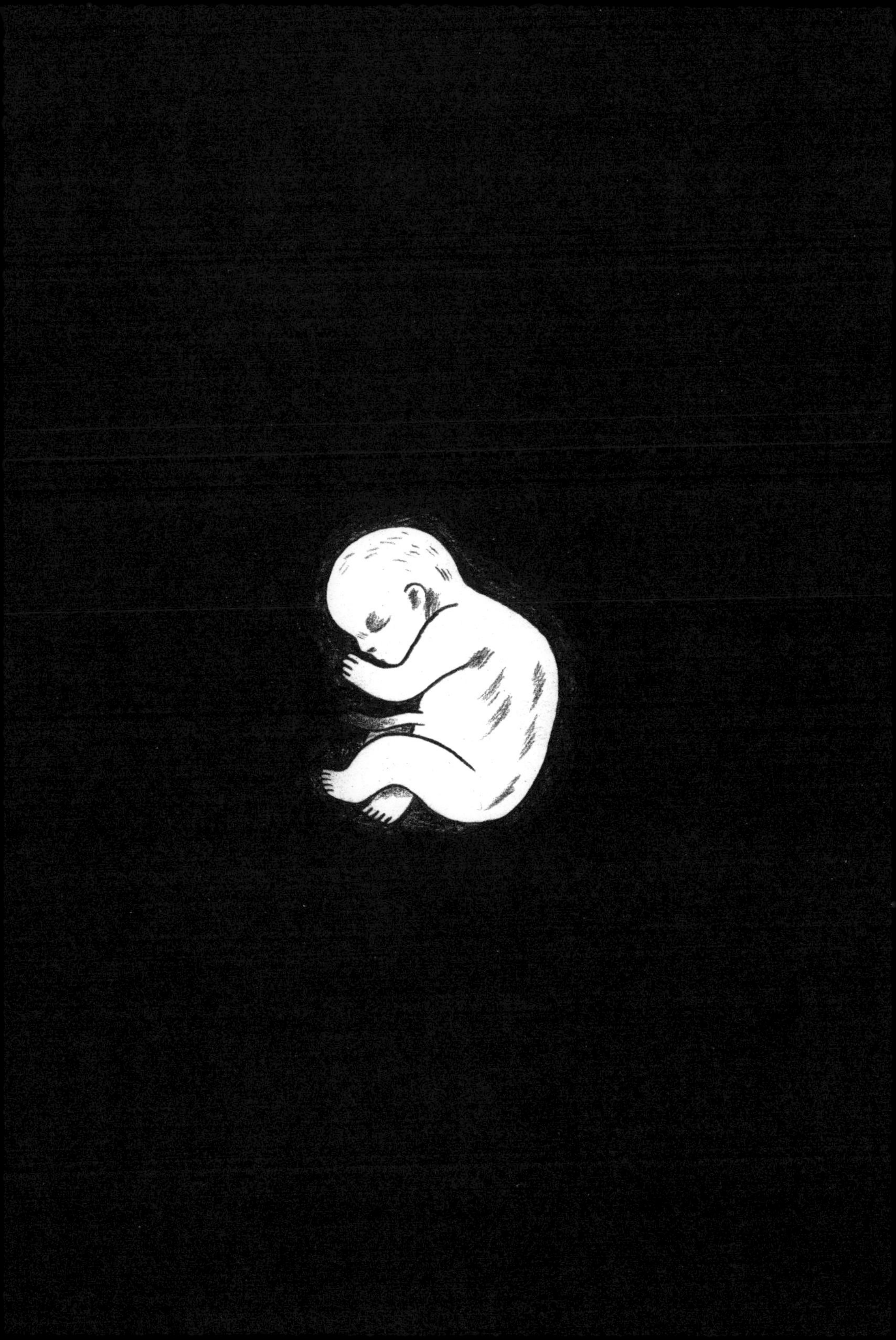

THE SLEEPY SECOND

Now that my long first-trimester hangover had abated, I felt like I'd come back to life.

Pancakesss

Welcome back, sweetie!

We drove up to Milwaukee to visit John's sister and her husband, Greg, and help them put together their nursery.

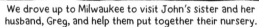

John's parents were there, too, for the big crib assembly.

Erika was about six months along at that point.

John pulled an ultrasound photo from under their coffee table.

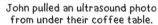

Hey, look!

Is this one of yours?

No?

Whose could it be, then?

It was ours.

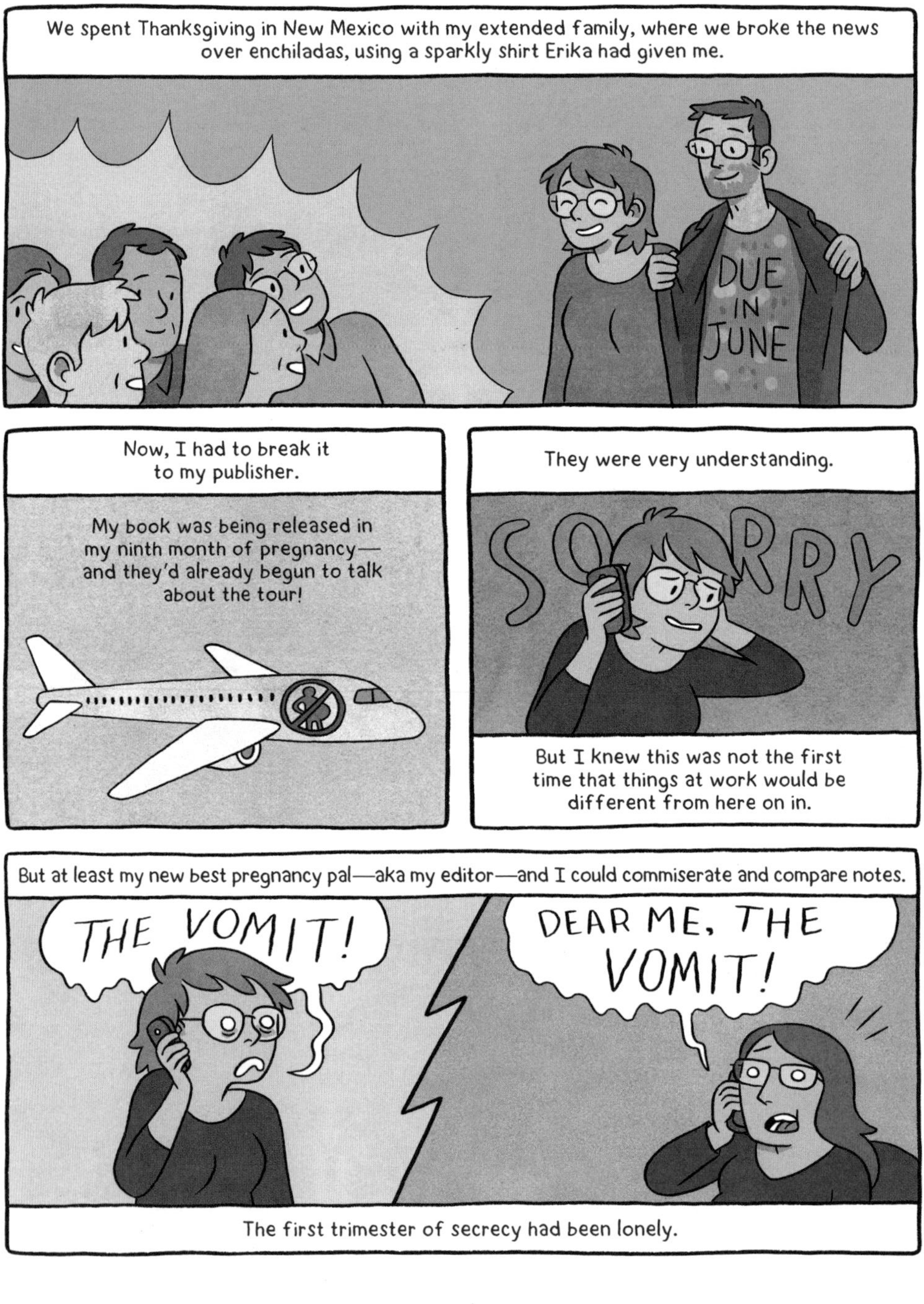
We spent Thanksgiving in New Mexico with my extended family, where we broke the news over enchiladas, using a sparkly shirt Erika had given me.
DUE IN JUNE
Now, I had to break it to my publisher.
My book was being released in my ninth month of pregnancy—and they'd already begun to talk about the tour!
They were very understanding.
SORRY
But I knew this was not the first time that things at work would be different from here on in.
But at least my new best pregnancy pal—aka my editor—and I could commiserate and compare notes.
THE VOMIT!
DEAR ME, THE VOMIT!
The first trimester of secrecy had been lonely.

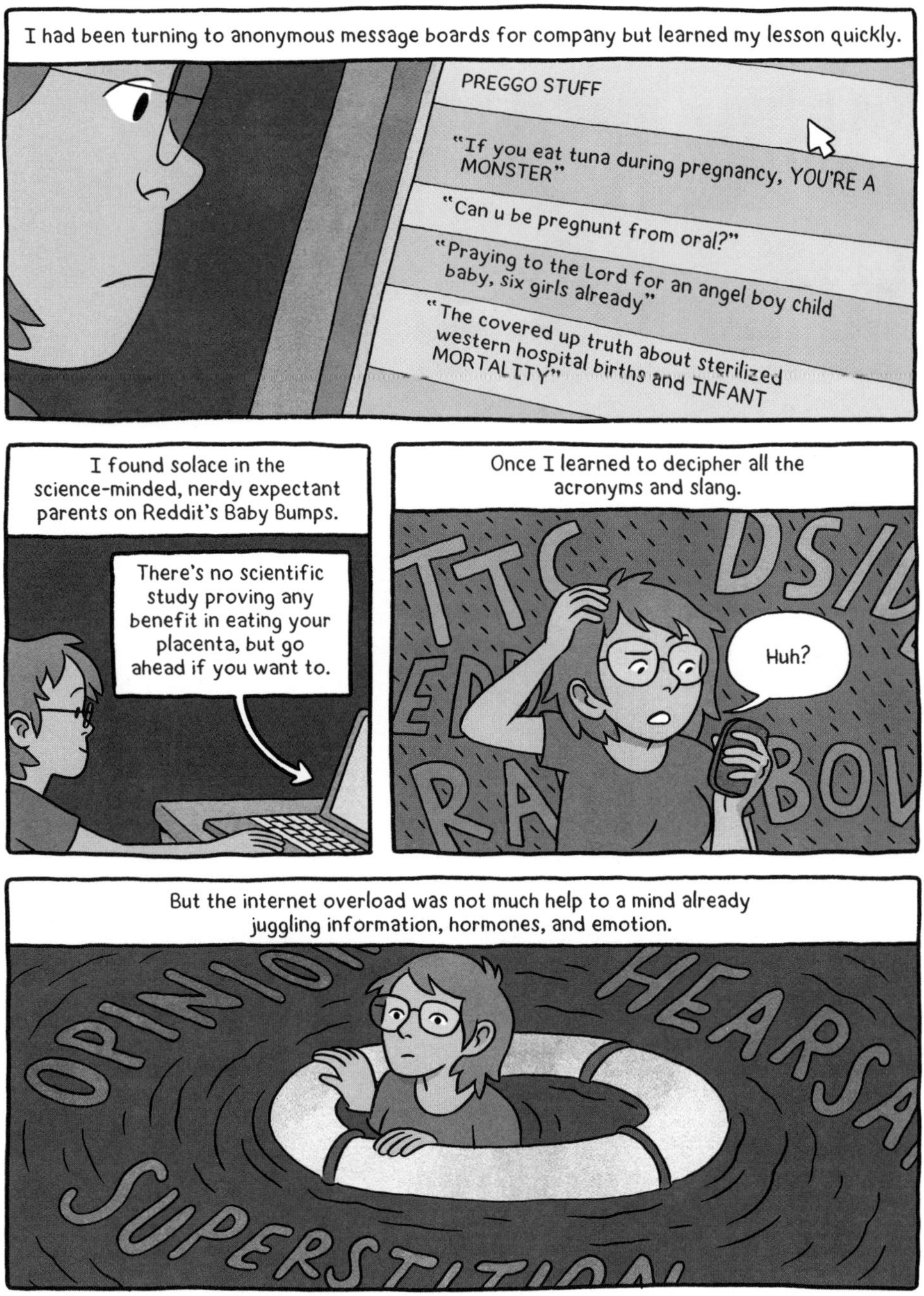
I had been turning to anonymous message boards for company but learned my lesson quickly.
PREGGO STUFF
"If you eat tuna during pregnancy, YOU'RE A MONSTER"
"Can u be pregnunt from oral?"
"Praying to the Lord for an angel boy child baby, six girls already"
"The covered up truth about sterilized western hospital births and INFANT MORTALITY"
I found solace in the science-minded, nerdy expectant parents on Reddit's Baby Bumps.
There's no scientific study proving any benefit in eating your placenta, but go ahead if you want to.
Once I learned to decipher all the acronyms and slang.
TTC
Huh?
But the internet overload was not much help to a mind already juggling information, hormones, and emotion.

A little before Christmas, and two weeks early, our niece, Hazel, was born.

She wore a tiny vest with bilirubin lights to help with a touch of jaundice.

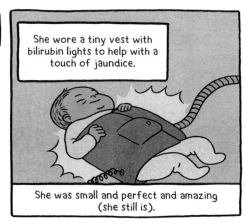

She was small and perfect and amazing (she still is).

I'd never been an aunt before and was surprised by how totally devoted I felt from the get-go.

PERFECT♥NIECE

But she was colicky. She cried for hours every day.

Erika developed recurrent bouts of mastitis* that nearly hospitalized her.

She and Greg were tired and sick and stressed out all the time.

UH-OH.

*A painful infection of the breast tissue, typically the result of blocked milk ducts.

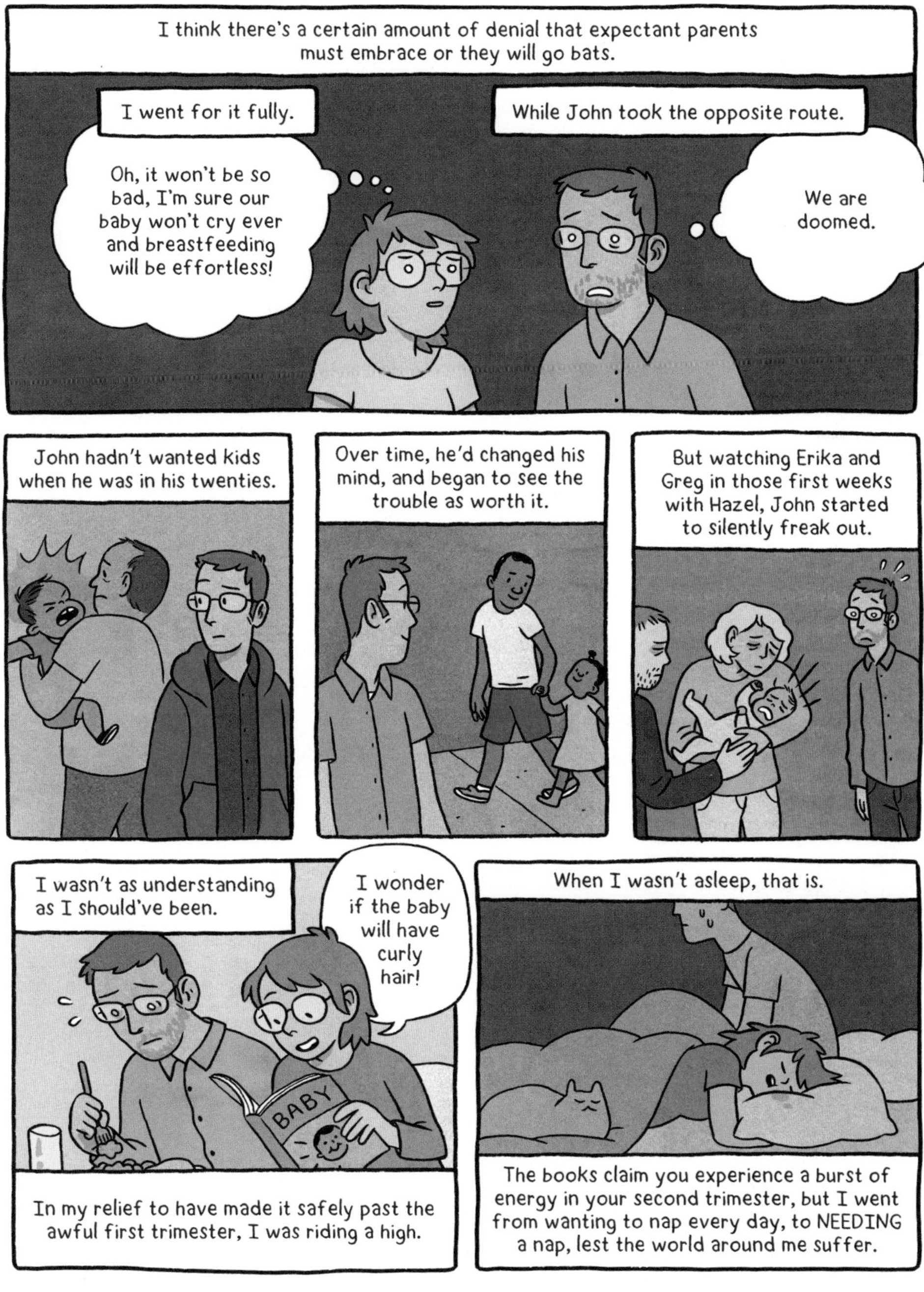

I think there's a certain amount of denial that expectant parents must embrace or they will go bats.
I went for it fully.
Oh, it won't be so bad, I'm sure our baby won't cry ever and breastfeeding will be effortless!
While John took the opposite route.
We are doomed.
John hadn't wanted kids when he was in his twenties.
Over time, he'd changed his mind, and began to see the trouble as worth it.
But watching Erika and Greg in those first weeks with Hazel, John started to silently freak out.
I wasn't as understanding as I should've been.
I wonder if the baby will have curly hair!
BABY
In my relief to have made it safely past the awful first trimester, I was riding a high.
When I wasn't asleep, that is.
The books claim you experience a burst of energy in your second trimester, but I went from wanting to nap every day, to NEEDING a nap, lest the world around me suffer.

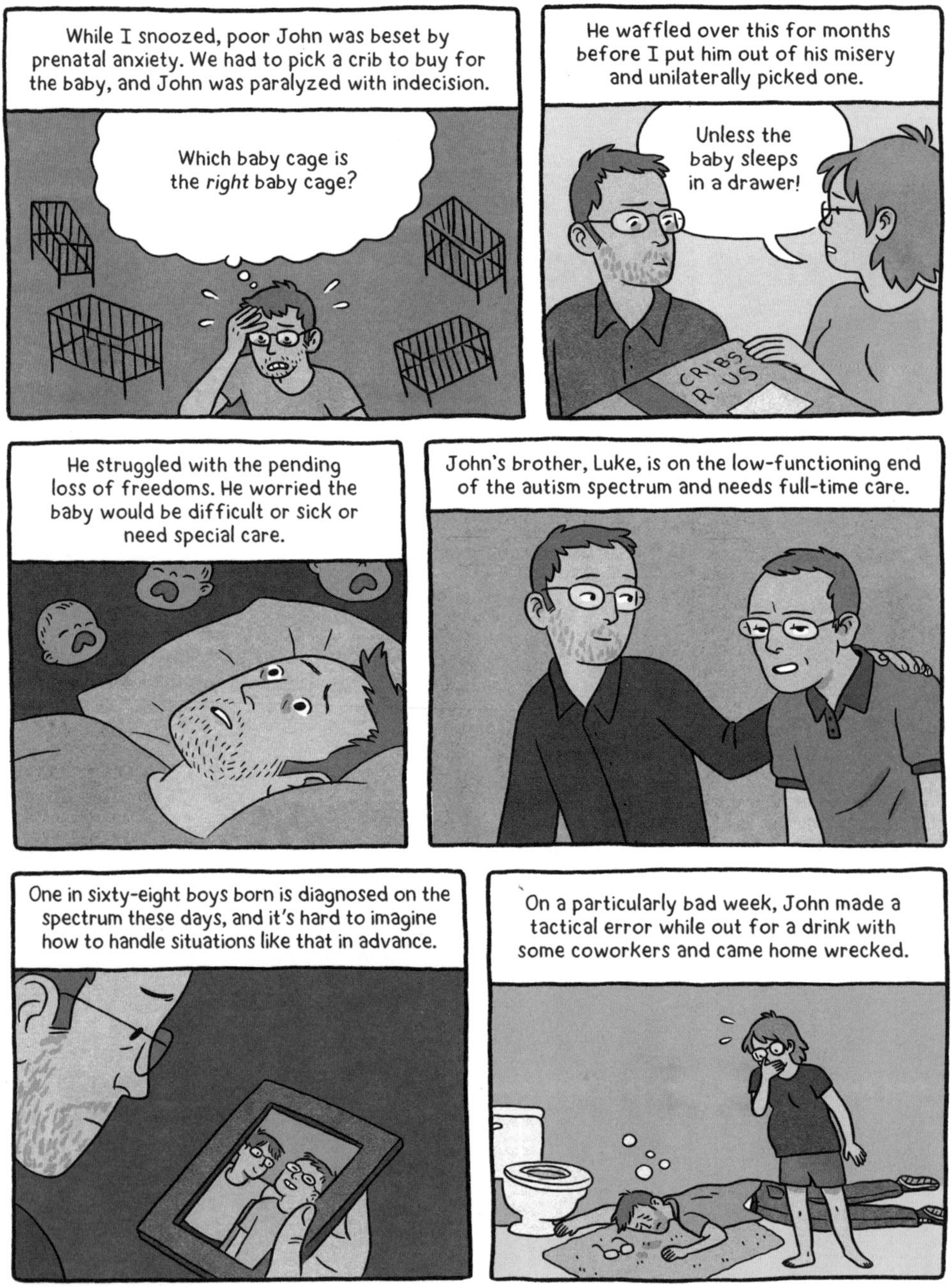
While I snoozed, poor John was beset by prenatal anxiety. We had to pick a crib to buy for the baby, and John was paralyzed with indecision.
Which baby cage is the *right* baby cage?
He waffled over this for months before I put him out of his misery and unilaterally picked one.
Unless the baby sleeps in a drawer!
CRIBS R-US
He struggled with the pending loss of freedoms. He worried the baby would be difficult or sick or need special care.
John's brother, Luke, is on the low-functioning end of the autism spectrum and needs full-time care.
One in sixty-eight boys born is diagnosed on the spectrum these days, and it's hard to imagine how to handle situations like that in advance.
On a particularly bad week, John made a tactical error while out for a drink with some coworkers and came home wrecked.

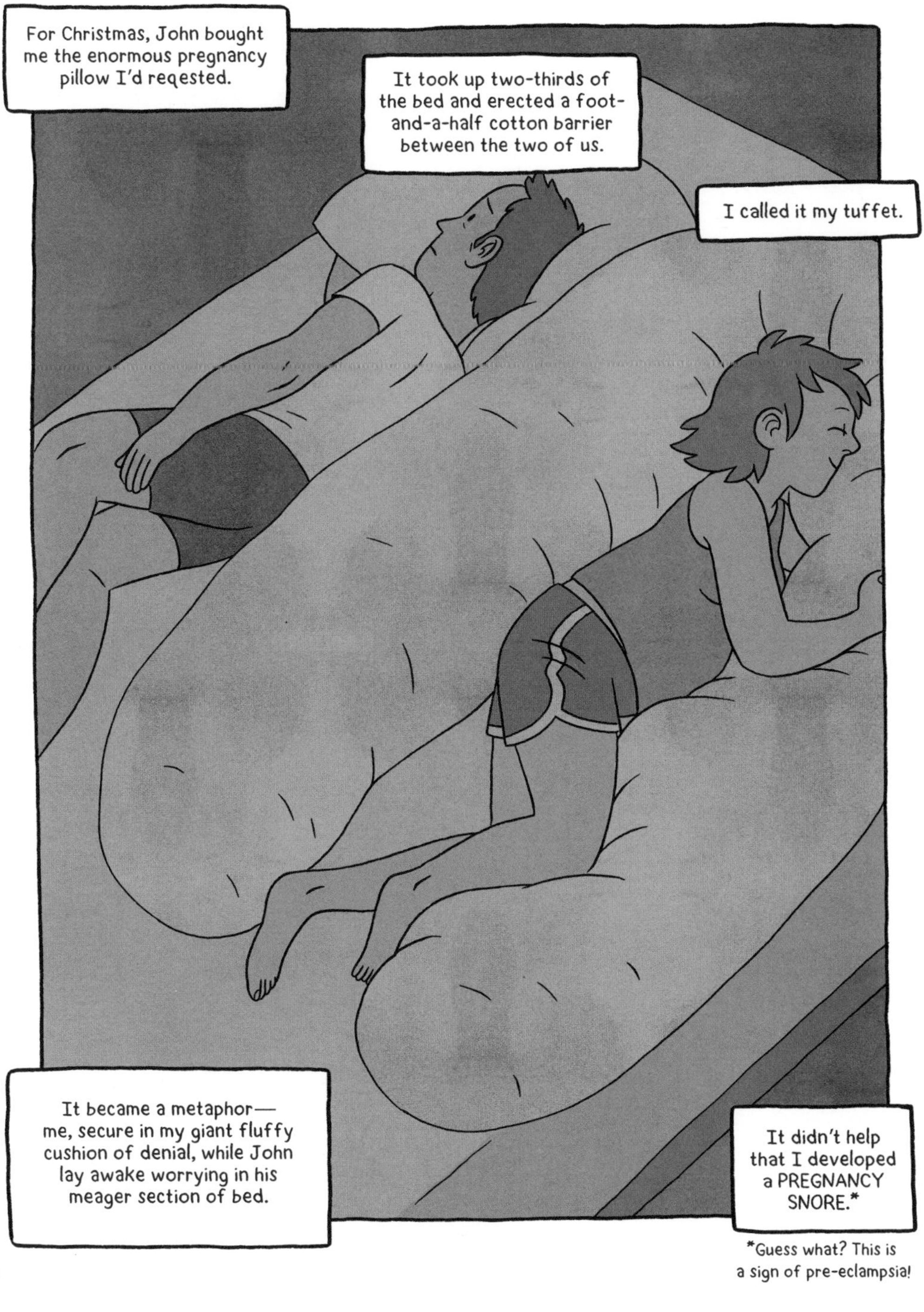
For Christmas, John bought me the enormous pregnancy pillow I'd reqested.
It took up two-thirds of the bed and erected a foot-and-a-half cotton barrier between the two of us.
I called it my tuffet.
It became a metaphor—me, secure in my giant fluffy cushion of denial, while John lay awake worrying in his meager section of bed.
It didn't help that I developed a PREGNANCY SNORE.*

*Guess what? This is a sign of pre-eclampsia!

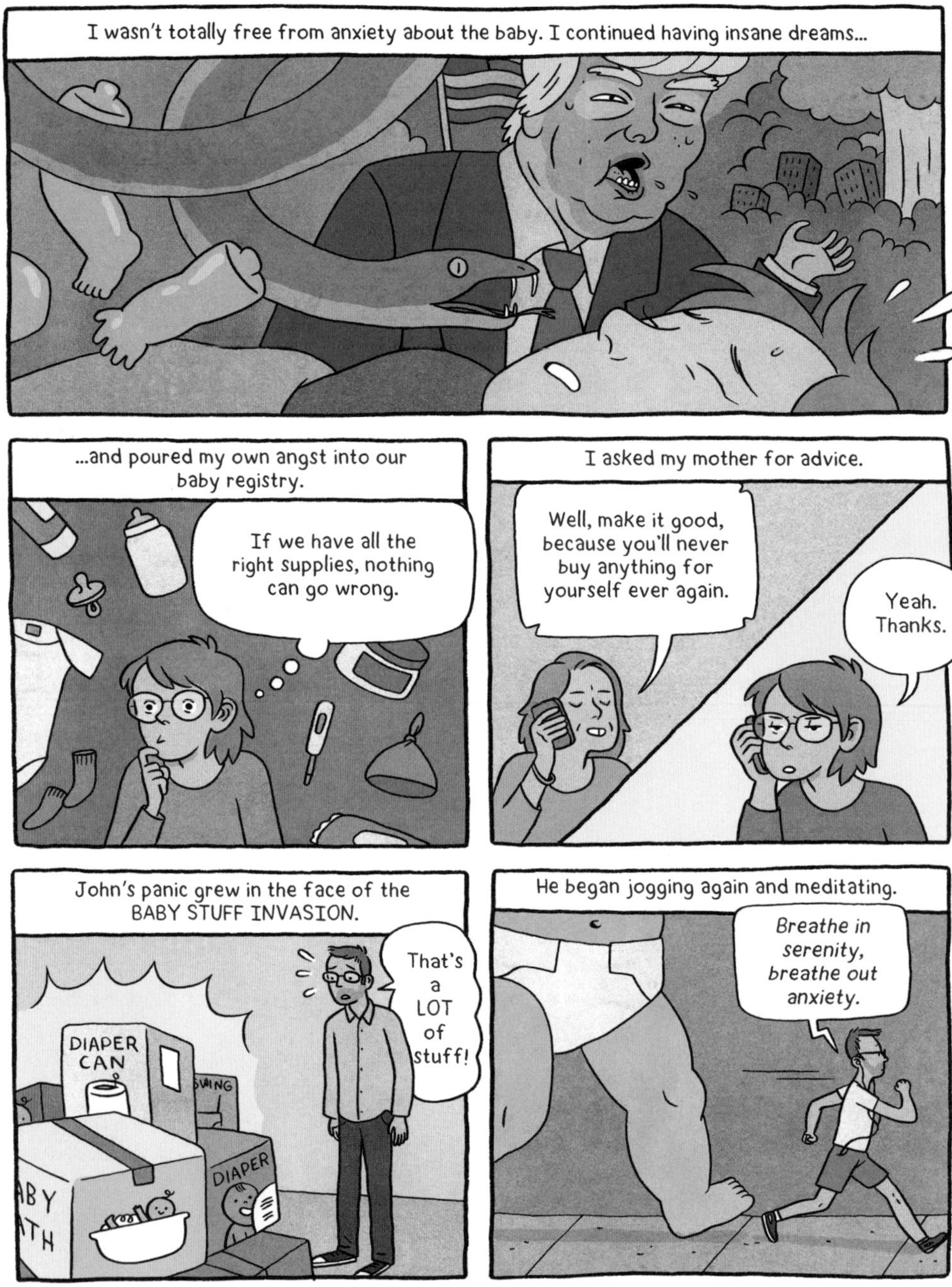
I wasn't totally free from anxiety about the baby. I continued having insane dreams...
...and poured my own angst into our baby registry.
If we have all the right supplies, nothing can go wrong.
I asked my mother for advice.
Well, make it good, because you'll never buy anything for yourself ever again.
Yeah. Thanks.
John's panic grew in the face of the BABY STUFF INVASION.
DIAPER CAN
DIAPER
That's a LOT of stuff!
He began jogging again and meditating.
Breathe in serenity, breathe out anxiety.

At our twenty-week ultrasound, we found out we were expecting a boy.

Well, he's not shy!

What?

You found out?!

Don't you want it to be a surprise??

No—having a kid was full of enough surprises for us already, thanks!

But is it a cat?

I can honestly say that the gender of my child makes no difference to me.

I'm perfectly happy to regard my child as their own little person, unhampered by gender norms.

And the sexist baby clothes really bum me out.

LADIES ♥ ME

But this discovery coincided with the Oscars.

And the WINNERS of EVERYTHING are a bunch of white guys who've dominated winning FOREVER!

I felt responsible to instill in my son the recognition and responsibility of his inherent privilege.

"If we do something over and over, it becomes normal. If we see the same thing over and over, it becomes normal."

CHIMAMANDA NGOZI ADICHIE
WE SHOULD ALL BE FEMINISTS

It was a lot to expect of a twenty-week fetus.

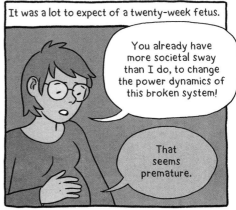

You already have more societal sway than I do, to change the power dynamics of this broken system!

That seems premature.

127

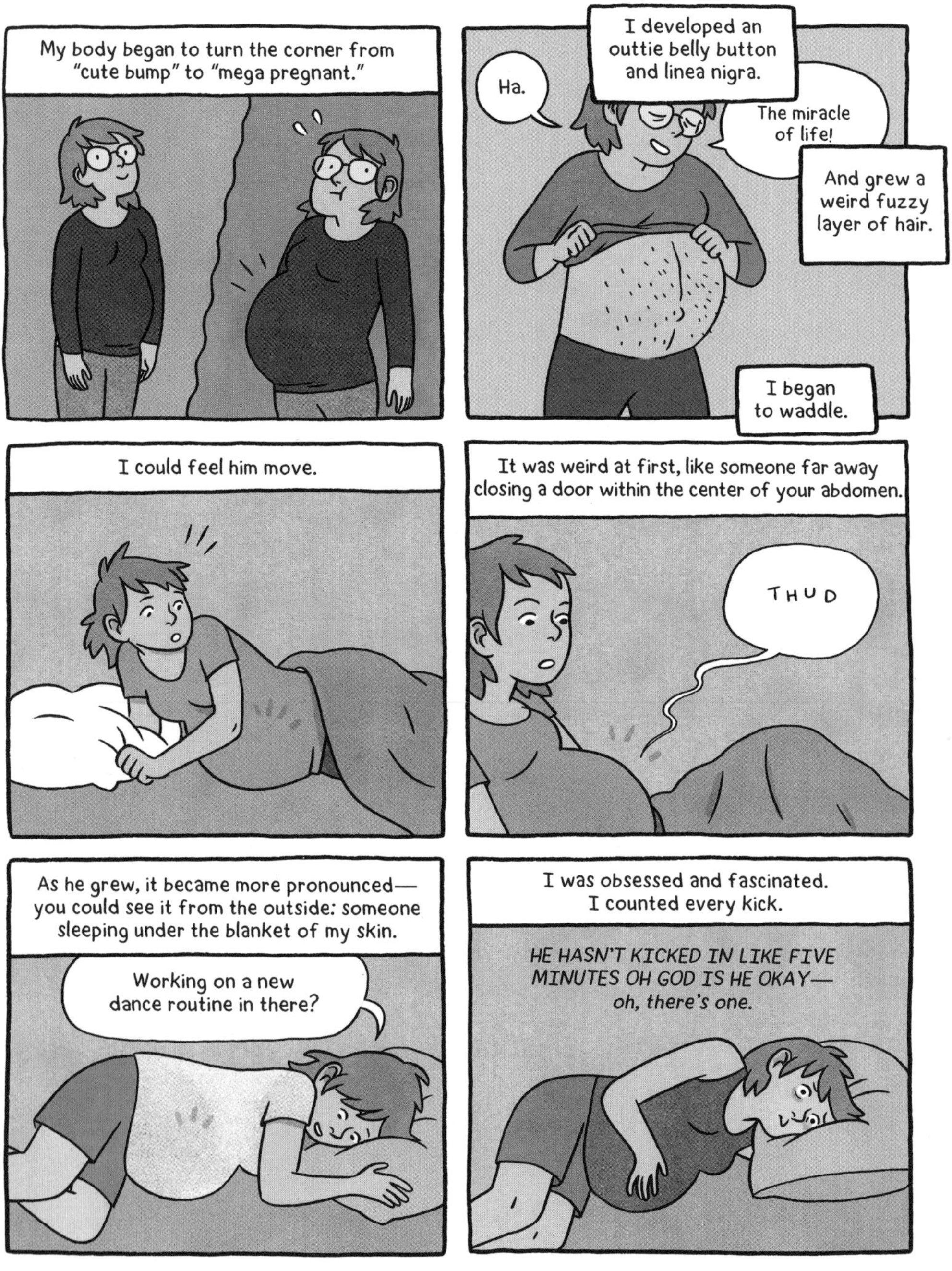
My body began to turn the corner from "cute bump" to "mega pregnant."
I developed an outtie belly button and linea nigra.
Ha.
The miracle of life!
And grew a weird fuzzy layer of hair.
I began to waddle.
I could feel him move.
It was weird at first, like someone far away closing a door within the center of your abdomen.
THUD
As he grew, it became more pronounced—you could see it from the outside: someone sleeping under the blanket of my skin.
Working on a new dance routine in there?
I was obsessed and fascinated. I counted every kick.
HE HASN'T KICKED IN LIKE FIVE MINUTES OH GOD IS HE OKAY—oh, there's one.

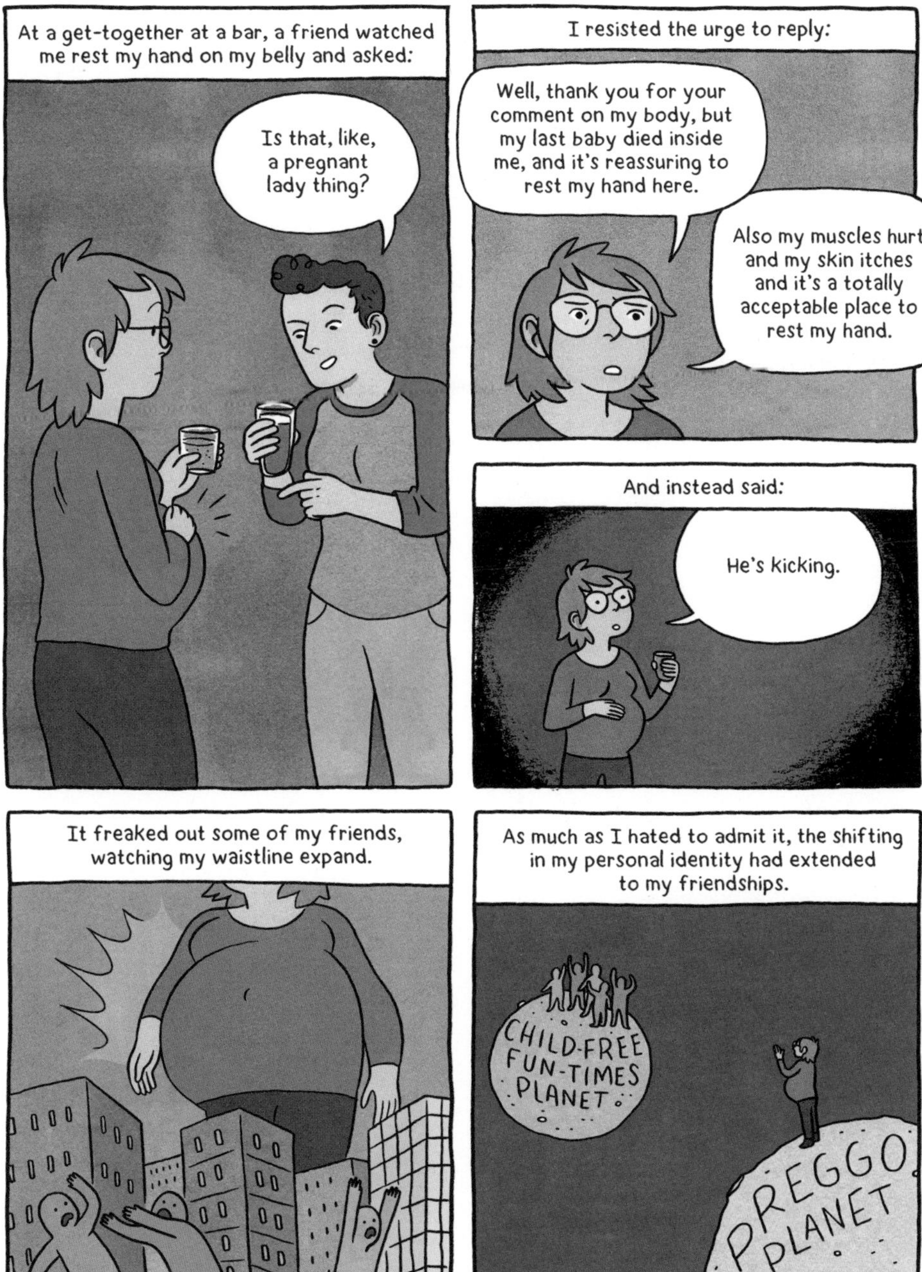
At a get-together at a bar, a friend watched me rest my hand on my belly and asked:
Is that, like, a pregnant lady thing?
I resisted the urge to reply:
Well, thank you for your comment on my body, but my last baby died inside me, and it's reassuring to rest my hand here.
Also my muscles hurt and my skin itches and it's a totally acceptable place to rest my hand.
And instead said:
He's kicking.
It freaked out some of my friends, watching my waistline expand.
As much as I hated to admit it, the shifting in my personal identity had extended to my friendships.
CHILD-FREE FUN-TIMES PLANET
PREGGO PLANET

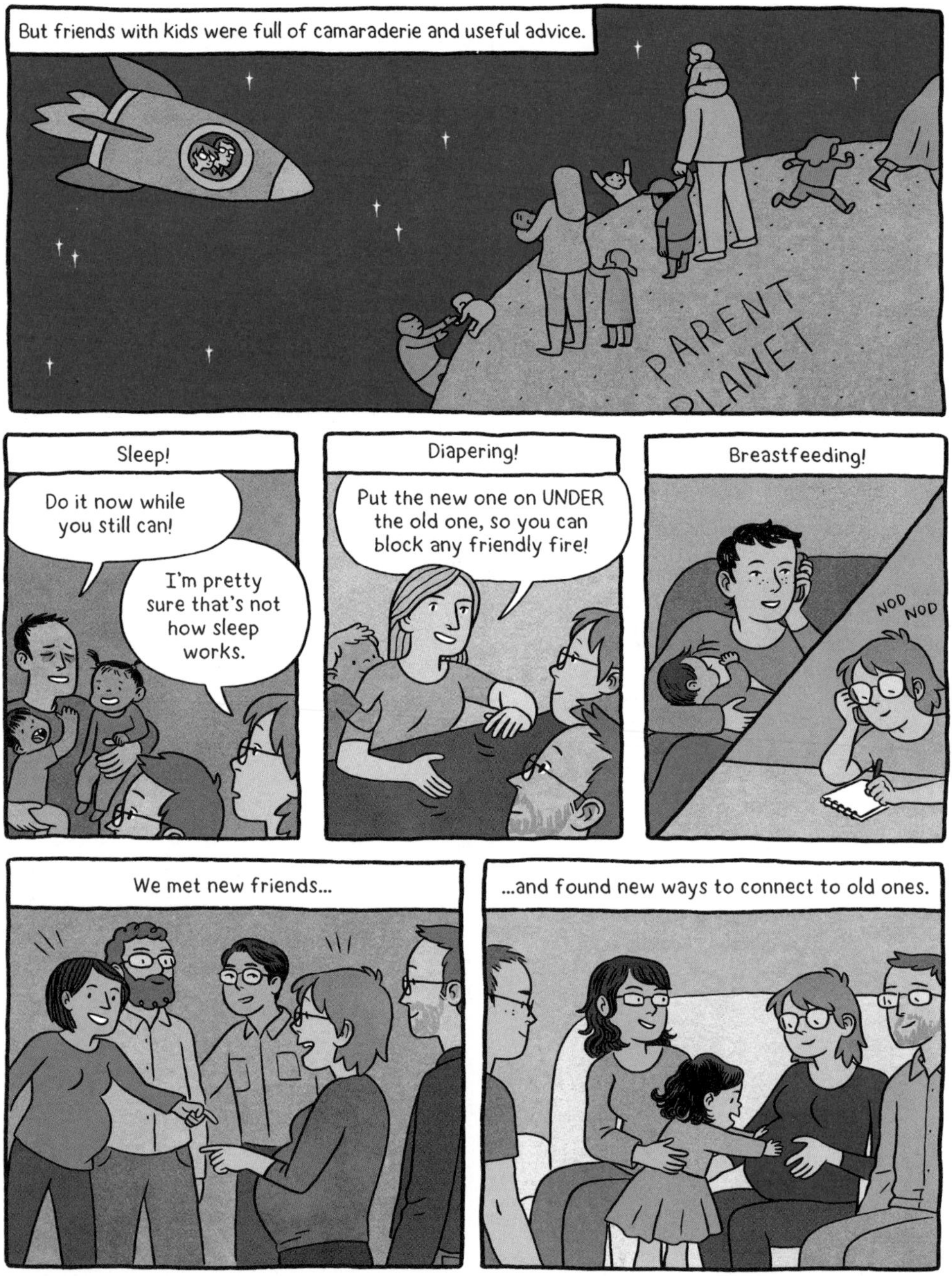
But friends with kids were full of camaraderie and useful advice.
PARENT PLANET
Sleep!
Do it now while you still can!
I'm pretty sure that's not how sleep works.
Diapering!
Put the new one on UNDER the old one, so you can block any friendly fire!
Breastfeeding!
NOD NOD
We met new friends...
...and found new ways to connect to old ones.

But not all advice for new parents is good.

Around this time, the CDC released a statement advising all women of childbearing age to avoid alcohol, lest one unwittingly harm an unrealized pregnancy.

Being pregnant, and visibly so, drove home the realization of how my body was seen as a commodity.

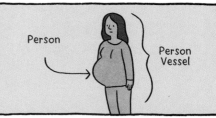

Person

Person Vessel

I was a vessel for the much more precious potential life I could bear, controlled by those who thought they Knew Better.

At the bus stop:

Aren't you worried about the Zika virus?

Well, sure, but—

STRANGER

Getting pregnant nowadays with all this Zika is child abuse!

At restaurants:

Can I have a sip of your beer?

Ma'am, should you be doing that?

I read stories on Baby Bumps about women being turned away from coffee shops for trying to order a latte...*

...or being ushered out the door of sushi restaurants.**

SHI

SLAM

*One cup of coffee a day is a totally acceptable amount of caffeine and won't harm the baby.
**As long as you're eating at a clean, reputable place, you probably won't get listeria from sushi.

131

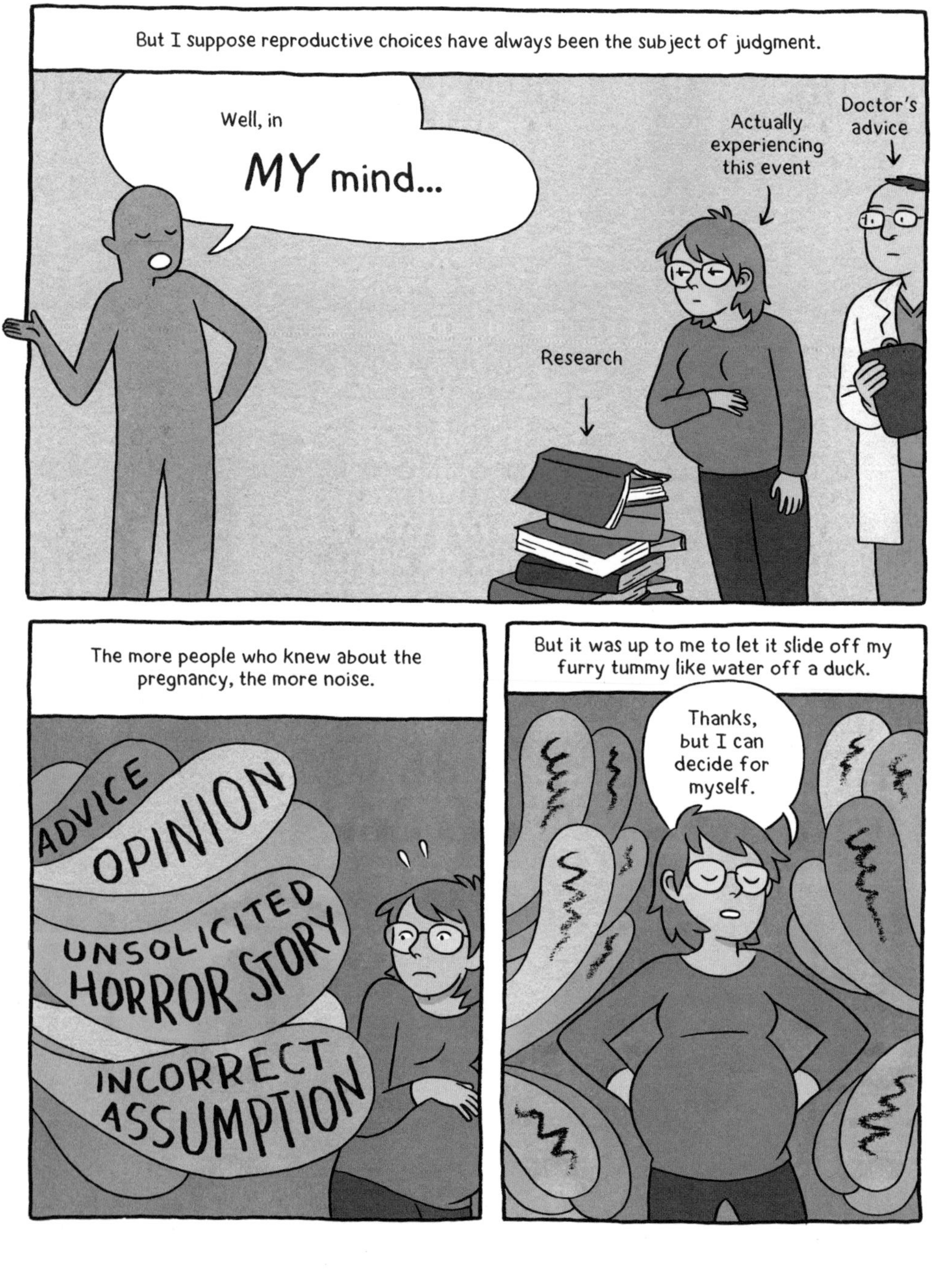
But I suppose reproductive choices have always been the subject of judgment.
Well, in MY mind...
Actually experiencing this event
Doctor's advice
Research
The more people who knew about the pregnancy, the more noise.
ADVICE
OPINION
UNSOLICITED HORROR STORY
INCORRECT ASSUMPTION
But it was up to me to let it slide off my furry tummy like water off a duck.
Thanks, but I can decide for myself.

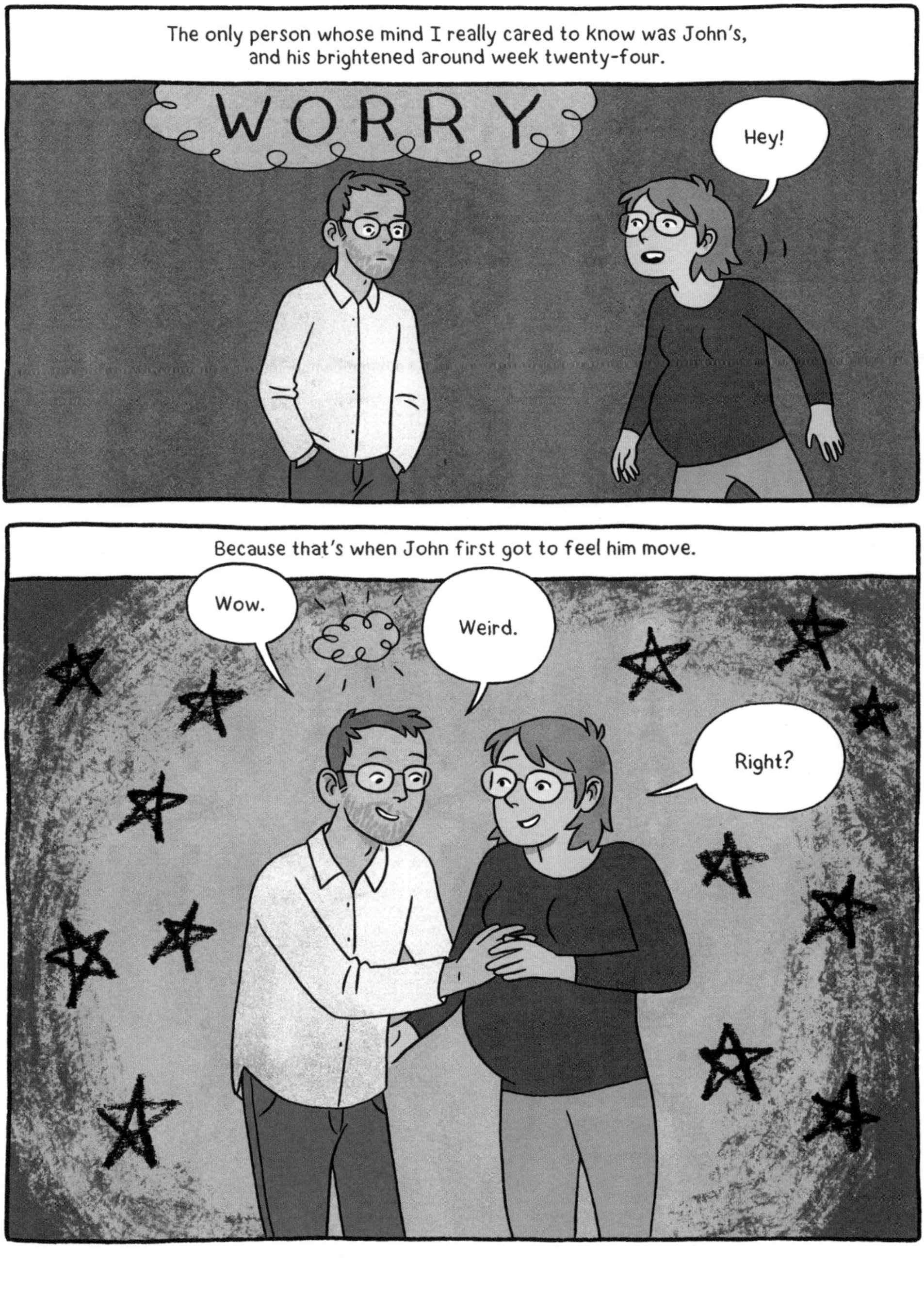
The only person whose mind I really cared to know was John's, and his brightened around week twenty-four.
WORRY
Hey!
Because that's when John first got to feel him move.
Wow.
Weird.
Right?

YIPPEE, IT'S PREGNANCY RESEARCH

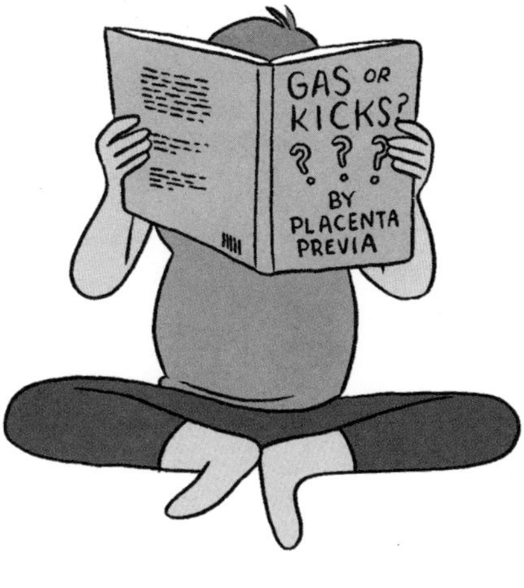
GAS OR KICKS?
???
BY PLACENTA PREVIA

NOT HAVING KIDS

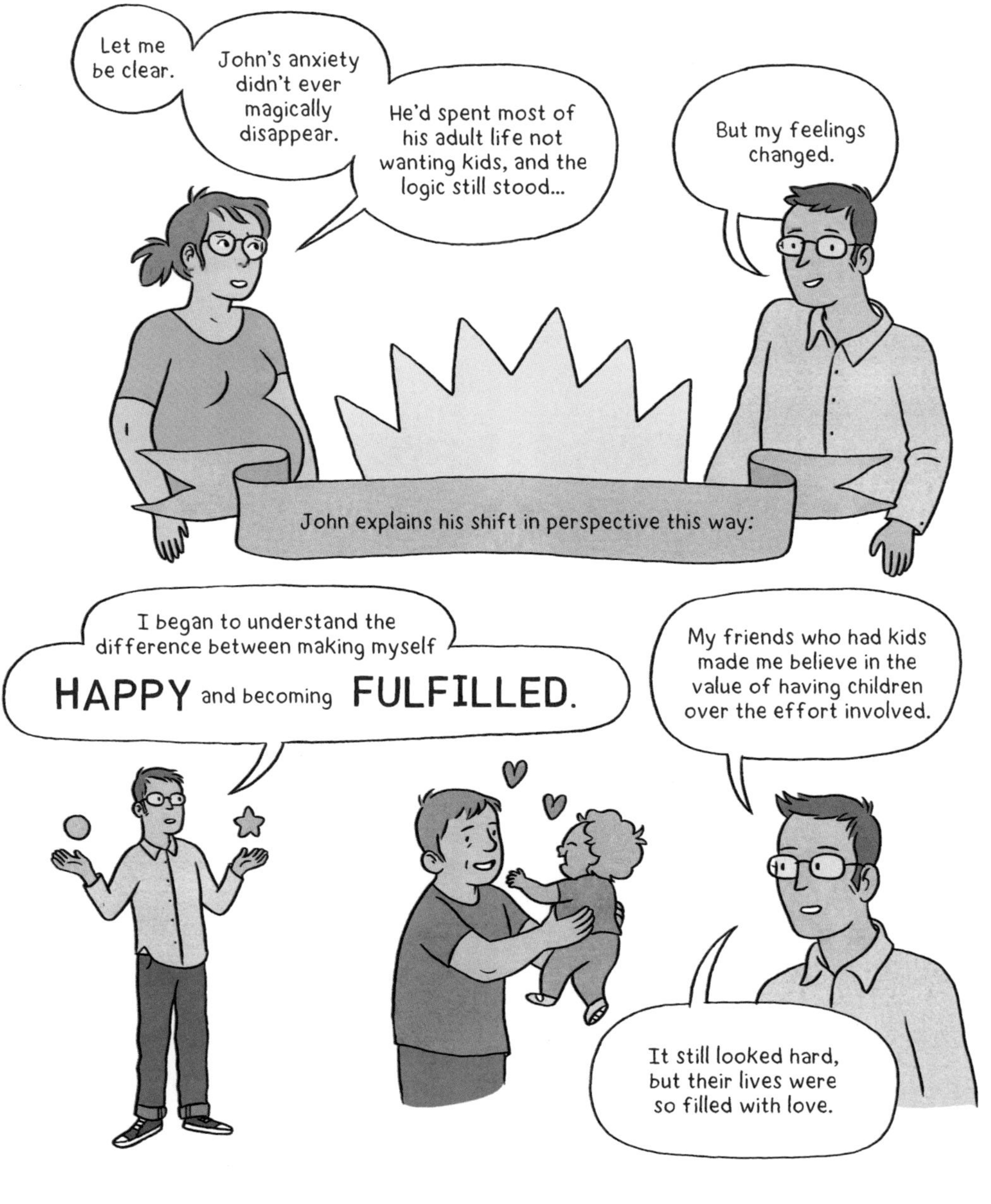
Let me be clear.
John's anxiety didn't ever magically disappear.
He'd spent most of his adult life not wanting kids, and the logic still stood...
But my feelings changed.
John explains his shift in perspective this way:
I began to understand the difference between making myself HAPPY and becoming FULFILLED.
My friends who had kids made me believe in the value of having children over the effort involved.
It still looked hard, but their lives were so filled with love.

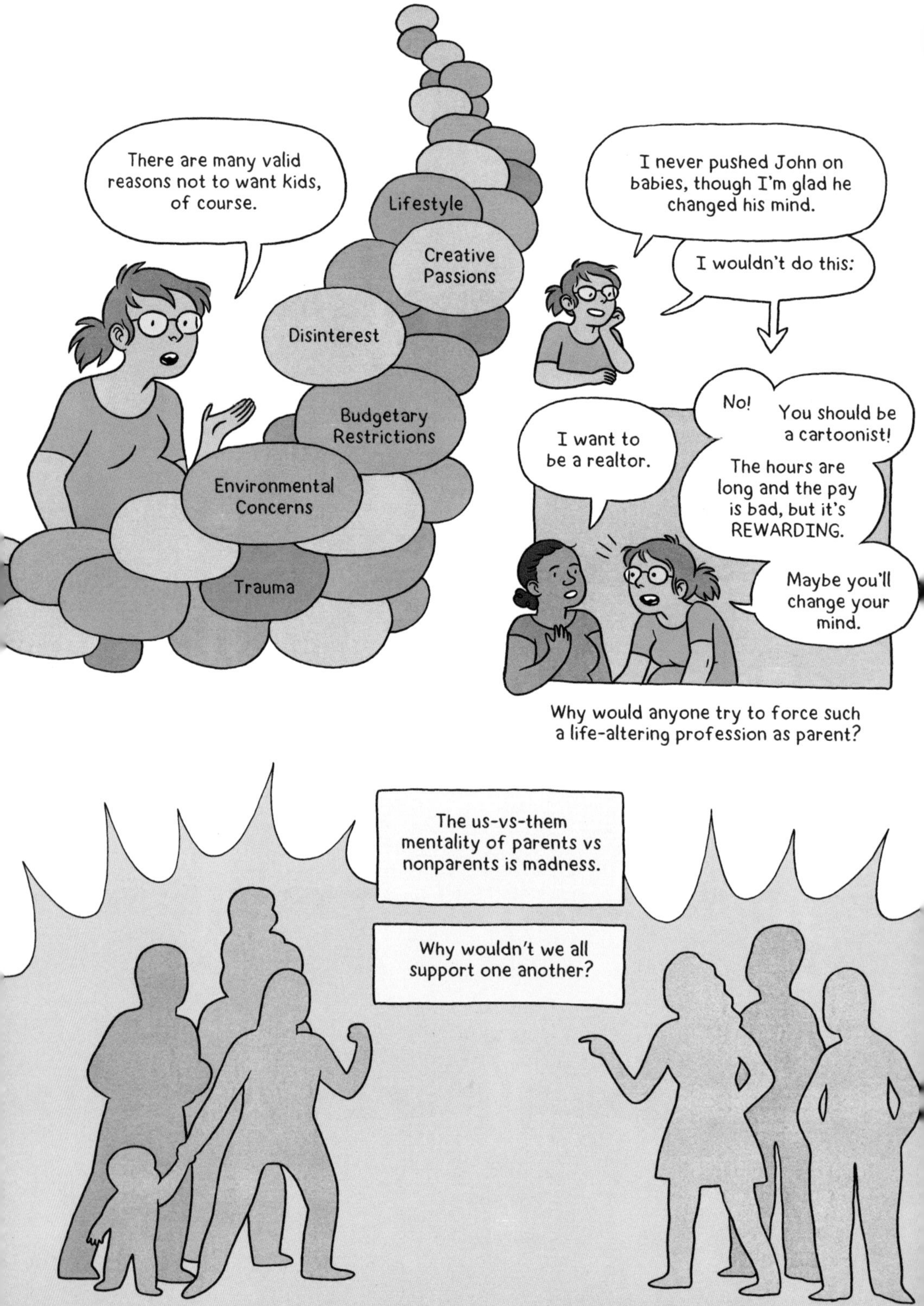
There are many valid reasons not to want kids, of course.
Lifestyle
Creative Passions
Disinterest
Budgetary Restrictions
Environmental Concerns
Trauma
I never pushed John on babies, though I'm glad he changed his mind.
I wouldn't do this:
I want to be a realtor.
No!
You should be a cartoonist!
The hours are long and the pay is bad, but it's REWARDING.
Maybe you'll change your mind.
Why would anyone try to force such a life-altering profession as parent?
The us-vs-them mentality of parents vs nonparents is madness.
Why wouldn't we all support one another?

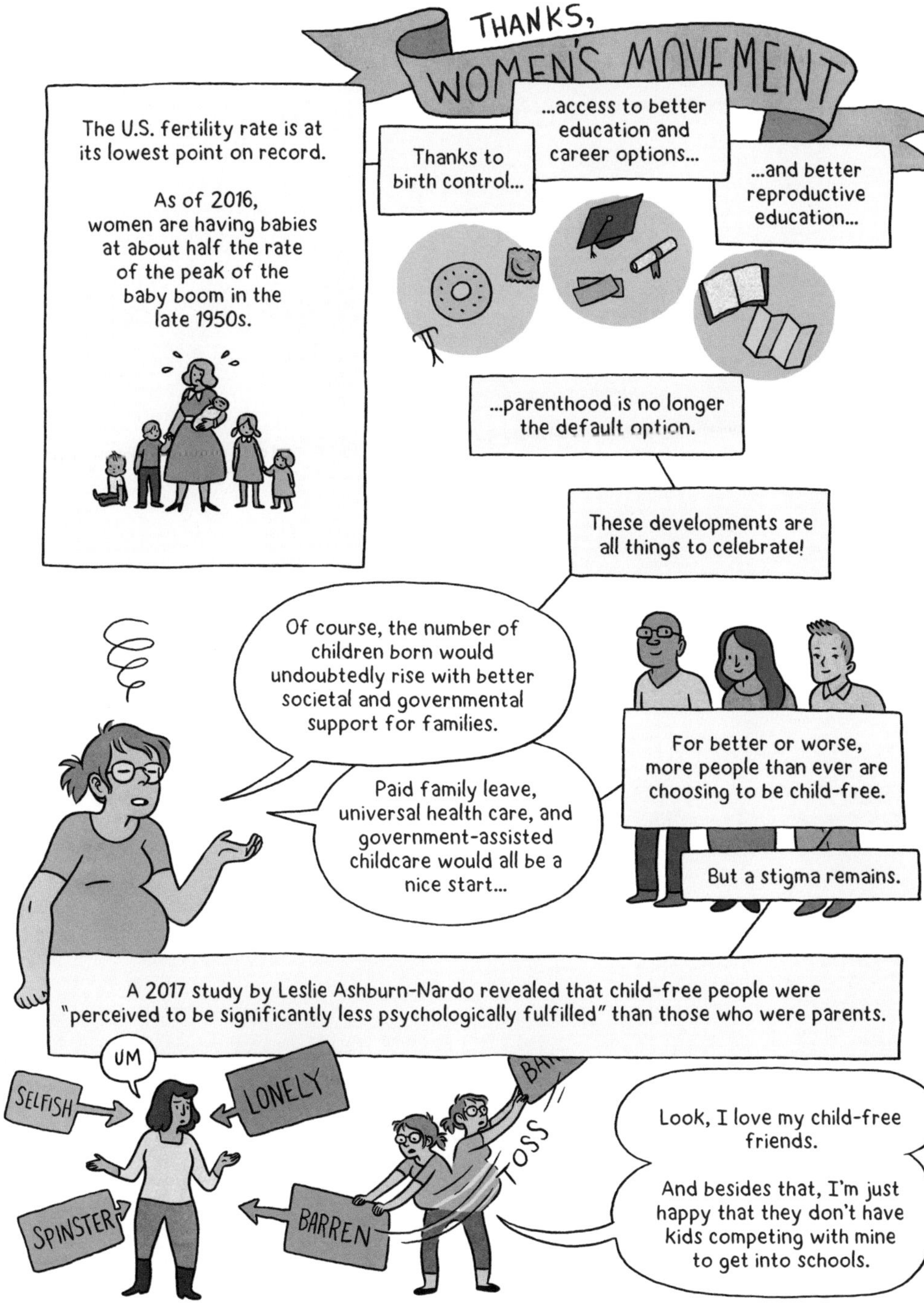
THANKS, WOMEN'S MOVEMENT
The U.S. fertility rate is at its lowest point on record.
As of 2016, women are having babies at about half the rate of the peak of the baby boom in the late 1950s.
Thanks to birth control...
...access to better education and career options...
...and better reproductive education...
...parenthood is no longer the default option.
These developments are all things to celebrate!
Of course, the number of children born would undoubtedly rise with better societal and governmental support for families.
Paid family leave, universal health care, and government-assisted childcare would all be a nice start...
For better or worse, more people than ever are choosing to be child-free.
But a stigma remains.
A 2017 study by Leslie Ashburn-Nardo revealed that child-free people were "perceived to be significantly less psychologically fulfilled" than those who were parents.
UM
SELFISH
LONELY
SPINSTER
BARREN
TOSS
Look, I love my child-free friends.
And besides that, I'm just happy that they don't have kids competing with mine to get into schools.

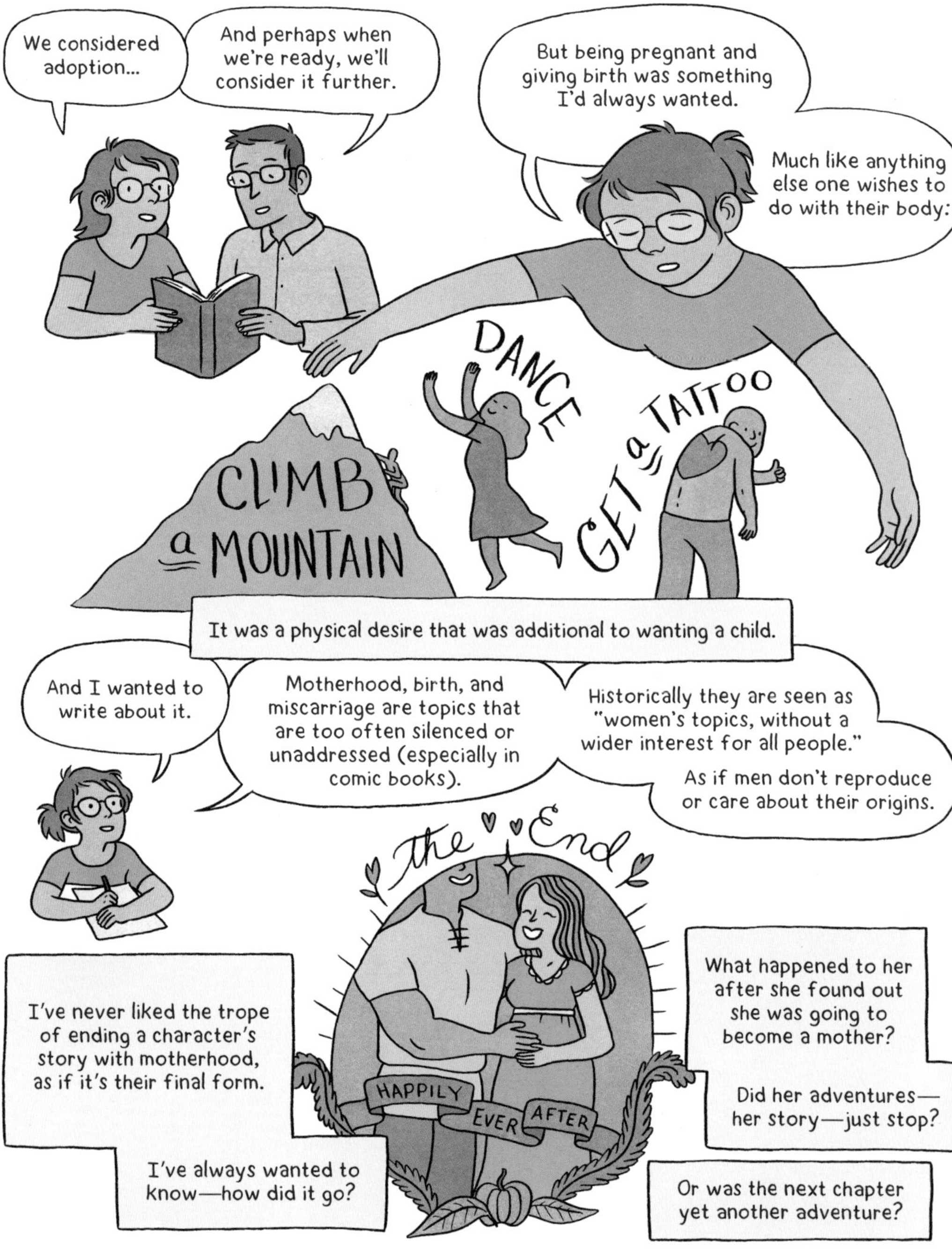
We considered adoption...
And perhaps when we're ready, we'll consider it further.
But being pregnant and giving birth was something I'd always wanted.
Much like anything else one wishes to do with their body:
DANCE
CLIMB a MOUNTAIN
GET a TATTOO
It was a physical desire that was additional to wanting a child.
And I wanted to write about it.
Motherhood, birth, and miscarriage are topics that are too often silenced or unaddressed (especially in comic books).
Historically they are seen as "women's topics, without a wider interest for all people."
As if men don't reproduce or care about their origins.
the End
HAPPILY EVER AFTER
I've never liked the trope of ending a character's story with motherhood, as if it's their final form.
I've always wanted to know—how did it go?
What happened to her after she found out she was going to become a mother?
Did her adventures—her story—just stop?
Or was the next chapter yet another adventure?

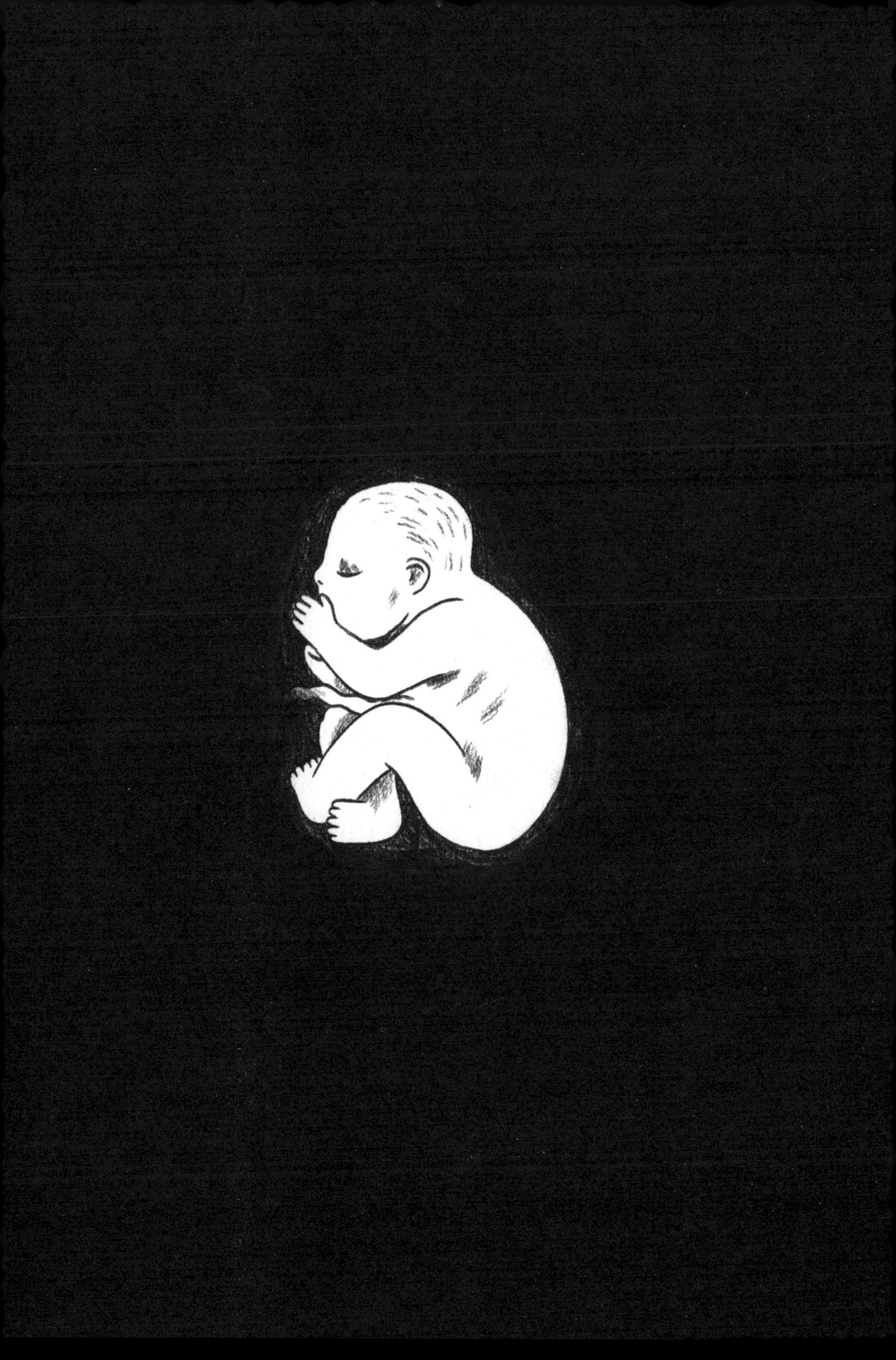

THE ETERNAL THIRD

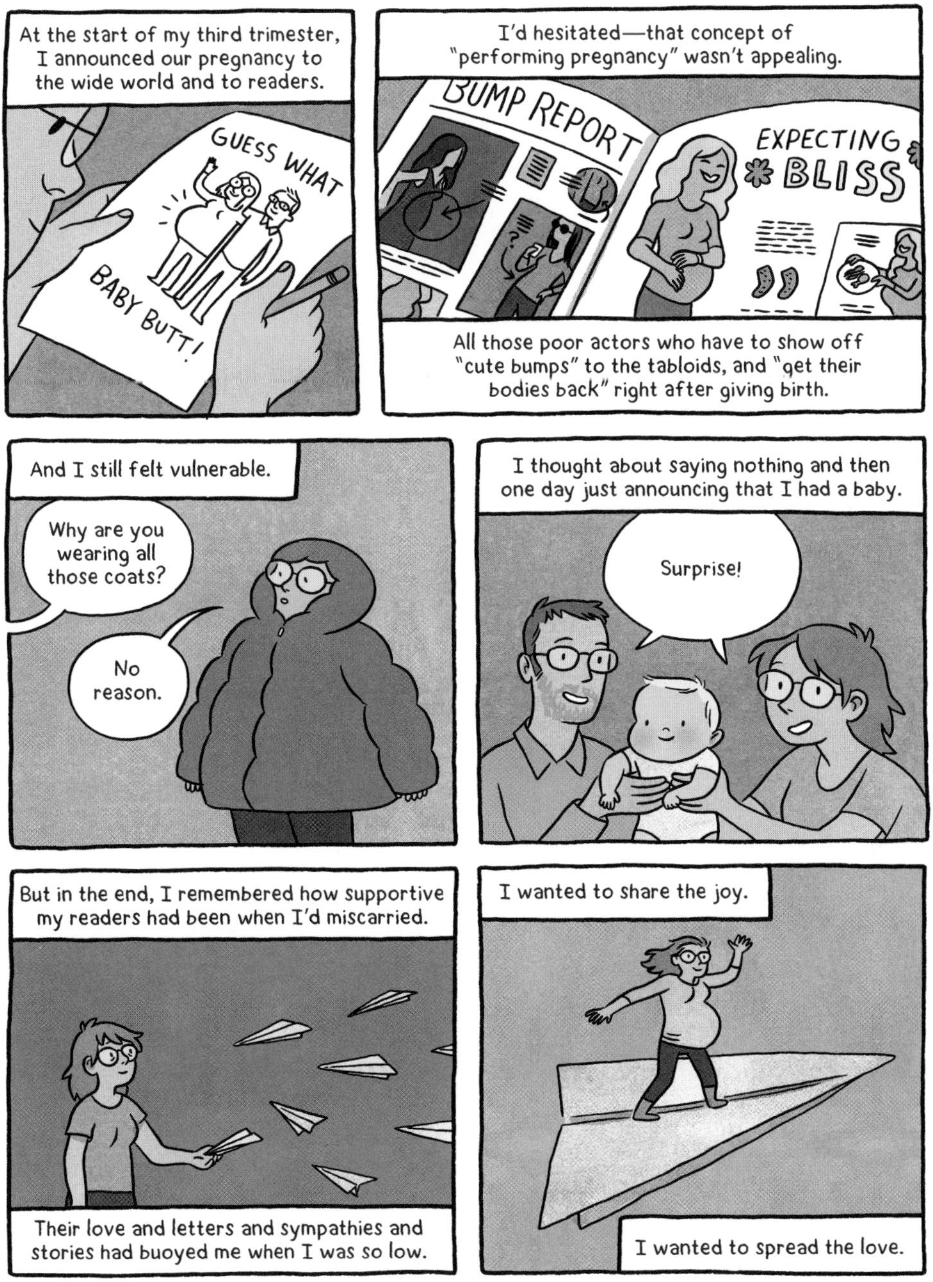

At the start of my third trimester, I announced our pregnancy to the wide world and to readers.
GUESS WHAT
BABY BUTT!
I'd hesitated—that concept of "performing pregnancy" wasn't appealing.
BUMP REPORT
EXPECTING BLISS
All those poor actors who have to show off "cute bumps" to the tabloids, and "get their bodies back" right after giving birth.
And I still felt vulnerable.
Why are you wearing all those coats?
No reason.
I thought about saying nothing and then one day just announcing that I had a baby.
Surprise!
But in the end, I remembered how supportive my readers had been when I'd miscarried.
Their love and letters and sympathies and stories had buoyed me when I was so low.
I wanted to share the joy.
I wanted to spread the love.

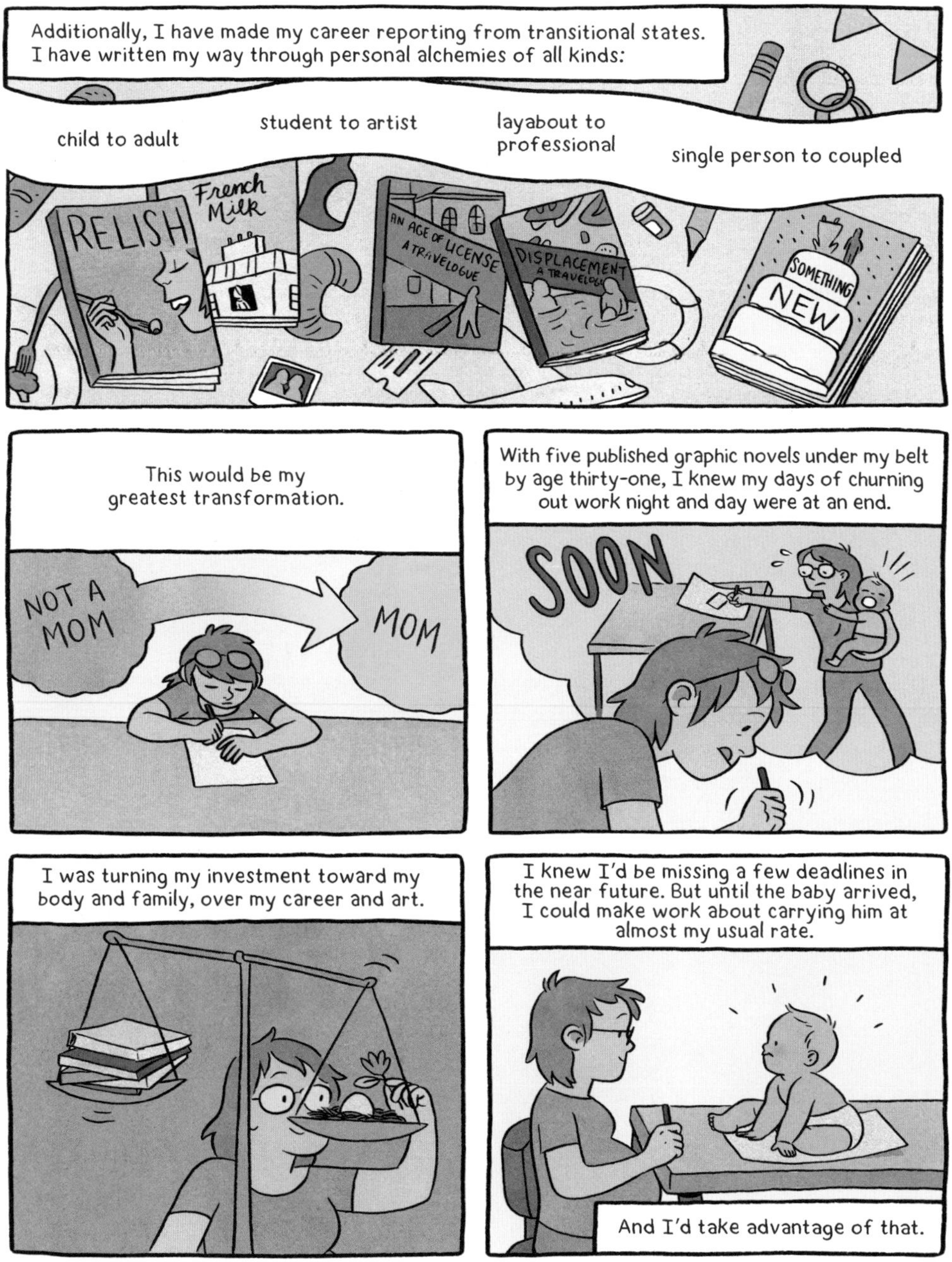
Additionally, I have made my career reporting from transitional states. I have written my way through personal alchemies of all kinds:
child to adult
student to artist
layabout to professional
single person to coupled
RELISH
French Milk
AN AGE OF LICENSE A TRAVELOGUE
DISPLACEMENT A TRAVELOGUE
SOMETHING NEW
This would be my greatest transformation.
NOT A MOM
MOM
With five published graphic novels under my belt by age thirty-one, I knew my days of churning out work night and day were at an end.
SOON
I was turning my investment toward my body and family, over my career and art.
I knew I'd be missing a few deadlines in the near future. But until the baby arrived, I could make work about carrying him at almost my usual rate.
And I'd take advantage of that.

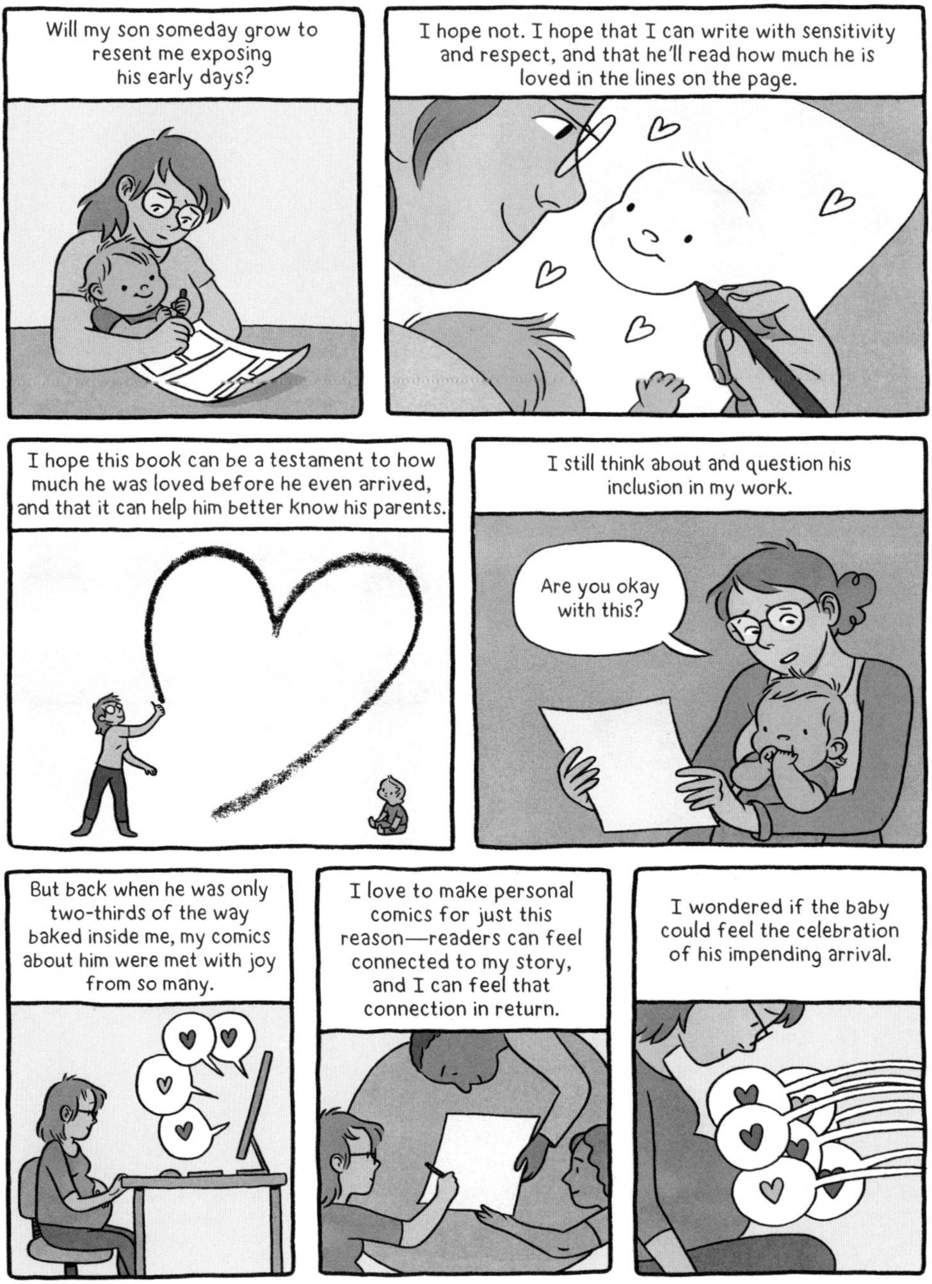
Will my son someday grow to resent me exposing his early days?
I hope not. I hope that I can write with sensitivity and respect, and that he'll read how much he is loved in the lines on the page.
I hope this book can be a testament to how much he was loved before he even arrived, and that it can help him better know his parents.
I still think about and question his inclusion in my work.
Are you okay with this?
But back when he was only two-thirds of the way baked inside me, my comics about him were met with joy from so many.
I love to make personal comics for just this reason—readers can feel connected to my story, and I can feel that connection in return.
I wondered if the baby could feel the celebration of his impending arrival.

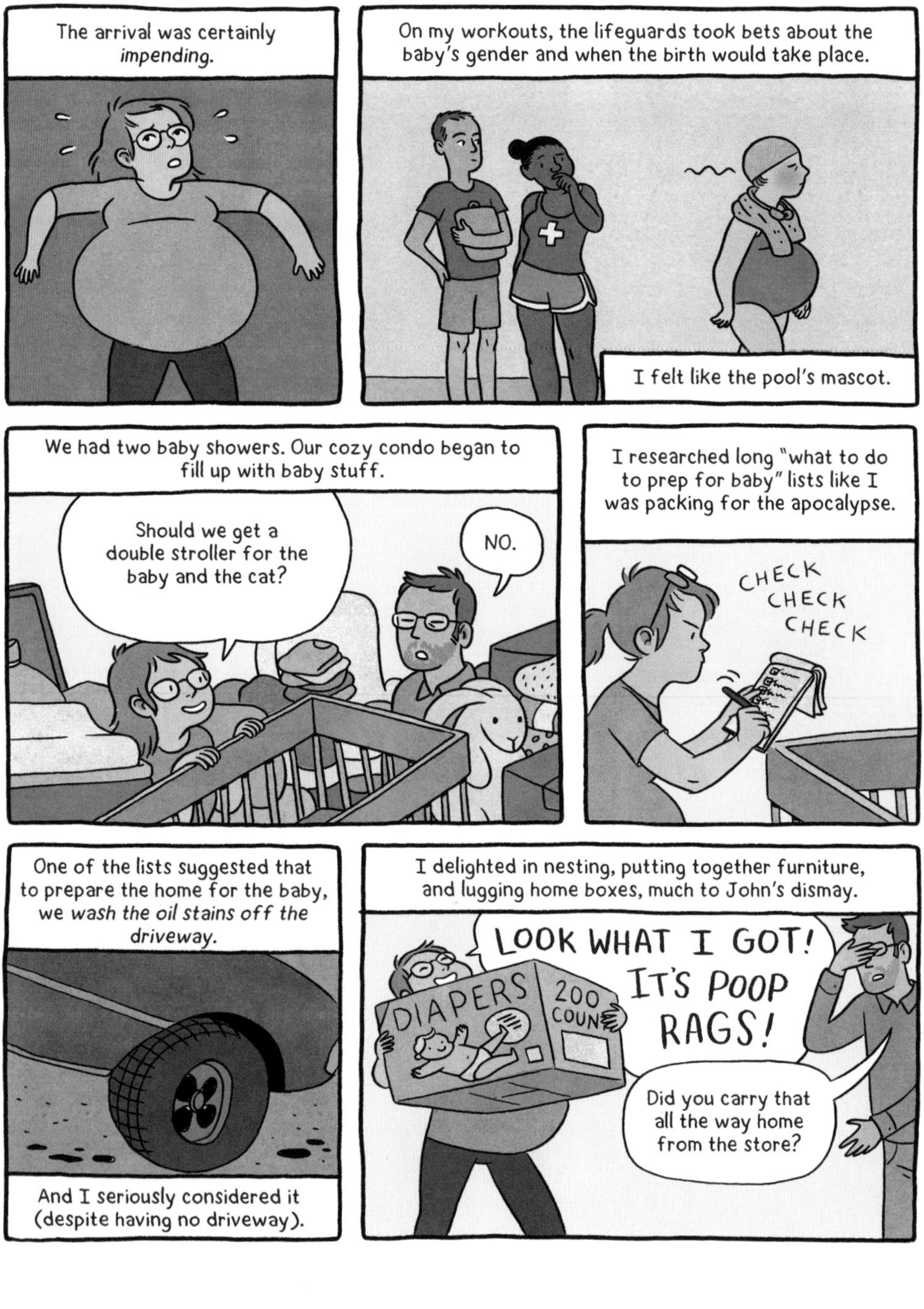
The arrival was certainly *impending.*
On my workouts, the lifeguards took bets about the baby's gender and when the birth would take place.
I felt like the pool's mascot.
We had two baby showers. Our cozy condo began to fill up with baby stuff.
Should we get a double stroller for the baby and the cat?
NO.
I researched long "what to do to prep for baby" lists like I was packing for the apocalypse.
CHECK
CHECK
CHECK
One of the lists suggested that to prepare the home for the baby, we *wash the oil stains off the driveway.*
And I seriously considered it (despite having no driveway).
I delighted in nesting, putting together furniture, and lugging home boxes, much to John's dismay.
LOOK WHAT I GOT! IT'S POOP RAGS!
DIAPERS
200 COUN
Did you carry that all the way home from the store?

We went to the hospital for infant care classes.

Note to anyone planning to take such courses: DON'T BEGIN WITH INFANT CPR. Work up to that one. Or face the insomnia.

Human babies are just trying to destroy themselves all the time! Animals don't have CPR! Elephants are born knowing how to walk! Human babies don't know that—human babies don't even know how to do ANYTHING! Maybe our pregnancy SHOULD be two years long, like an elephant!

During my mother's hospital tour, she fainted and had to be tended by the nurses.

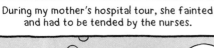

Oh, dear...

I stayed conscious, though I did get ooky during the episiotomy portion of birth class.

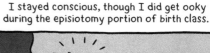

151

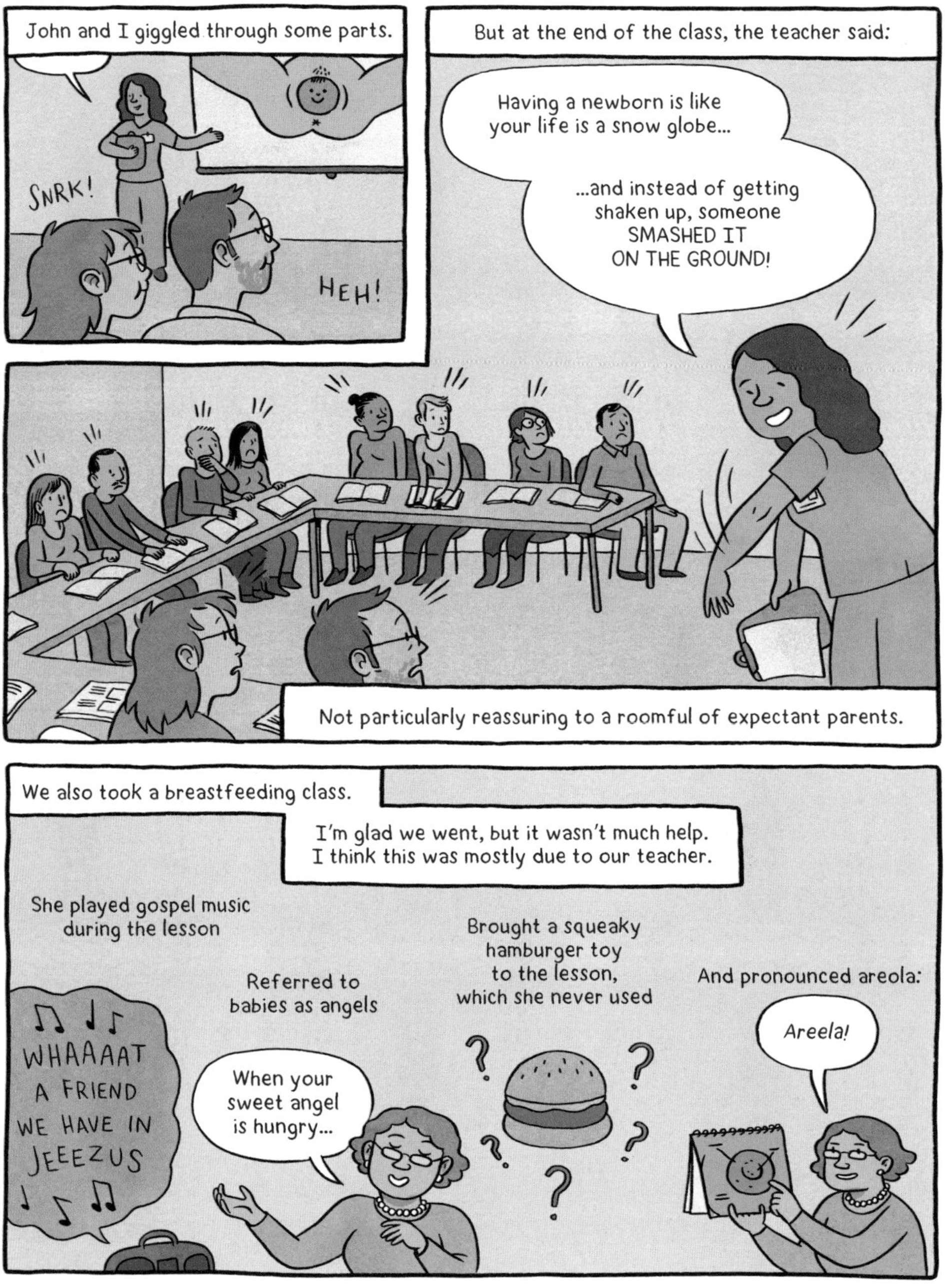

John and I giggled through some parts.
SNRK!
HEH!
But at the end of the class, the teacher said:
Having a newborn is like your life is a snow globe...
...and instead of getting shaken up, someone SMASHED IT ON THE GROUND!
Not particularly reassuring to a roomful of expectant parents.
We also took a breastfeeding class.
I'm glad we went, but it wasn't much help. I think this was mostly due to our teacher.
She played gospel music during the lesson
WHAAAAT A FRIEND WE HAVE IN JEEEZUS
Referred to babies as angels
When your sweet angel is hungry...
Brought a squeaky hamburger toy to the lesson, which she never used
And pronounced areola:
Areela!

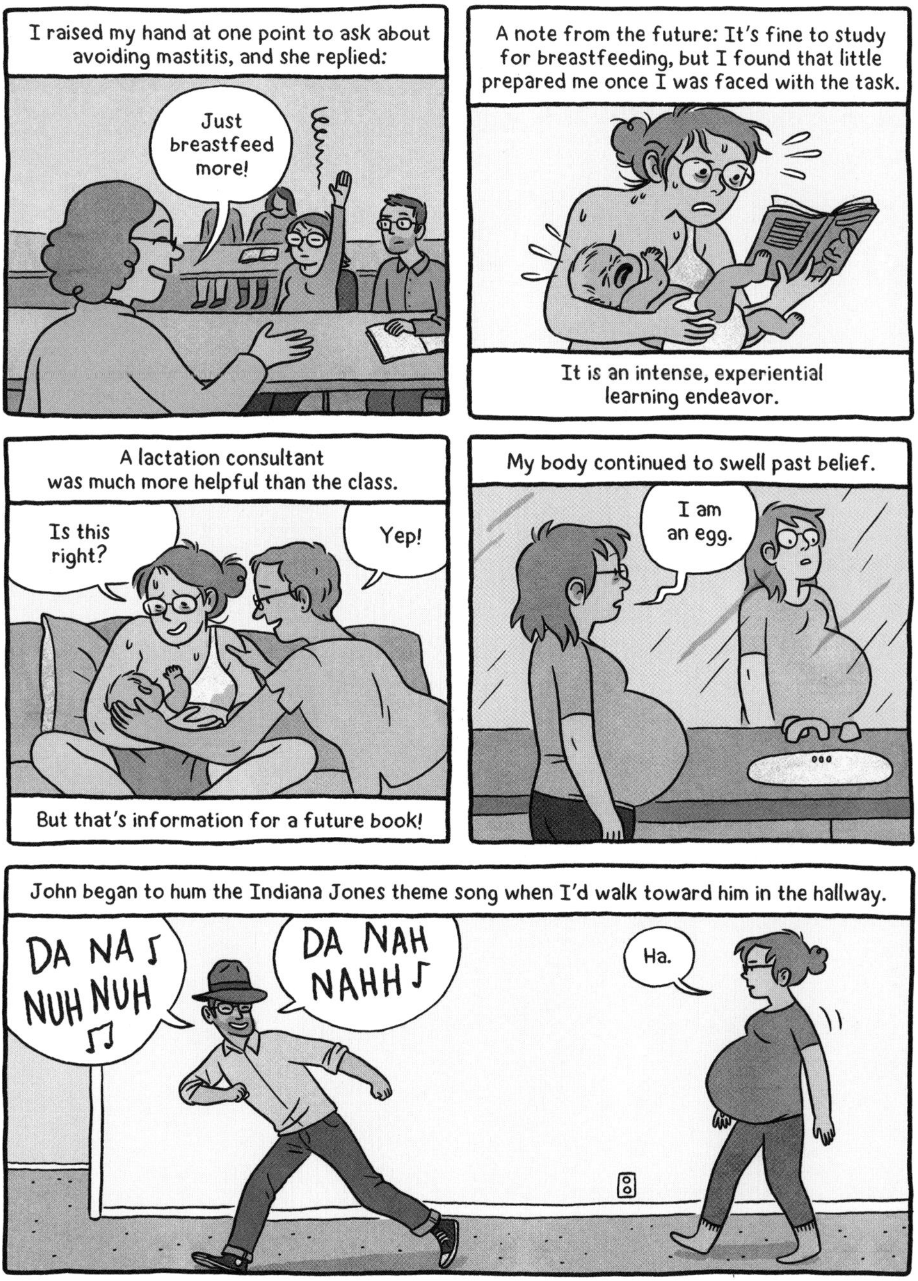
I raised my hand at one point to ask about avoiding mastitis, and she replied:
Just breastfeed more!
A note from the future: It's fine to study for breastfeeding, but I found that little prepared me once I was faced with the task.
It is an intense, experiential learning endeavor.
A lactation consultant was much more helpful than the class.
Is this right?
Yep!
But that's information for a future book!
My body continued to swell past belief.
I am an egg.
John began to hum the Indiana Jones theme song when I'd walk toward him in the hallway.
DA NA NUH NUH
DA NAH NAHH
Ha.

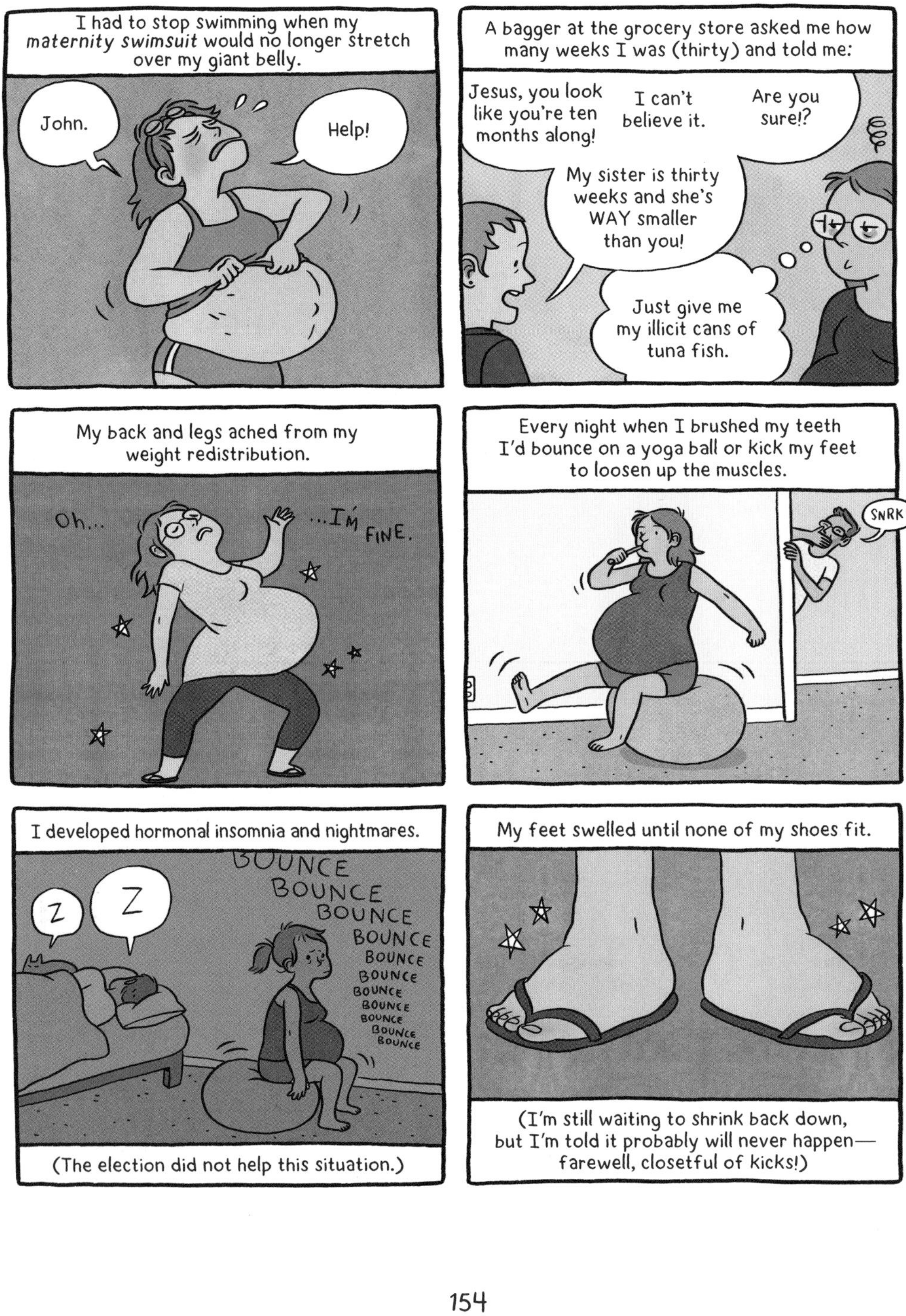
I had to stop swimming when my *maternity swimsuit* would no longer stretch over my giant belly.
John.
Help!
A bagger at the grocery store asked me how many weeks I was (thirty) and told me:
Jesus, you look like you're ten months along!
I can't believe it.
Are you sure!?
My sister is thirty weeks and she's WAY smaller than you!
Just give me my illicit cans of tuna fish.
My back and legs ached from my weight redistribution.
Oh...
...I'M FINE.
Every night when I brushed my teeth I'd bounce on a yoga ball or kick my feet to loosen up the muscles.
SNRK!
I developed hormonal insomnia and nightmares.
Z
Z
BOUNCE
BOUNCE
BOUNCE
BOUNCE
BOUNCE
BOUNCE
BOUNCE
BOUNCE
BOUNCE
BOUNCE
BOUNCE
(The election did not help this situation.)
My feet swelled until none of my shoes fit.
(I'm still waiting to shrink back down, but I'm told it probably will never happen— farewell, closetful of kicks!)

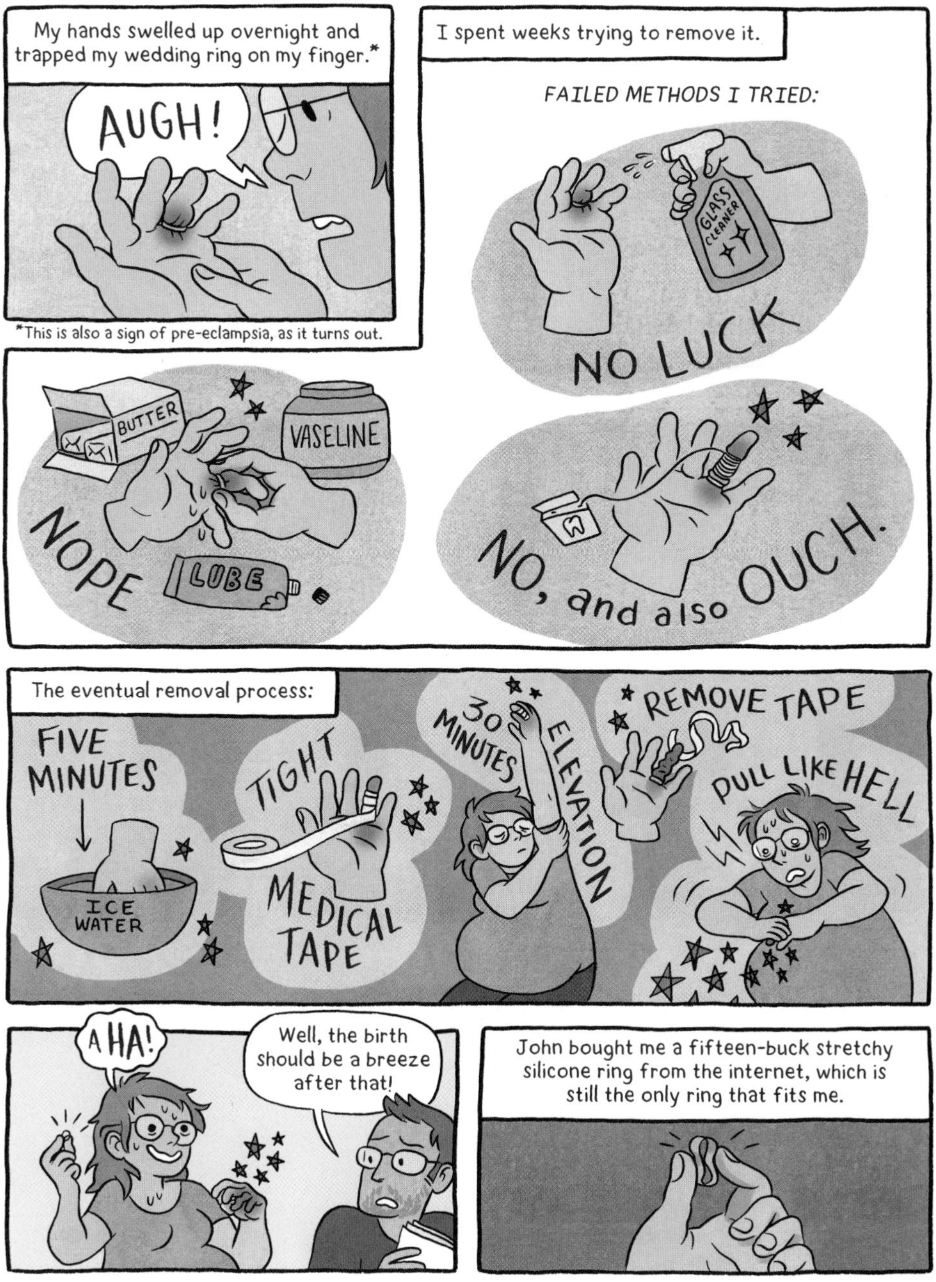

My hands swelled up overnight and trapped my wedding ring on my finger.*
AUGH!
*This is also a sign of pre-eclampsia, as it turns out.
I spent weeks trying to remove it.
FAILED METHODS I TRIED:
GLASS CLEANER
NO LUCK
BUTTER
VASELINE
NOPE
LUBE
NO, and also OUCH.
The eventual removal process:
FIVE MINUTES
ICE WATER
TIGHT
MEDICAL TAPE
30 MINUTES
ELEVATION
REMOVE TAPE
PULL LIKE HELL
AHA!
Well, the birth should be a breeze after that!
John bought me a fifteen-buck stretchy silicone ring from the internet, which is still the only ring that fits me.

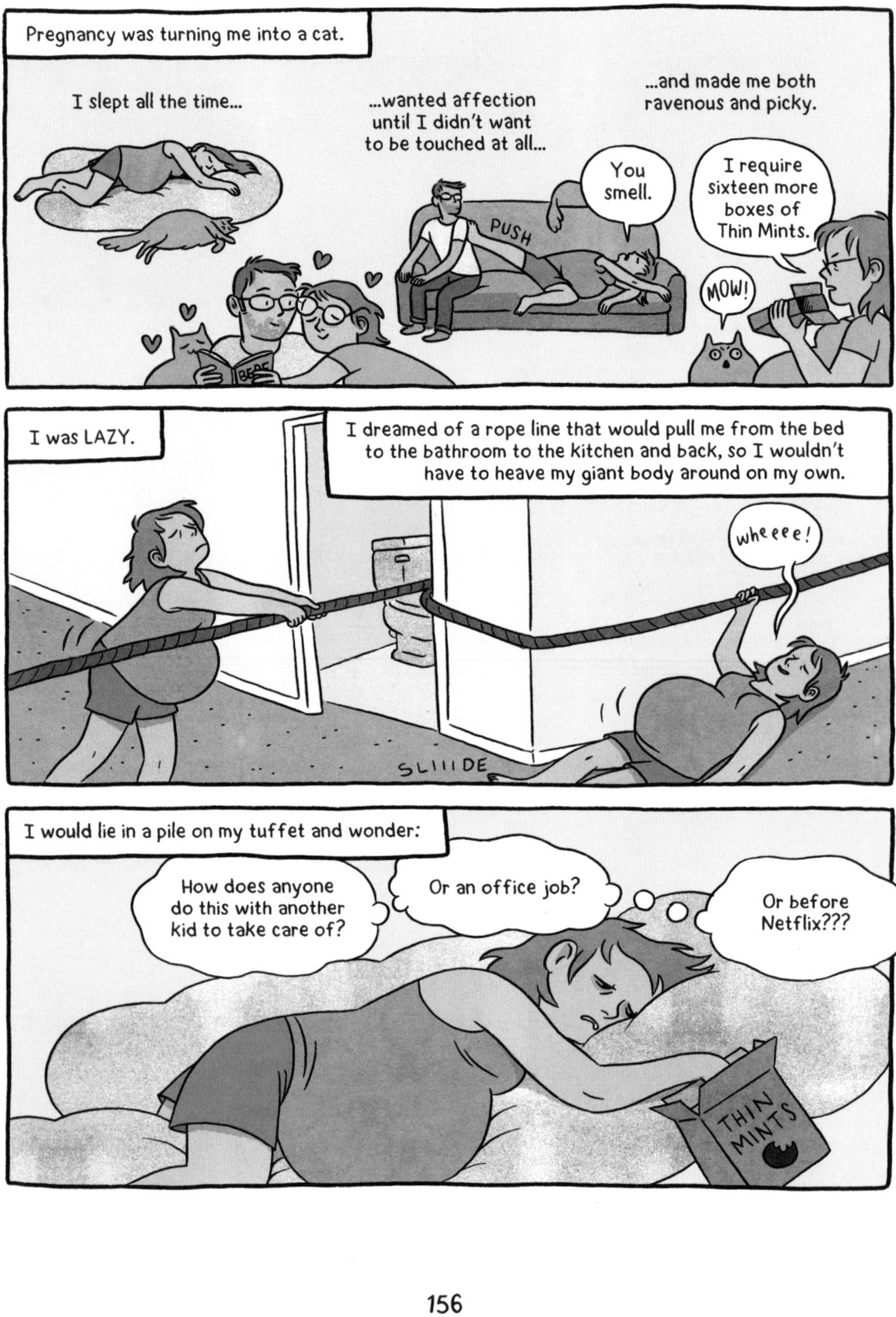
Pregnancy was turning me into a cat.
I slept all the time...
...wanted affection until I didn't want to be touched at all...
PUSH
You smell.
...and made me both ravenous and picky.
I require sixteen more boxes of Thin Mints.
MOW!
I was LAZY.
I dreamed of a rope line that would pull me from the bed to the bathroom to the kitchen and back, so I wouldn't have to heave my giant body around on my own.
wheeee!
SLIIIDE
I would lie in a pile on my tuffet and wonder:
How does anyone do this with another kid to take care of?
Or an office job?
Or before Netflix???
THIN MINTS

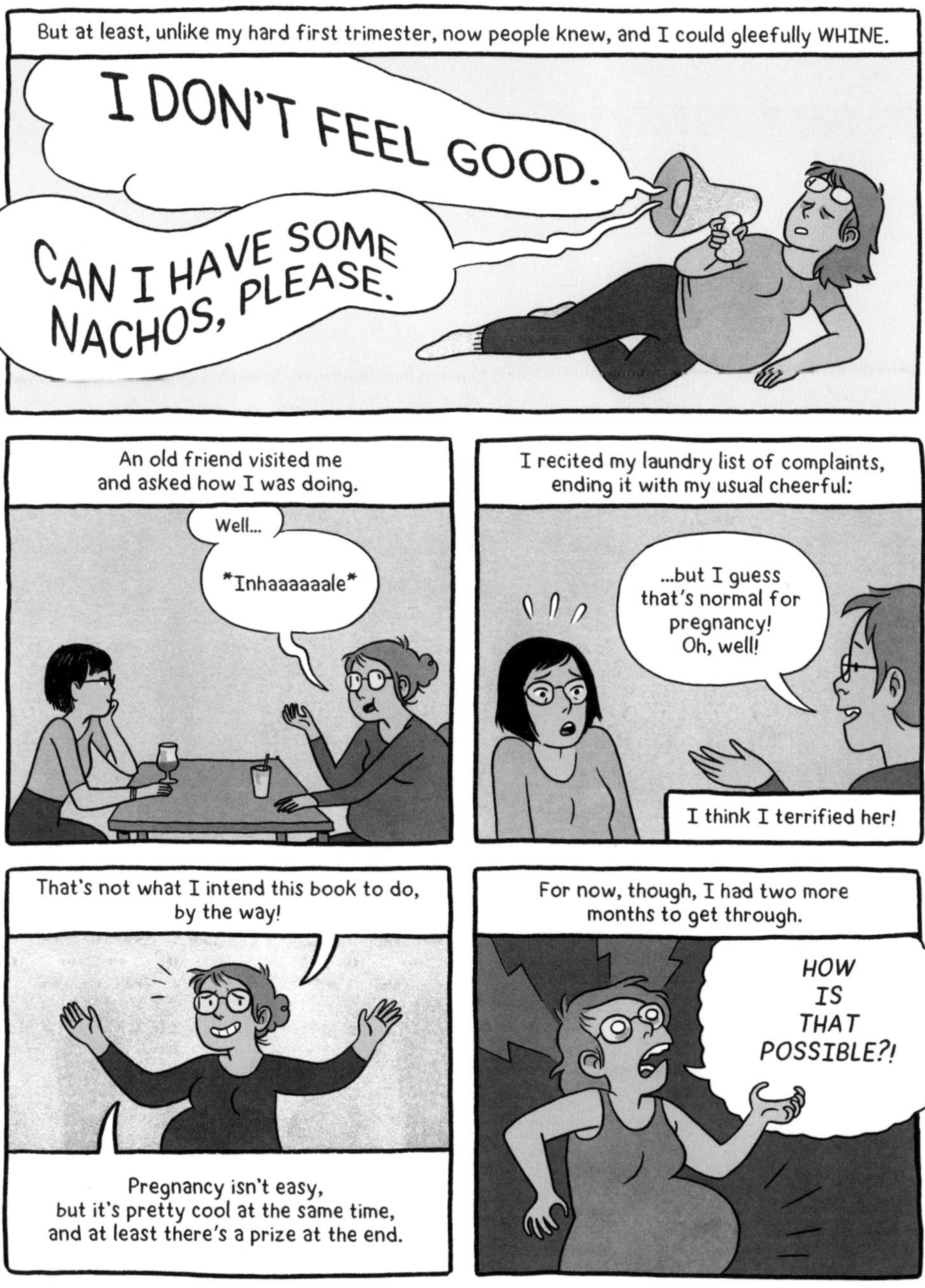

But at least, unlike my hard first trimester, now people knew, and I could gleefully WHINE.
I DON'T FEEL GOOD.
CAN I HAVE SOME NACHOS, PLEASE.
An old friend visited me and asked how I was doing.
Well...
Inhaaaaaale
I recited my laundry list of complaints, ending it with my usual cheerful:
...but I guess that's normal for pregnancy! Oh, well!
I think I terrified her!
That's not what I intend this book to do, by the way!
Pregnancy isn't easy, but it's pretty cool at the same time, and at least there's a prize at the end.
For now, though, I had two more months to get through.
HOW IS THAT POSSIBLE?!

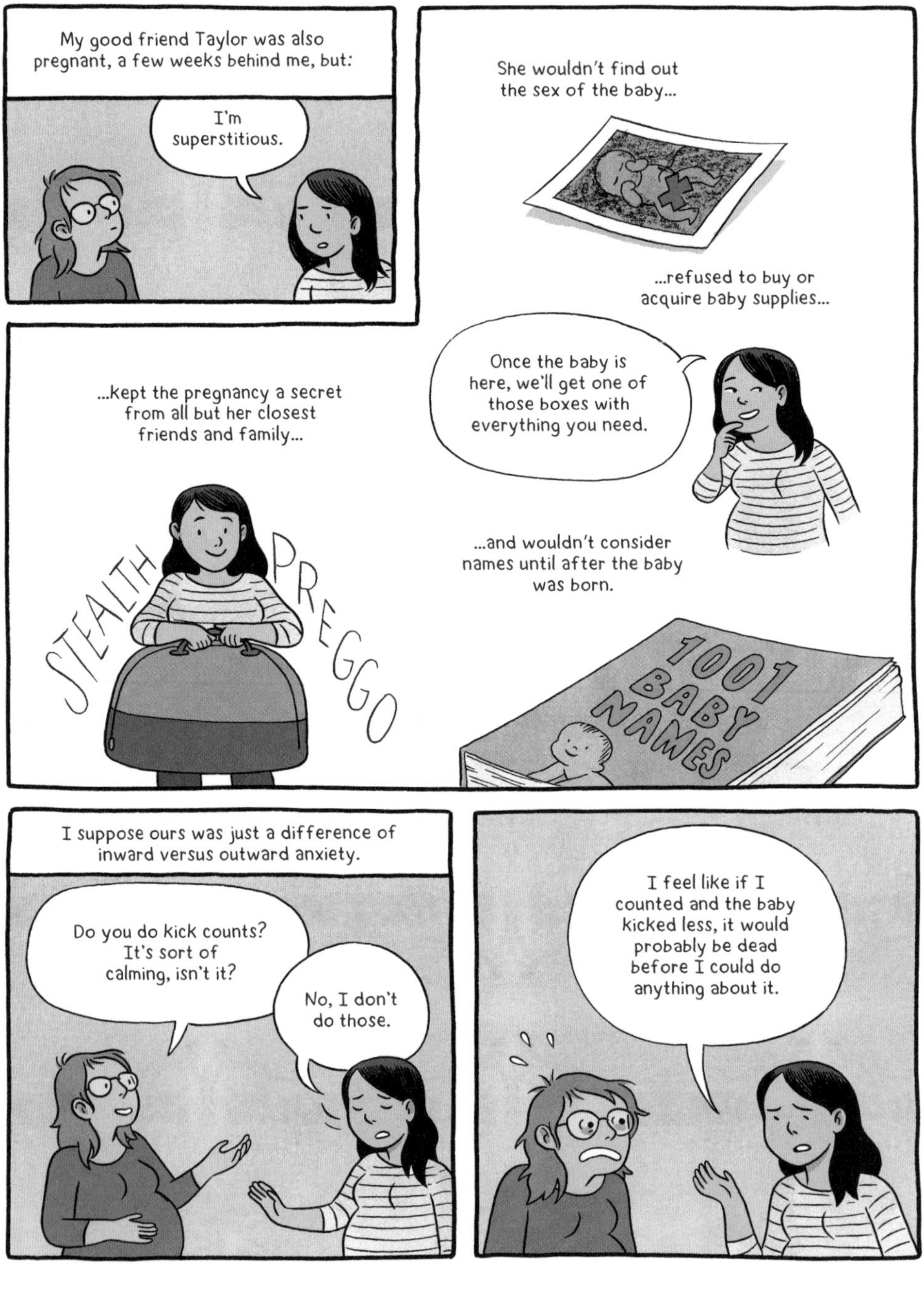
My good friend Taylor was also pregnant, a few weeks behind me, but:
I'm superstitious.
She wouldn't find out the sex of the baby...
...refused to buy or acquire baby supplies...
Once the baby is here, we'll get one of those boxes with everything you need.
...kept the pregnancy a secret from all but her closest friends and family...
STEALTH PREGGO
...and wouldn't consider names until after the baby was born.
1001 BABY NAMES
I suppose ours was just a difference of inward versus outward anxiety.
Do you do kick counts? It's sort of calming, isn't it?
No, I don't do those.
I feel like if I counted and the baby kicked less, it would probably be dead before I could do anything about it.

I developed a burning pain under my right ribs, causing me to be unable to lie on that side or breathe deeply.*

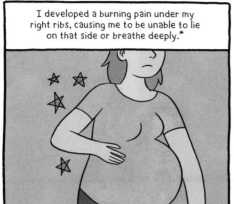

My doctor shrugged this off.

It's probably the baby kicking you!

(It wasn't.)

Eventually, I was in too much pain when I drew, which required me to take an early maternity leave.

What are you doing?

This is the only position I can draw in.

It made me sad and listless to be unable to work.

If this is what pregnancy does to me, will having a BABY blow my work to smithereens?

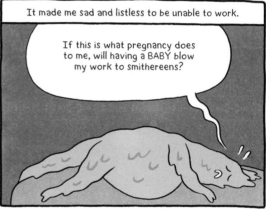

It helped that our niece, Hazel, got over her colic one day and turned into a smiling, cooing sweetie.

Four months of screaming suddenly abated.

What happened?

Don't question it!

*Another sign of pre-eclampsia.

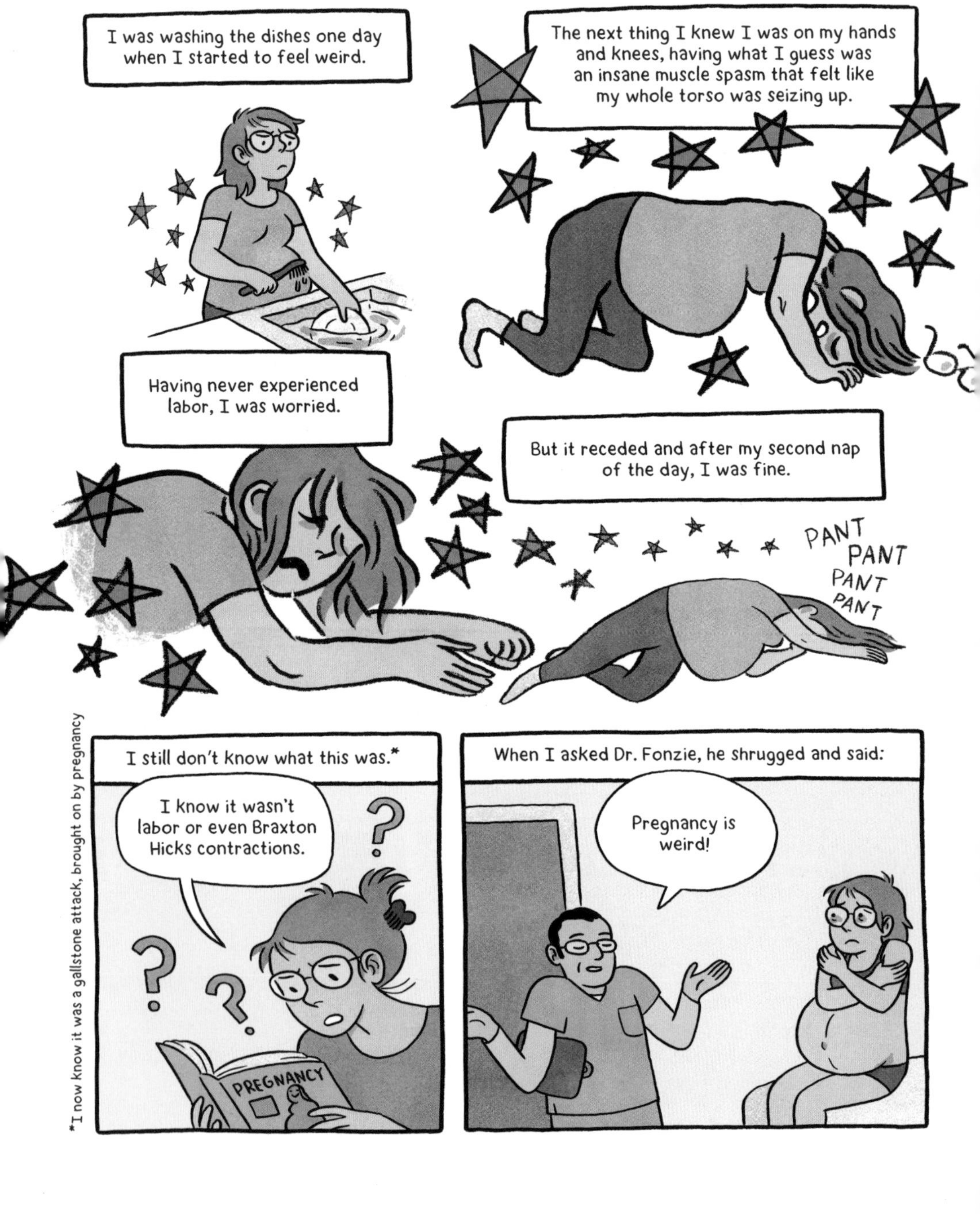

I was washing the dishes one day when I started to feel weird.
The next thing I knew I was on my hands and knees, having what I guess was an insane muscle spasm that felt like my whole torso was seizing up.
Having never experienced labor, I was worried.
But it receded and after my second nap of the day, I was fine.
PANT PANT PANT PANT
I still don't know what this was.*
I know it wasn't labor or even Braxton Hicks contractions.
PREGNANCY
When I asked Dr. Fonzie, he shrugged and said:
Pregnancy is weird!
*I now know it was a gallstone attack, brought on by pregnancy

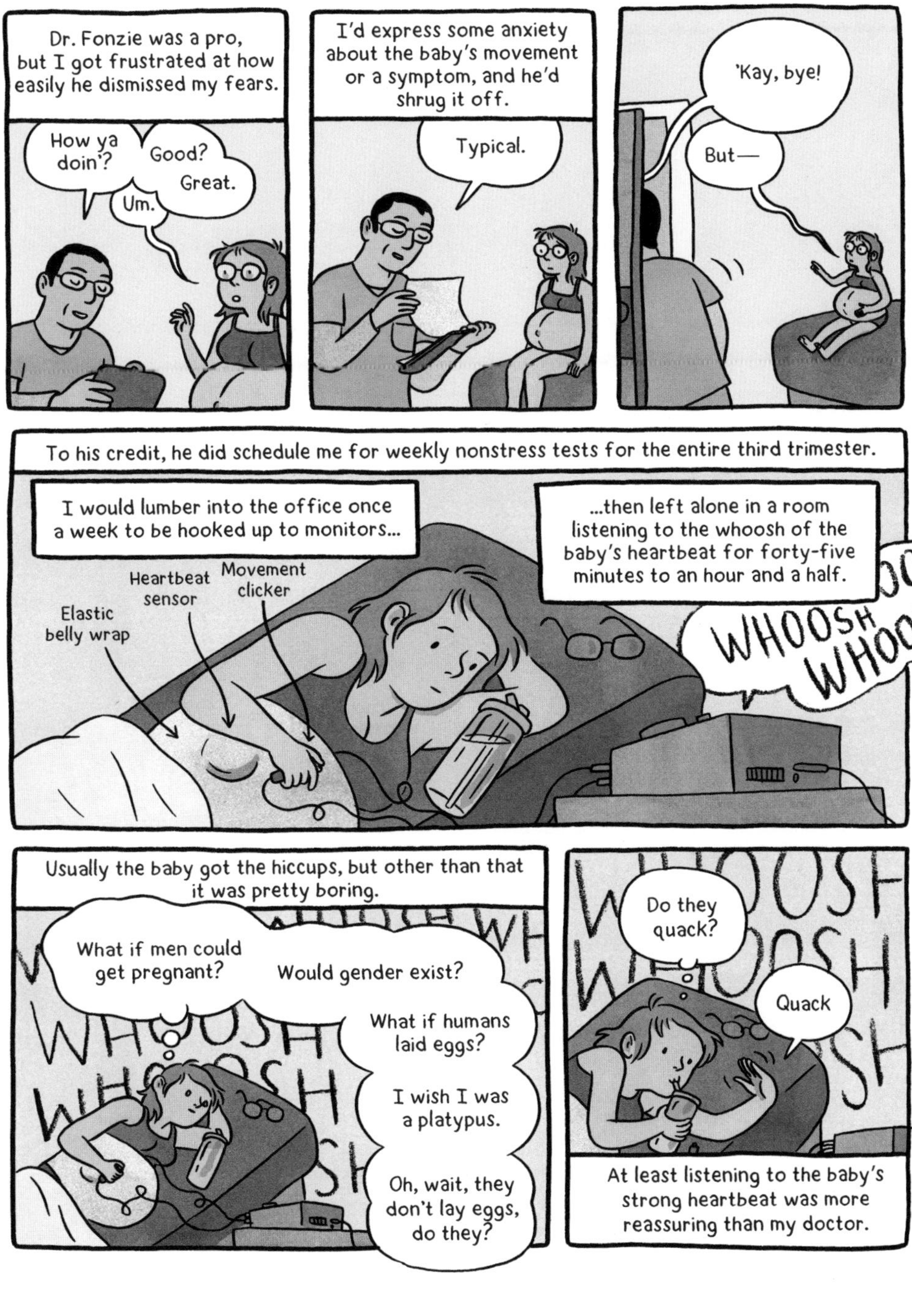

Dr. Fonzie was a pro, but I got frustrated at how easily he dismissed my fears.
How ya doin'?
Good?
Um.
Great.
I'd express some anxiety about the baby's movement or a symptom, and he'd shrug it off.
Typical.
'Kay, bye!
But—
To his credit, he did schedule me for weekly nonstress tests for the entire third trimester.
I would lumber into the office once a week to be hooked up to monitors...
Heartbeat sensor
Movement clicker
Elastic belly wrap
...then left alone in a room listening to the whoosh of the baby's heartbeat for forty-five minutes to an hour and a half.
WHOOSH WHOOSH WHOOSH
Usually the baby got the hiccups, but other than that it was pretty boring.
What if men could get pregnant?
Would gender exist?
What if humans laid eggs?
I wish I was a platypus.
Oh, wait, they don't lay eggs, do they?
Do they quack?
Quack
At least listening to the baby's strong heartbeat was more reassuring than my doctor.

At thirty-one weeks, my ultrasound tech insisted on having me lie flat on my back during an exam.

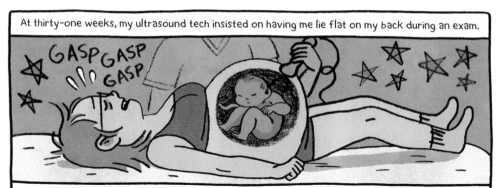

GASP GASP GASP

Heavily pregnant women aren't supposed to do this, because the baby presses on the vena cava and stops blood flow to her brain and heart.

I spent twenty minutes prone, and by the time she was done, I felt like I was going to throw up and pass out.

GASP GASP

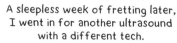

Just from *LYING ON MY BACK.*

The same tech told us the baby was measuring small, and that he was in the transverse position.

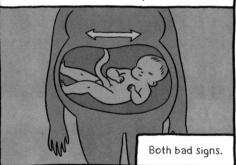

Both bad signs.

A sleepless week of fretting later, I went in for another ultrasound with a different tech.

Great news! The baby is measuring *BIG*, and he's head down.

What?

DOES ANYONE KNOW WHAT THEY'RE DOING HERE??

SEE YOU NEXT WEEK

BECAUSE I DON'T AND SOMEONE PROBABLY SHOULD!

Good news, right?

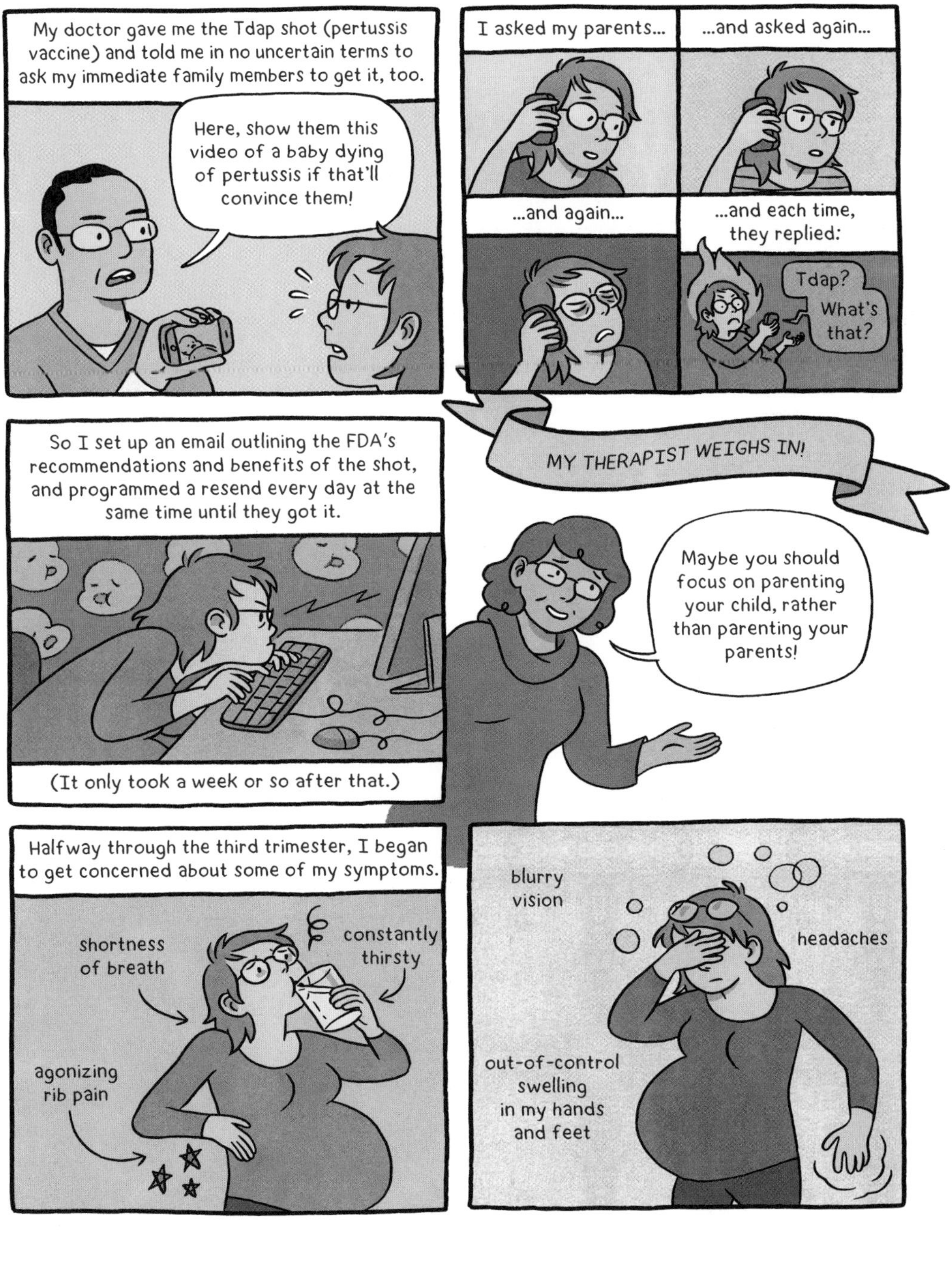

My doctor gave me the Tdap shot (pertussis vaccine) and told me in no uncertain terms to ask my immediate family members to get it, too.
Here, show them this video of a baby dying of pertussis if that'll convince them!
I asked my parents...
...and asked again...
...and again...
...and each time, they replied:
Tdap? What's that?
So I set up an email outlining the FDA's recommendations and benefits of the shot, and programmed a resend every day at the same time until they got it.
(It only took a week or so after that.)
MY THERAPIST WEIGHS IN!
Maybe you should focus on parenting your child, rather than parenting your parents!
Halfway through the third trimester, I began to get concerned about some of my symptoms.
shortness of breath
constantly thirsty
agonizing rib pain
blurry vision
headaches
out-of-control swelling in my hands and feet

The symptom list for pre-eclampsia:

- ☑ Increased thirst
- ☑ Shortness of breath and snoring
- ☑ Upper abdominal pain, usually under your ribs on the right side
- ☑ Blurry vision
- ☑ Headaches and fatigue
- ☑ Sudden weight gain in your hands
- ☐ High blood pressure

*Lady Sybil died, violently, of pre-eclampsia on the show.

But I'd seen *Downton Abbey.**

Are you *sure* it's not pre-eclampsia?

Your blood pressure isn't that high.

(As he's leaving)

Still, I guess I'd trust in my doctor.

I wouldn't want to seem like some hysterical first-timer!

But my doctor shrugged me off.

Welcome to being pregnant in the summertime!

I had relatively low blood pressure before pregnancy, though, so to have slightly above average was pretty high for me.

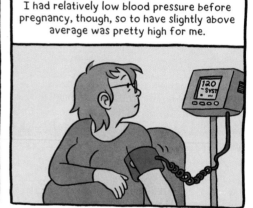

120
SYST

FORBODING DOOM

Yep, I sure wouldn't want to seem like that.

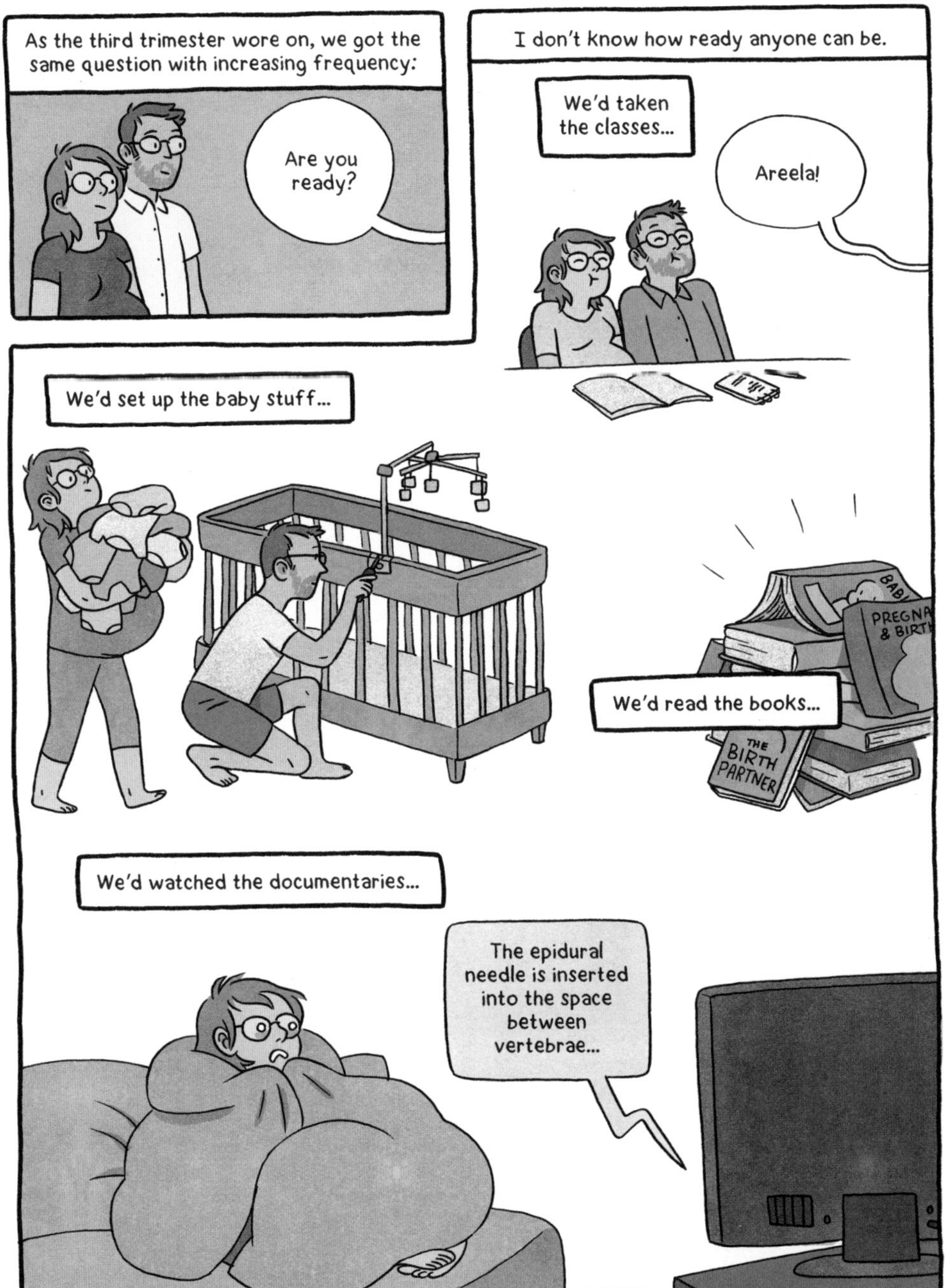
As the third trimester wore on, we got the same question with increasing frequency:
Are you ready?
I don't know how ready anyone can be.
We'd taken the classes...
Areela!
We'd set up the baby stuff...
We'd read the books...
THE BIRTH PARTNER
We'd watched the documentaries...
The epidural needle is inserted into the space between vertebrae...

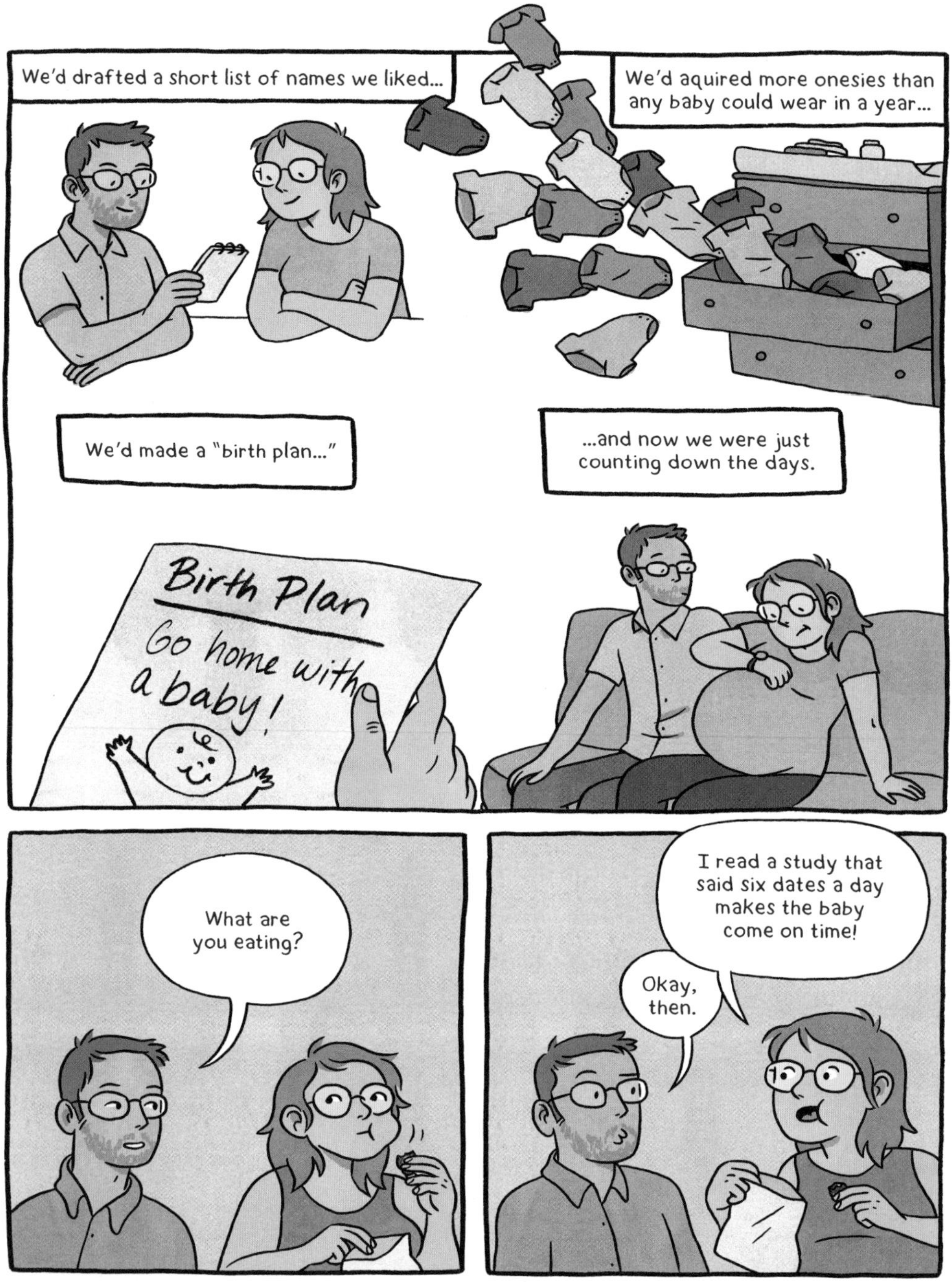
We'd drafted a short list of names we liked...
We'd aquired more onesies than any baby could wear in a year...
We'd made a "birth plan..."
Birth Plan
Go home with a baby!
...and now we were just counting down the days.
What are you eating?
I read a study that said six dates a day makes the baby come on time!
Okay, then.

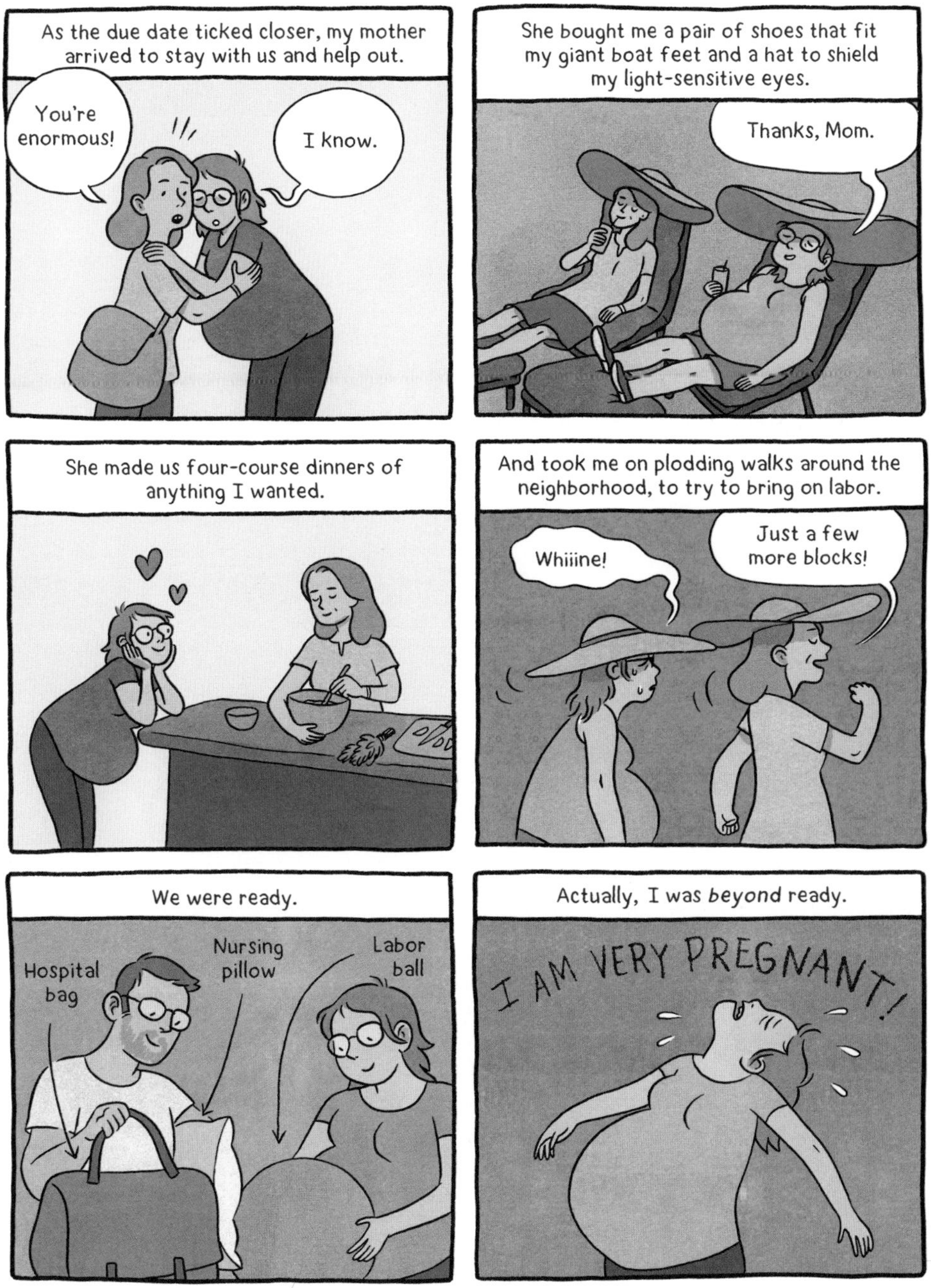
As the due date ticked closer, my mother arrived to stay with us and help out.
You're enormous!
I know.
She bought me a pair of shoes that fit my giant boat feet and a hat to shield my light-sensitive eyes.
Thanks, Mom.
She made us four-course dinners of anything I wanted.
And took me on plodding walks around the neighborhood, to try to bring on labor.
Whiiine!
Just a few more blocks!
We were ready.
Hospital bag
Nursing pillow
Labor ball
Actually, I was *beyond* ready.
I AM VERY PREGNANT!

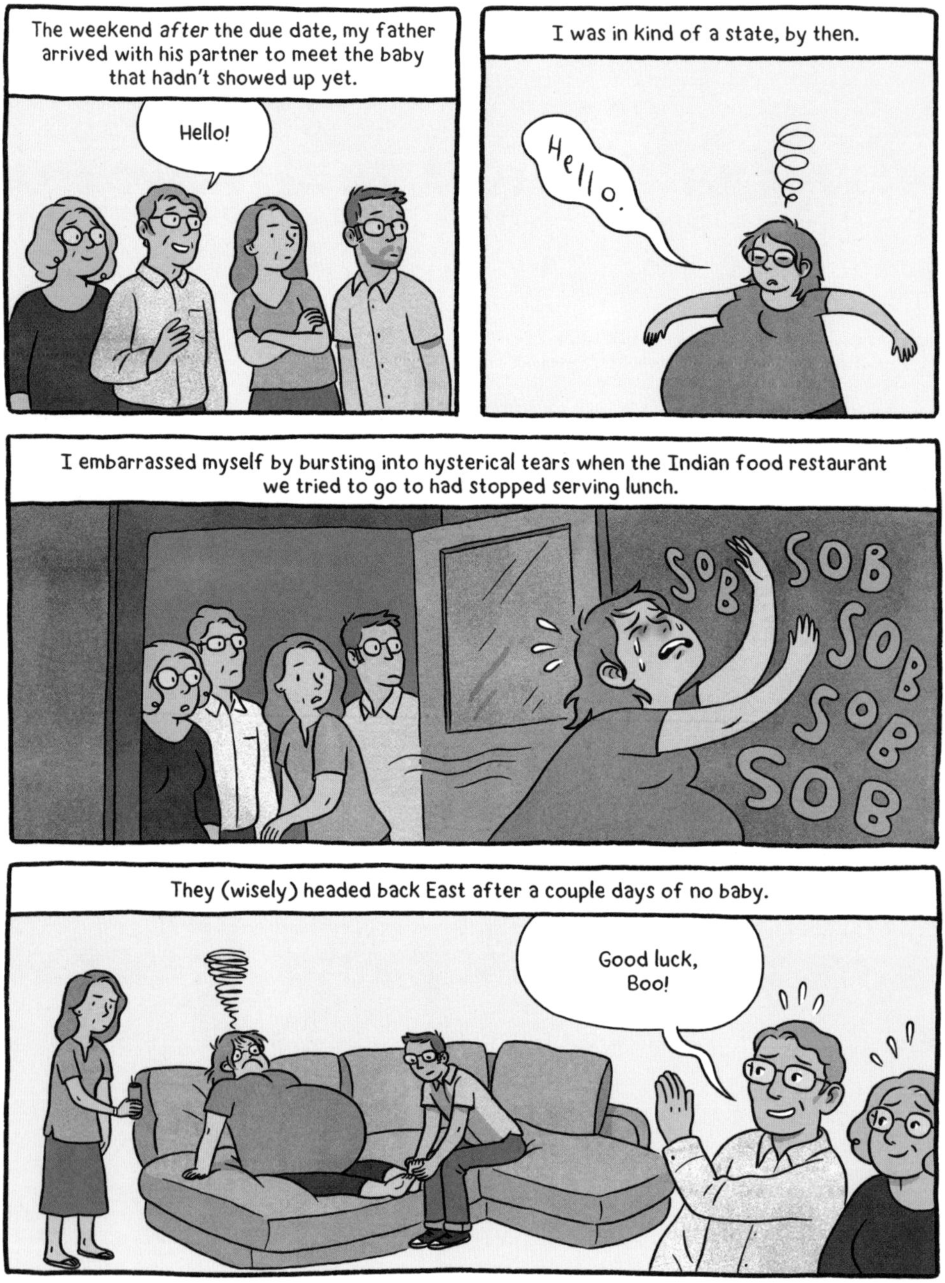
The weekend *after* the due date, my father arrived with his partner to meet the baby that hadn't showed up yet.
Hello!
I was in kind of a state, by then.
Hello.
I embarrassed myself by bursting into hysterical tears when the Indian food restaurant we tried to go to had stopped serving lunch.
SOB SOB SOB SOB SOB
They (wisely) headed back East after a couple days of no baby.
Good luck, Boo!

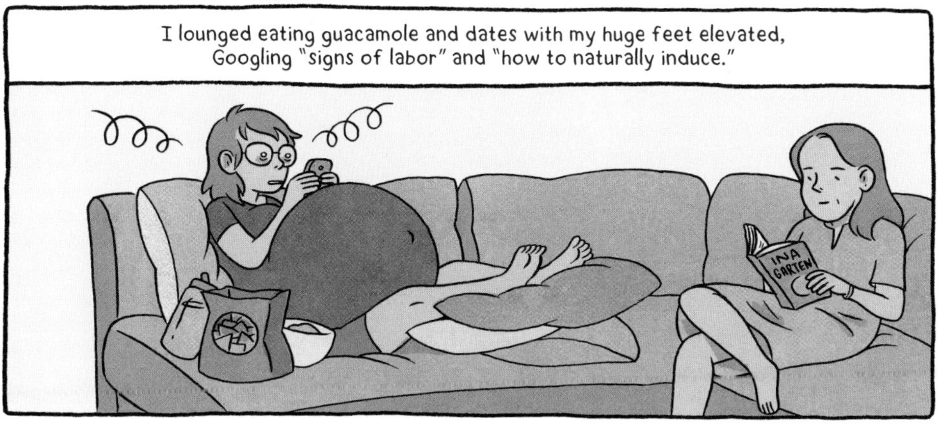
I lounged eating guacamole and dates with my huge feet elevated, Googling "signs of labor" and "how to naturally induce."
INA GARTEN

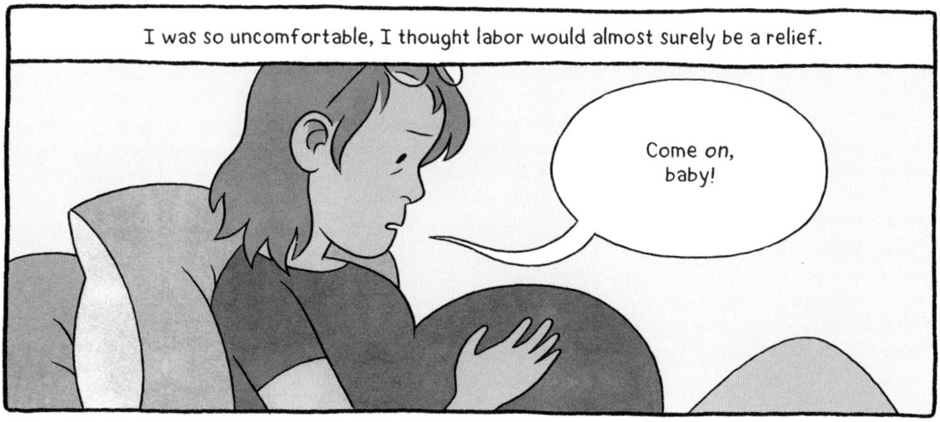
I was so uncomfortable, I thought labor would almost surely be a relief.
Come *on*, baby!

Almost exactly a week past the due date,
I was proven seriously wrong.

LOOK AT ALL THIS PREGNANCY RESEARCH

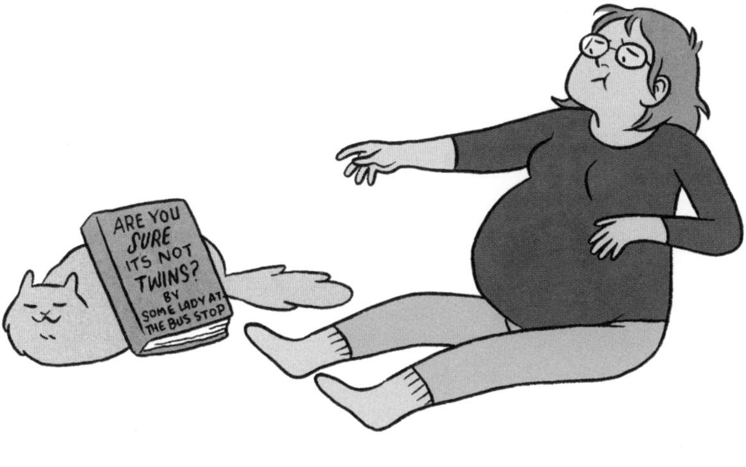
ARE YOU SURE IT'S NOT TWINS?
BY SOME LADY AT THE BUS STOP

THE HISTORICAL PREGGO

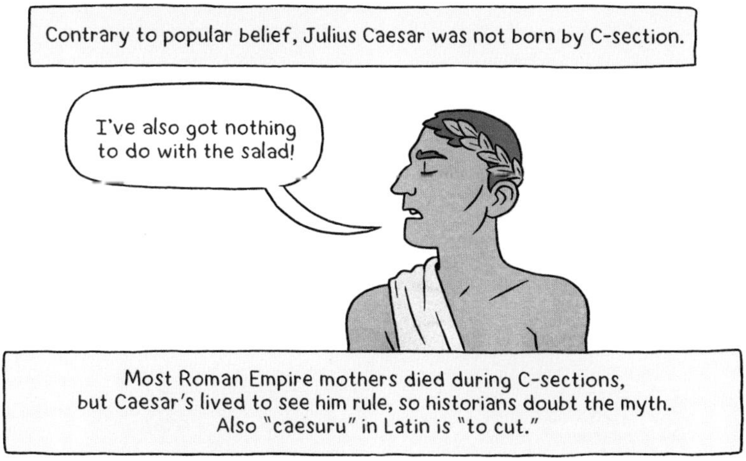

Contrary to popular belief, Julius Caesar was not born by C-section.

I've also got nothing to do with the salad!

Most Roman Empire mothers died during C-sections, but Caesar's lived to see him rule, so historians doubt the myth. Also "caesuru" in Latin is "to cut."

In 1522, a doctor was sentenced to death for dressing as a woman and sneaking into a delivery room to observe a birth.

ARREST HIM!

It was considered obscene for a man to be present, despite the fact that they were the ones writing the birth books.

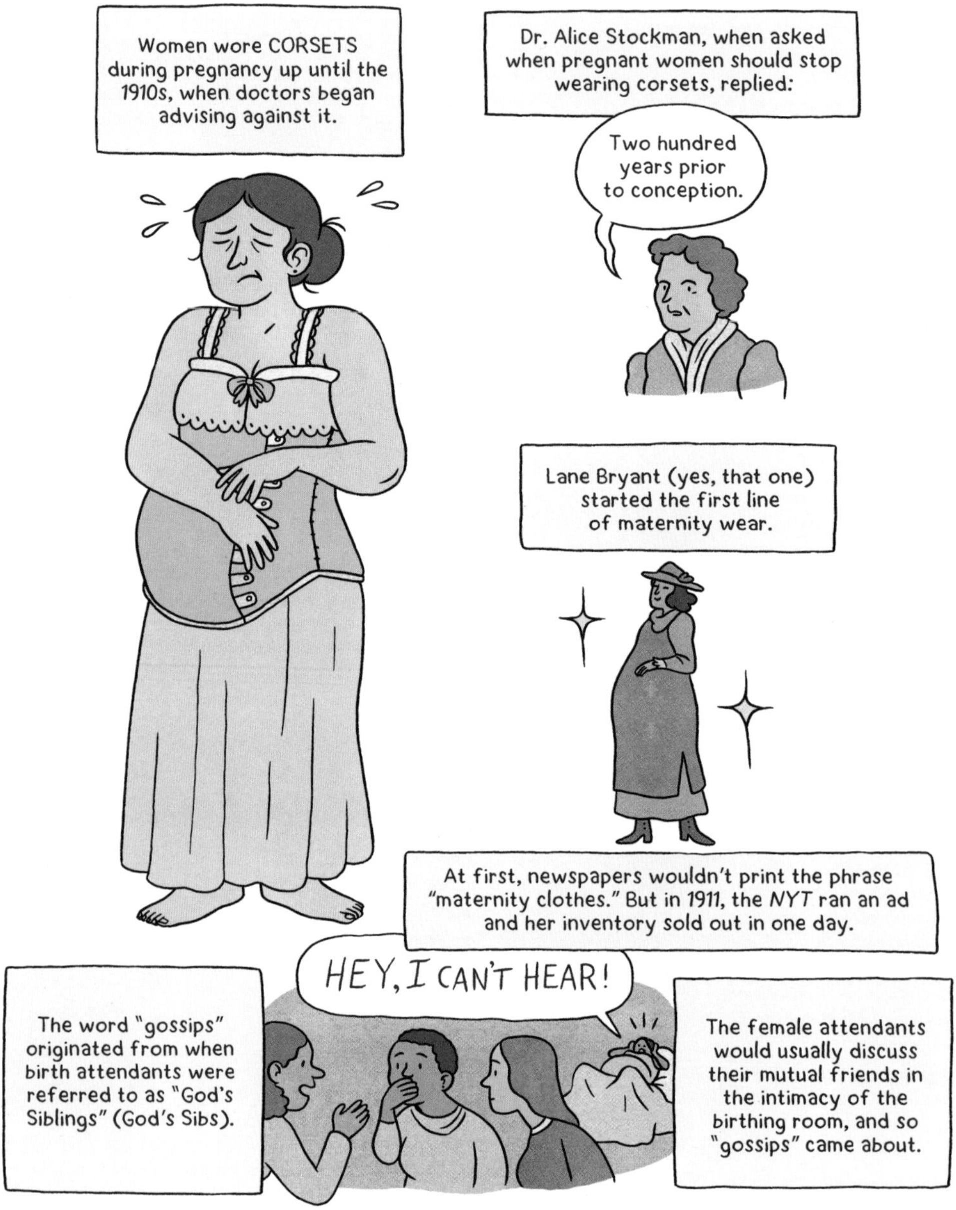
Women wore CORSETS during pregnancy up until the 1910s, when doctors began advising against it.
Dr. Alice Stockman, when asked when pregnant women should stop wearing corsets, replied:
Two hundred years prior to conception.
Lane Bryant (yes, that one) started the first line of maternity wear.
At first, newspapers wouldn't print the phrase "maternity clothes." But in 1911, the *NYT* ran an ad and her inventory sold out in one day.
The word "gossips" originated from when birth attendants were referred to as "God's Siblings" (God's Sibs).
HEY, I CAN'T HEAR!
The female attendants would usually discuss their mutual friends in the intimacy of the birthing room, and so "gossips" came about.

Ultrasounds were invented to spot German subs during WWI.
It's the same technology as sonar.

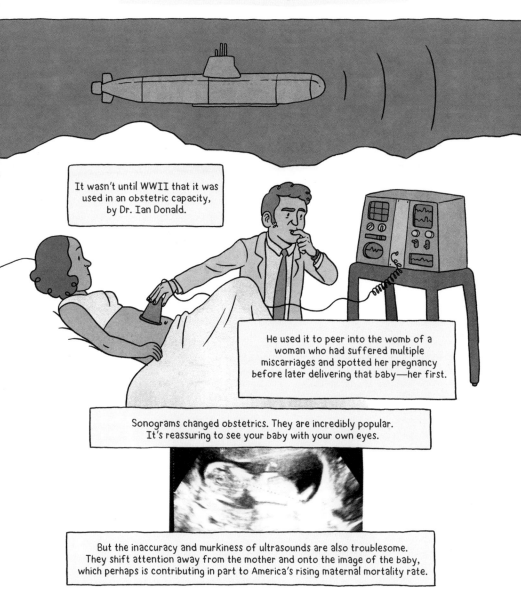

It wasn't until WWII that it was used in an obstetric capacity, by Dr. Ian Donald.

He used it to peer into the womb of a woman who had suffered multiple miscarriages and spotted her pregnancy before later delivering that baby—her first.

Sonograms changed obstetrics. They are incredibly popular.
It's reassuring to see your baby with your own eyes.

But the inaccuracy and murkiness of ultrasounds are also troublesome.
They shift attention away from the mother and onto the image of the baby,
which perhaps is contributing in part to America's rising maternal mortality rate.

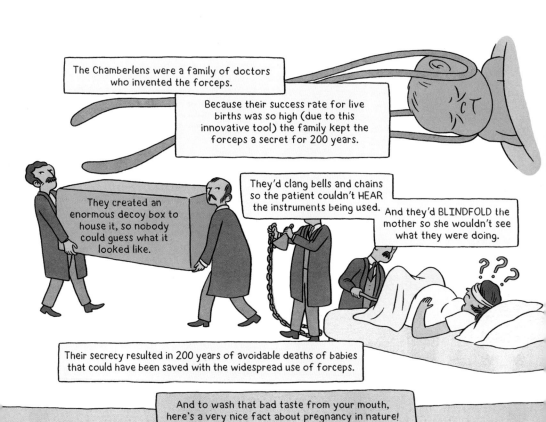

The Chamberlens were a family of doctors who invented the forceps.

Because their success rate for live births was so high (due to this innovative tool) the family kept the forceps a secret for 200 years.

They created an enormous decoy box to house it, so nobody could guess what it looked like.

They'd clang bells and chains so the patient couldn't HEAR the instruments being used.

And they'd BLINDFOLD the mother so she wouldn't see what they were doing.

Their secrecy resulted in 200 years of avoidable deaths of babies that could have been saved with the widespread use of forceps.

And to wash that bad taste from your mouth, here's a very nice fact about pregnancy in nature!

Elephants—my guide animal in pregnancy— are matriarchal and hold birth rituals!

After their twenty-two-month pregnancy (the longest of any mammal), the other elephants huddle around a laboring mother elephant, swaying with her.

They comfort her and keep predators at bay. They even help the baby out of the birth canal.

And then...

BABY ELEPHANT

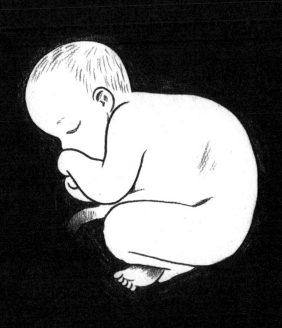

BIRTH STORY

I have always wondered what labor feels like.

Bad menstrual cramps!

Knife stabs.

Like someone squeezing your insides!

For a state often referenced as the standard of pain ("more painful than childbirth") it seems pretty difficult to nail down exactly what it feels like.

It was hard to wrap my head around when I was staring down the runway of my own birth experience.

My first contractions were like rolling, condensed period cramps that came and went.

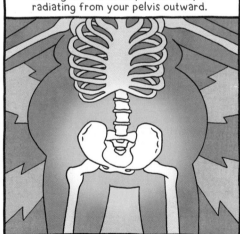

For non-period-havers, let's say it's like having severe constipation cramps radiating from your pelvis outward.

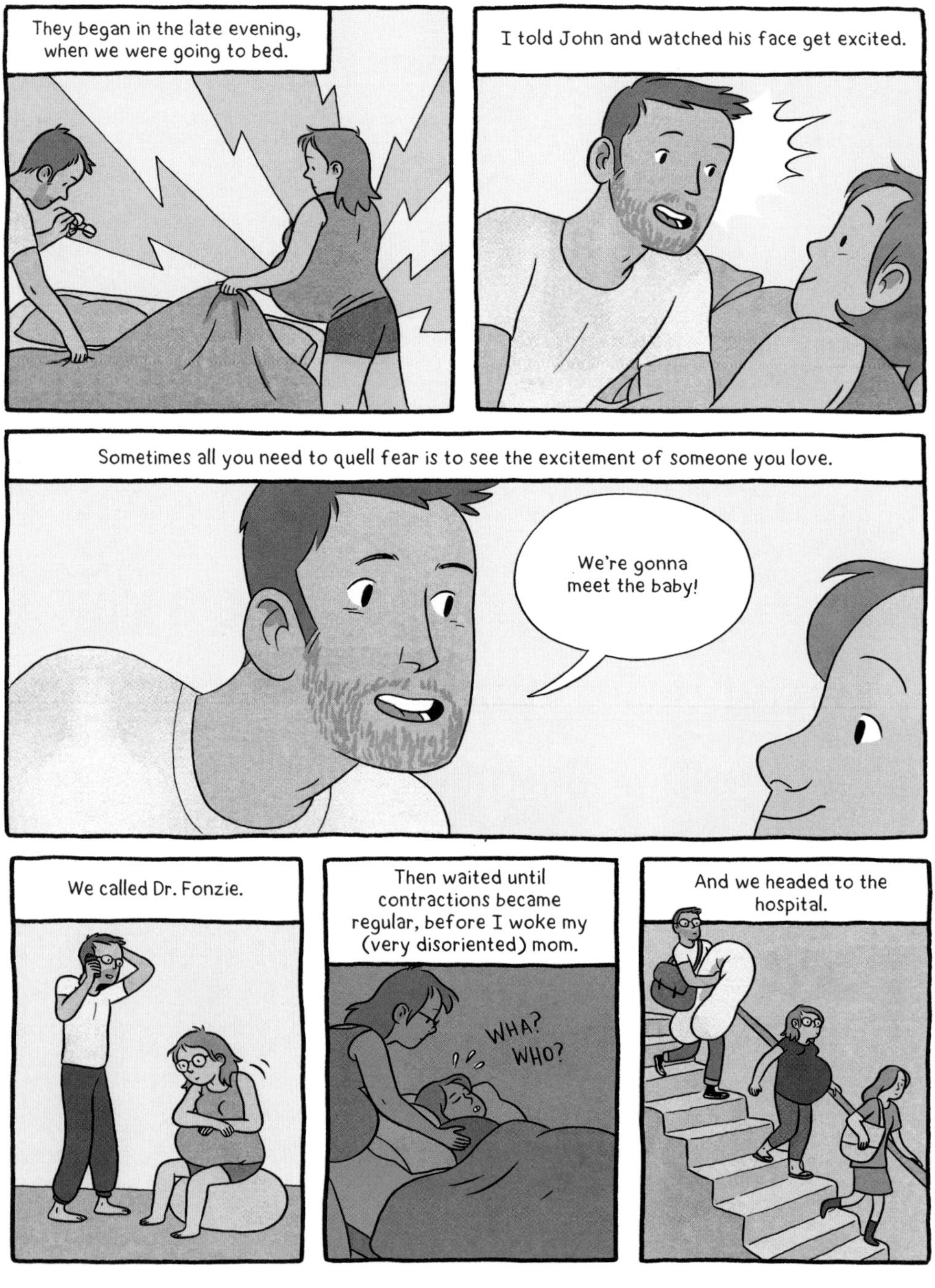
They began in the late evening, when we were going to bed.
I told John and watched his face get excited.
Sometimes all you need to quell fear is to see the excitement of someone you love.
We're gonna meet the baby!
We called Dr. Fonzie.
Then waited until contractions became regular, before I woke my (very disoriented) mom.
WHA? WHO?
And we headed to the hospital.

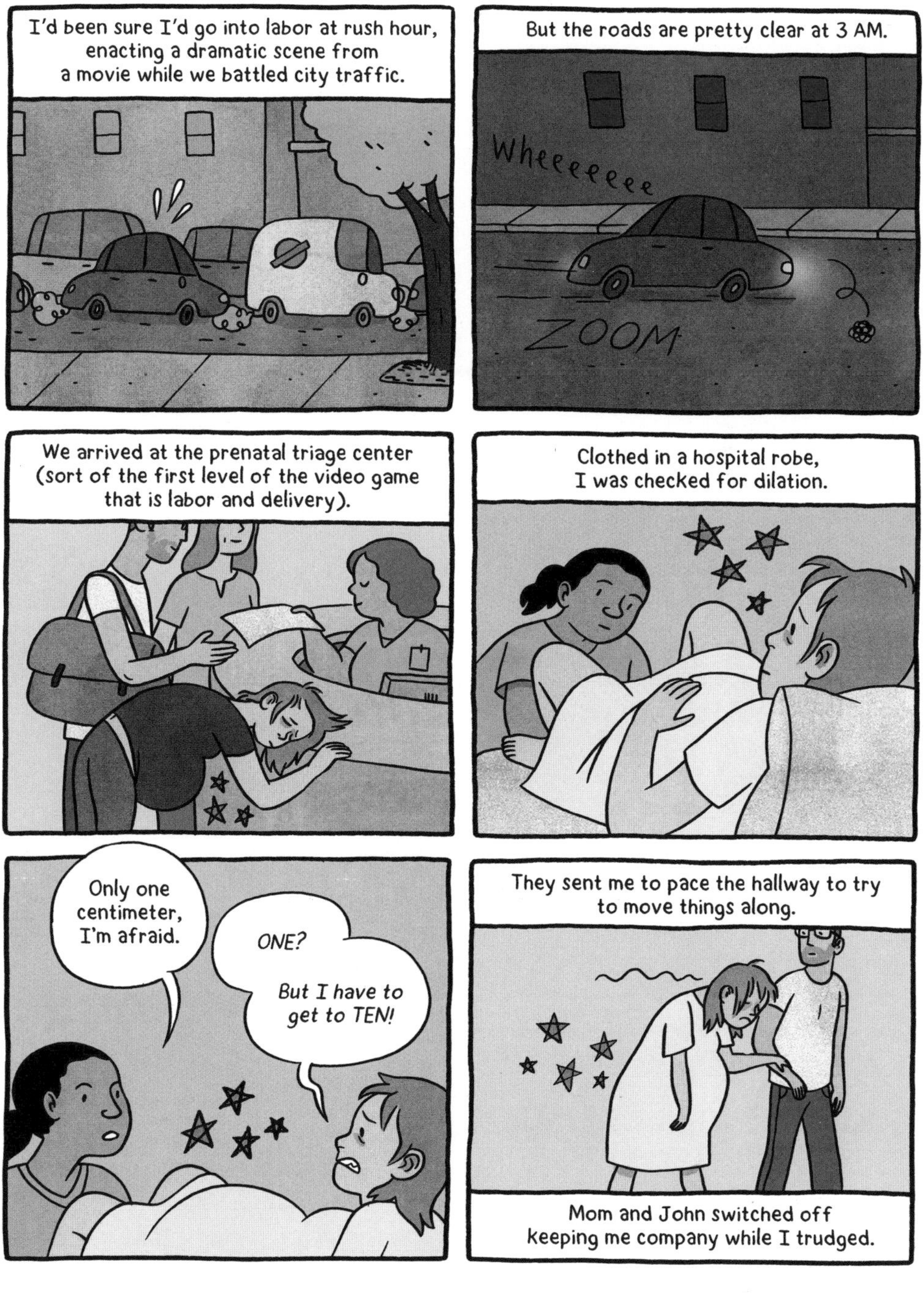
I'd been sure I'd go into labor at rush hour, enacting a dramatic scene from a movie while we battled city traffic.
But the roads are pretty clear at 3 AM.
Wheeeeeeee
ZOOM
We arrived at the prenatal triage center (sort of the first level of the video game that is labor and delivery).
Clothed in a hospital robe, I was checked for dilation.
Only one centimeter, I'm afraid.
ONE?
But I have to get to TEN!
They sent me to pace the hallway to try to move things along.
Mom and John switched off keeping me company while I trudged.

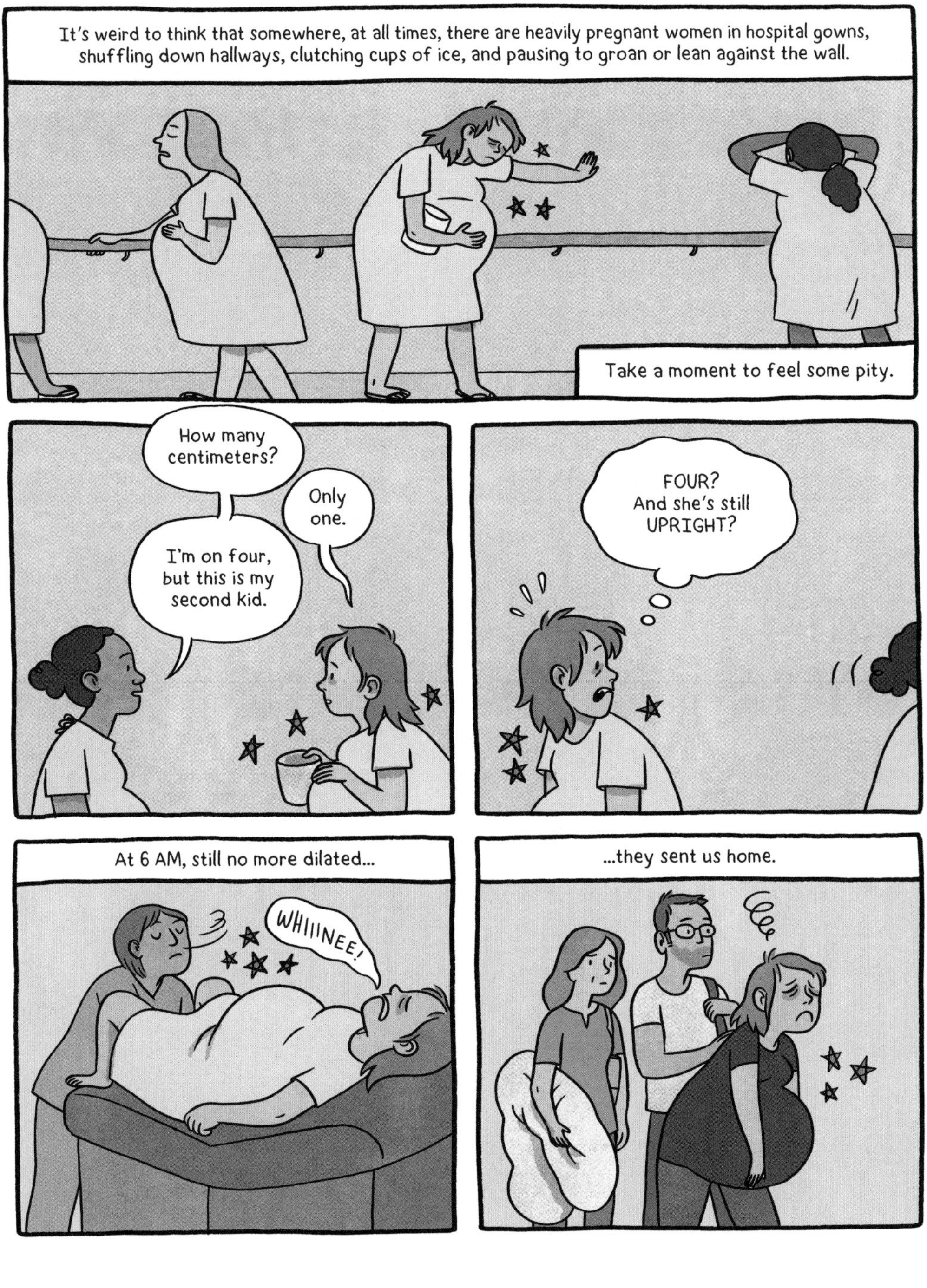
It's weird to think that somewhere, at all times, there are heavily pregnant women in hospital gowns, shuffling down hallways, clutching cups of ice, and pausing to groan or lean against the wall.
Take a moment to feel some pity.
How many centimeters?
I'm on four, but this is my second kid.
Only one.
FOUR? And she's still UPRIGHT?
At 6 AM, still no more dilated...
WHIIINEE!
...they sent us home.

I labored irregularly throughout the day while we all tried to rest.

That evening, I watched the Tonys while contractions rolled through me.

Hamilton wins EVERYTHING!

We drove back to the hospital again at 4 AM.

Surely, surely, after more than twenty-four hours of early labor, I would be further along!

NOPE, ONLY A CENTIMETER AND A HALF.

HOW

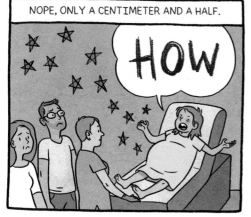

The nurse took one look at my face and offered to pull some strings and have me admitted anyway and given an epidural.

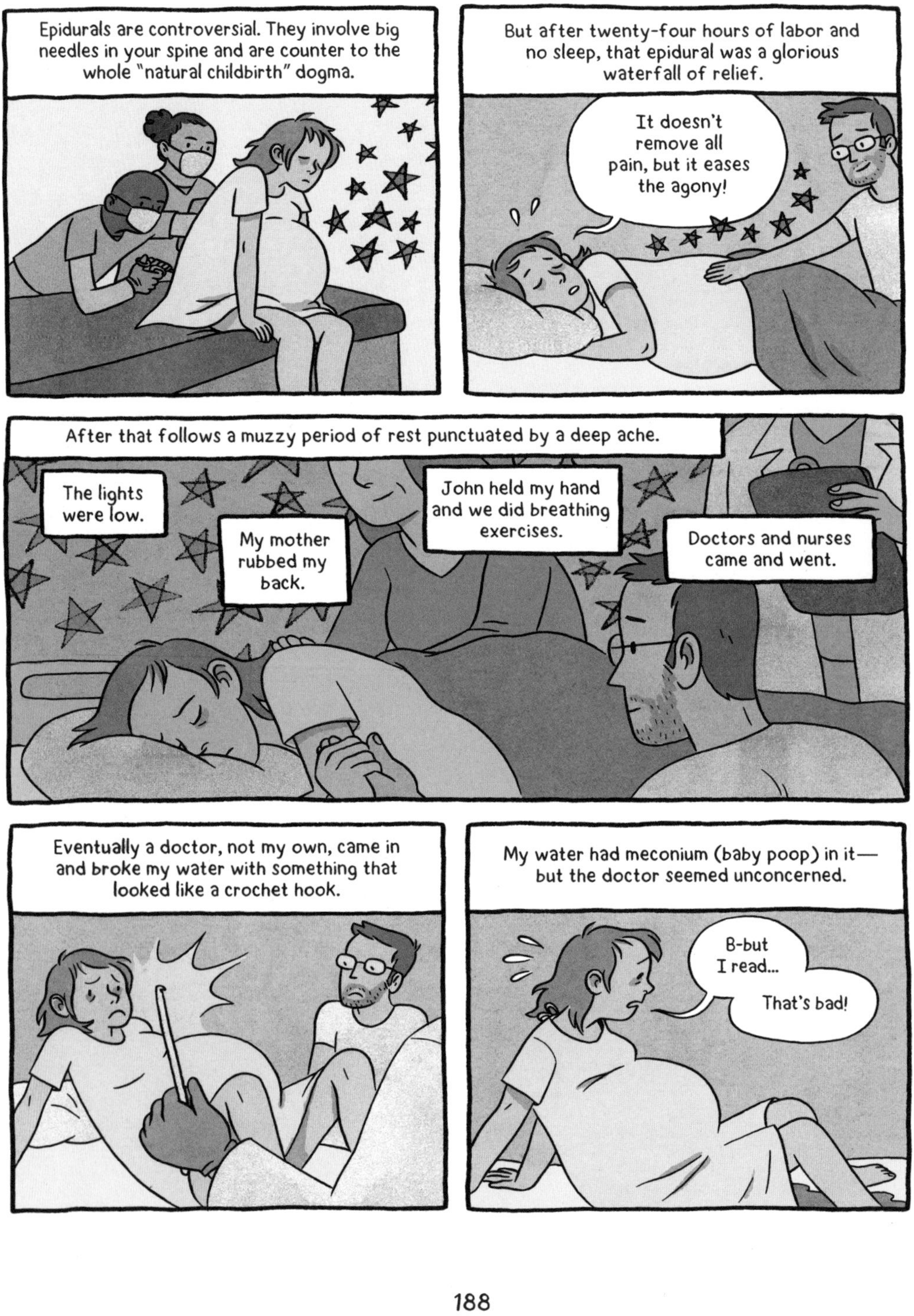
Epidurals are controversial. They involve big needles in your spine and are counter to the whole "natural childbirth" dogma.
But after twenty-four hours of labor and no sleep, that epidural was a glorious waterfall of relief.
It doesn't remove all pain, but it eases the agony!
After that follows a muzzy period of rest punctuated by a deep ache.
The lights were low.
My mother rubbed my back.
John held my hand and we did breathing exercises.
Doctors and nurses came and went.
Eventually a doctor, not my own, came in and broke my water with something that looked like a crochet hook.
My water had meconium (baby poop) in it—but the doctor seemed unconcerned.
B-but I read...
That's bad!

Despite it all, dilation stalled, and they recommended Pitocin (a drug used to increase contractions and speed labor).

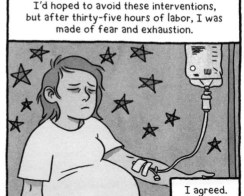

I'd hoped to avoid these interventions, but after thirty-five hours of labor, I was made of fear and exhaustion.

I agreed.

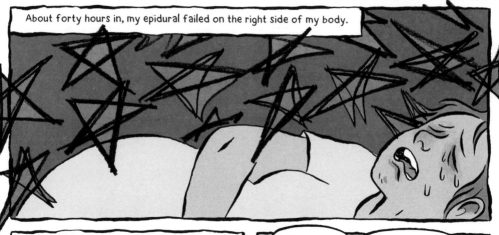

About forty hours in, my epidural failed on the right side of my body.

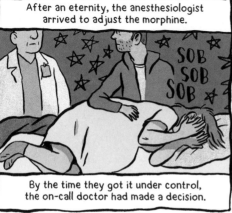

After an eternity, the anesthesiologist arrived to adjust the morphine.

SOB
SOB
SOB

By the time they got it under control, the on-call doctor had made a decision.

The baby isn't engaging.

You're not progressing past five centimeters.

You're too tired to continue.

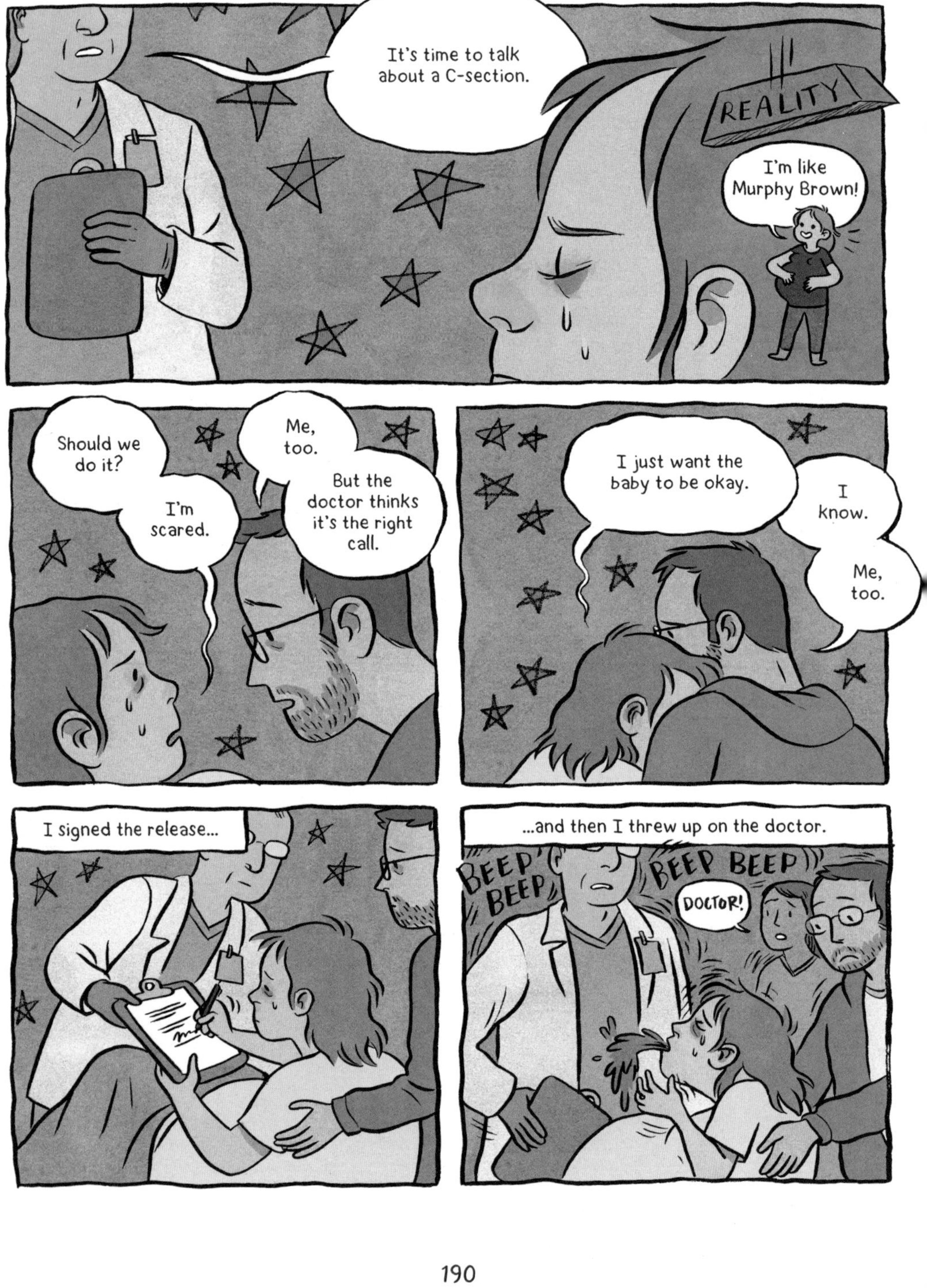
It's time to talk about a C-section.
REALITY
I'm like Murphy Brown!
Should we do it?
I'm scared.
Me, too.
But the doctor thinks it's the right call.
I just want the baby to be okay.
I know.
Me, too.
I signed the release...
...and then I threw up on the doctor.
BEEP BEEP
BEEP BEEP
DOCTOR!

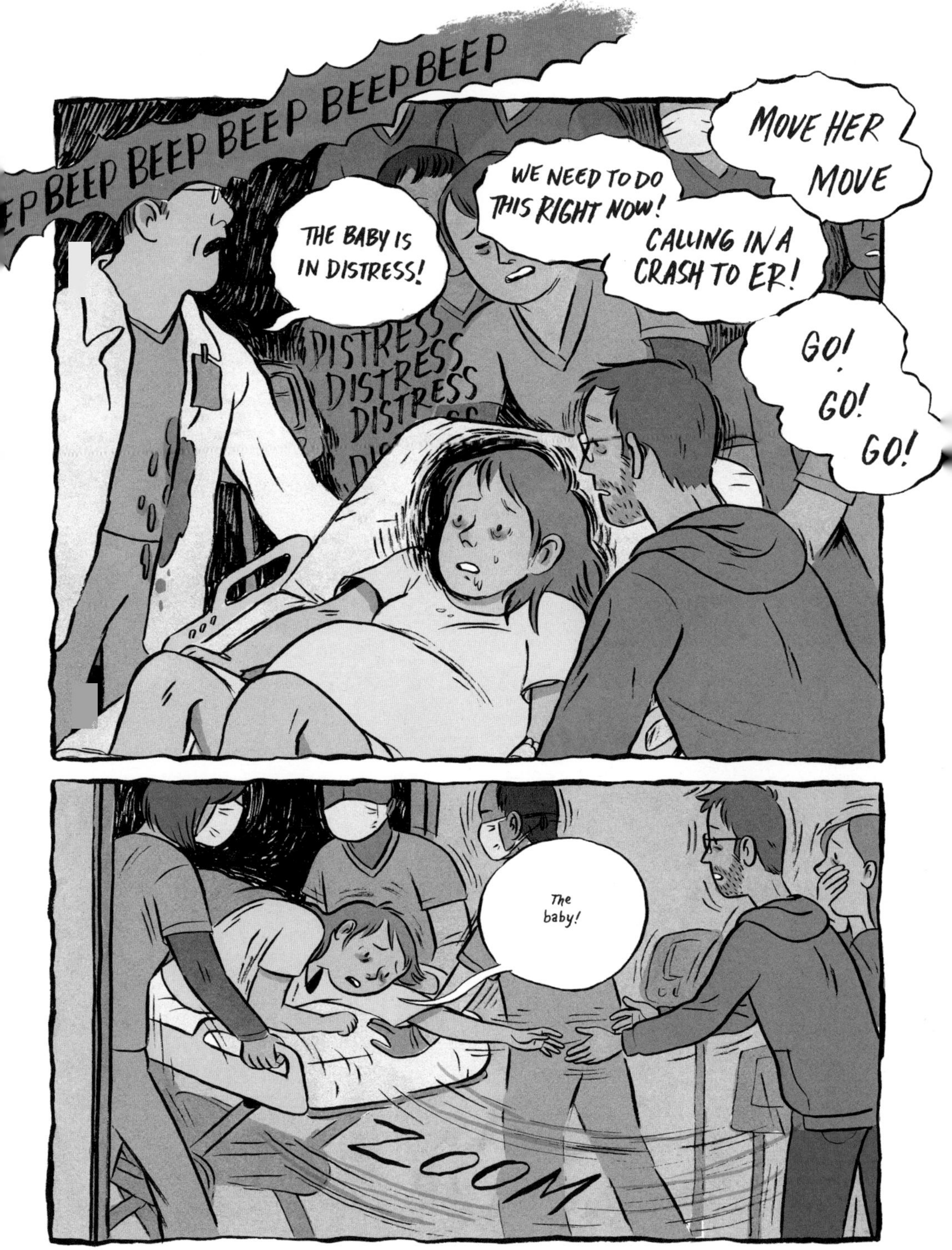
BEEP BEEP BEEP BEEP BEEP
THE BABY IS IN DISTRESS!
DISTRESS
DISTRESS
DISTRESS
WE NEED TO DO THIS RIGHT NOW!
CALLING IN A CRASH TO ER!
MOVE HER MOVE
GO! GO! GO!
The baby!
ZOOM

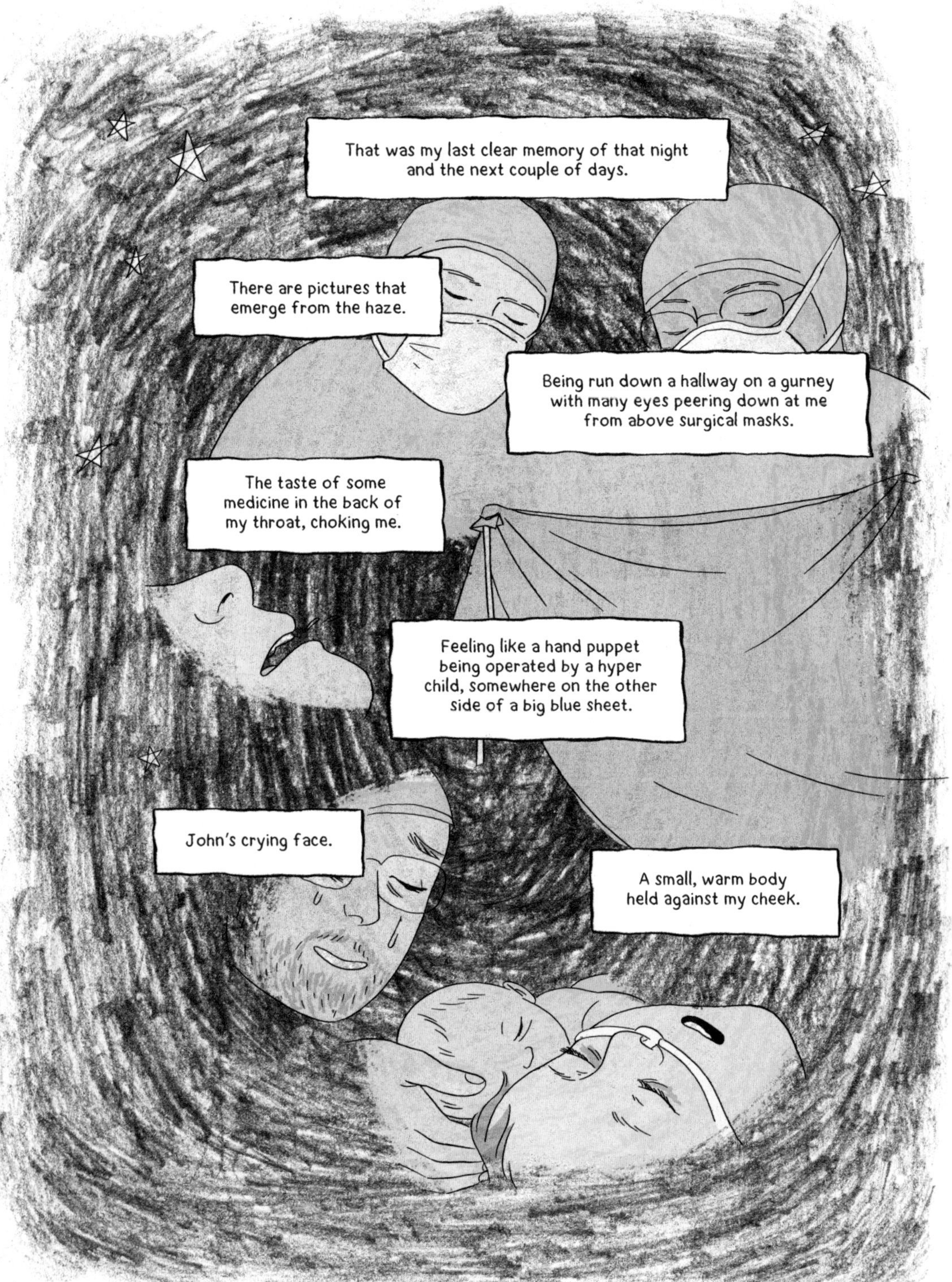
That was my last clear memory of that night and the next couple of days.
There are pictures that emerge from the haze.
Being run down a hallway on a gurney with many eyes peering down at me from above surgical masks.
The taste of some medicine in the back of my throat, choking me.
Feeling like a hand puppet being operated by a hyper child, somewhere on the other side of a big blue sheet.
John's crying face.
A small, warm body held against my cheek.

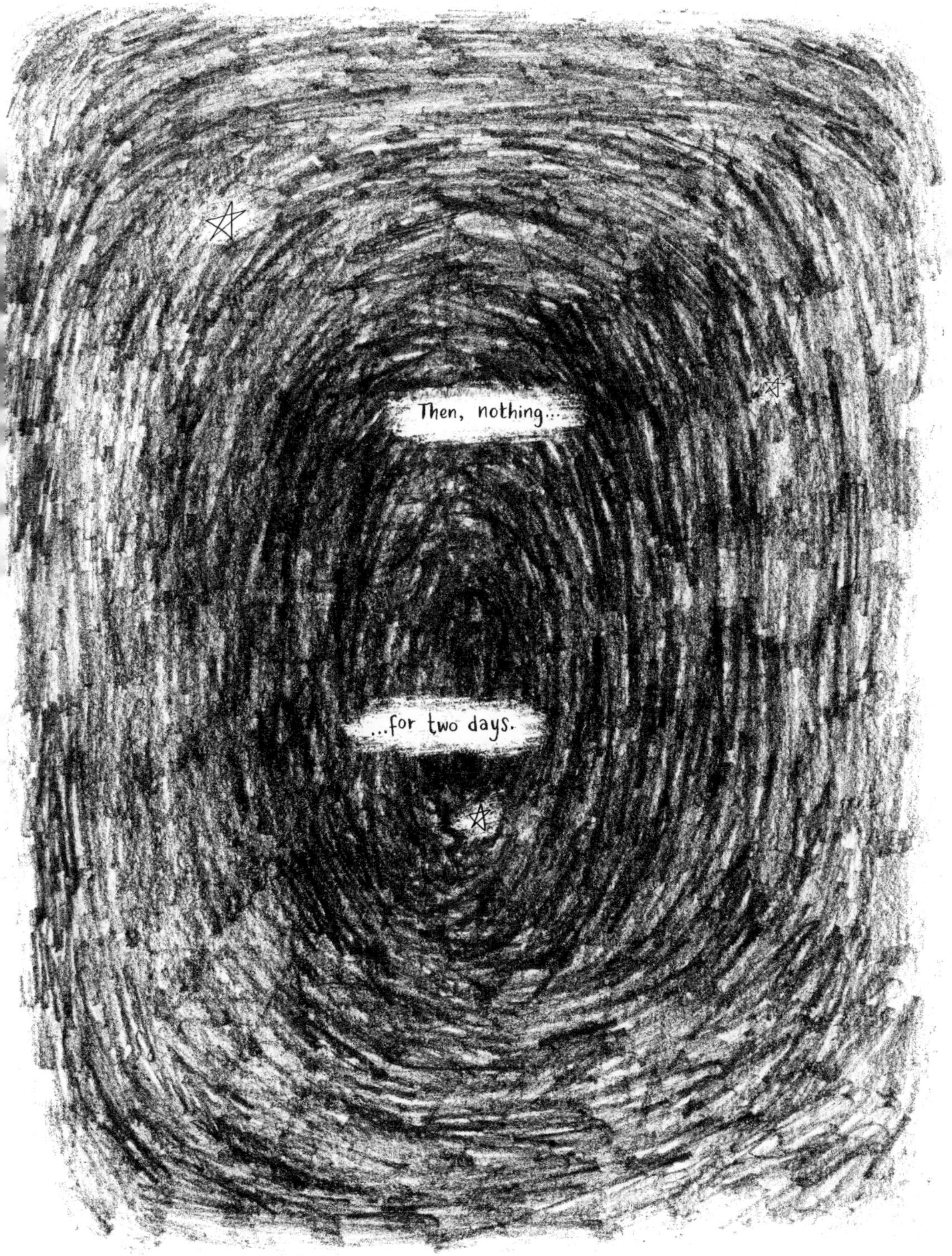
Then, nothing...
...for two days.

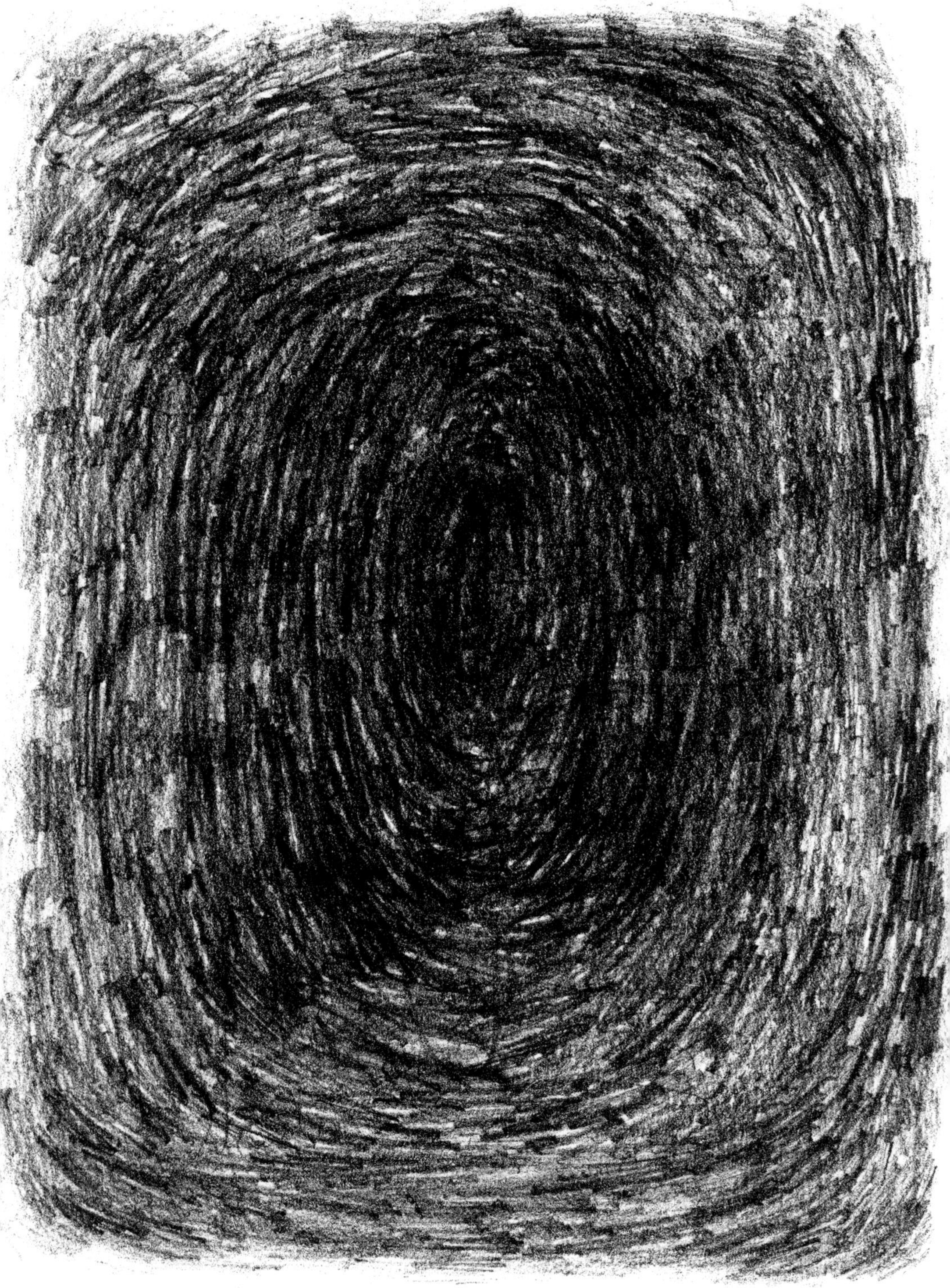

THE FOLLOWING PORTION
IS WRITTEN FROM JOHN'S PERSPECTIVE
because I do not remember it.

The baby!

I'm left in the waiting room alone, wringing my hands for a few minutes.

One of the nurses comes back.

You're John?

Here, put these on and come with me!

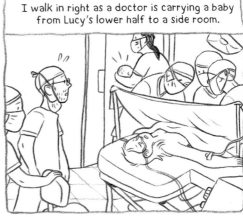

I walk in right as a doctor is carrying a baby from Lucy's lower half to a side room.

Lucy looks yellow and out of it.
We talk while she's still being operated upon.

Did you see him?

Is he okay?

I don't know.

Would you like to meet your son?

Come with me.

go please

I lay eyes on Pal and break down sobbing.

WEHHH!

I rejoin Lucy with Pal in my hands.

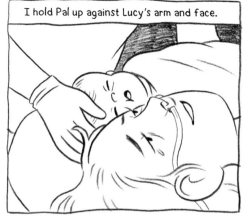

I hold Pal up against Lucy's arm and face.

196

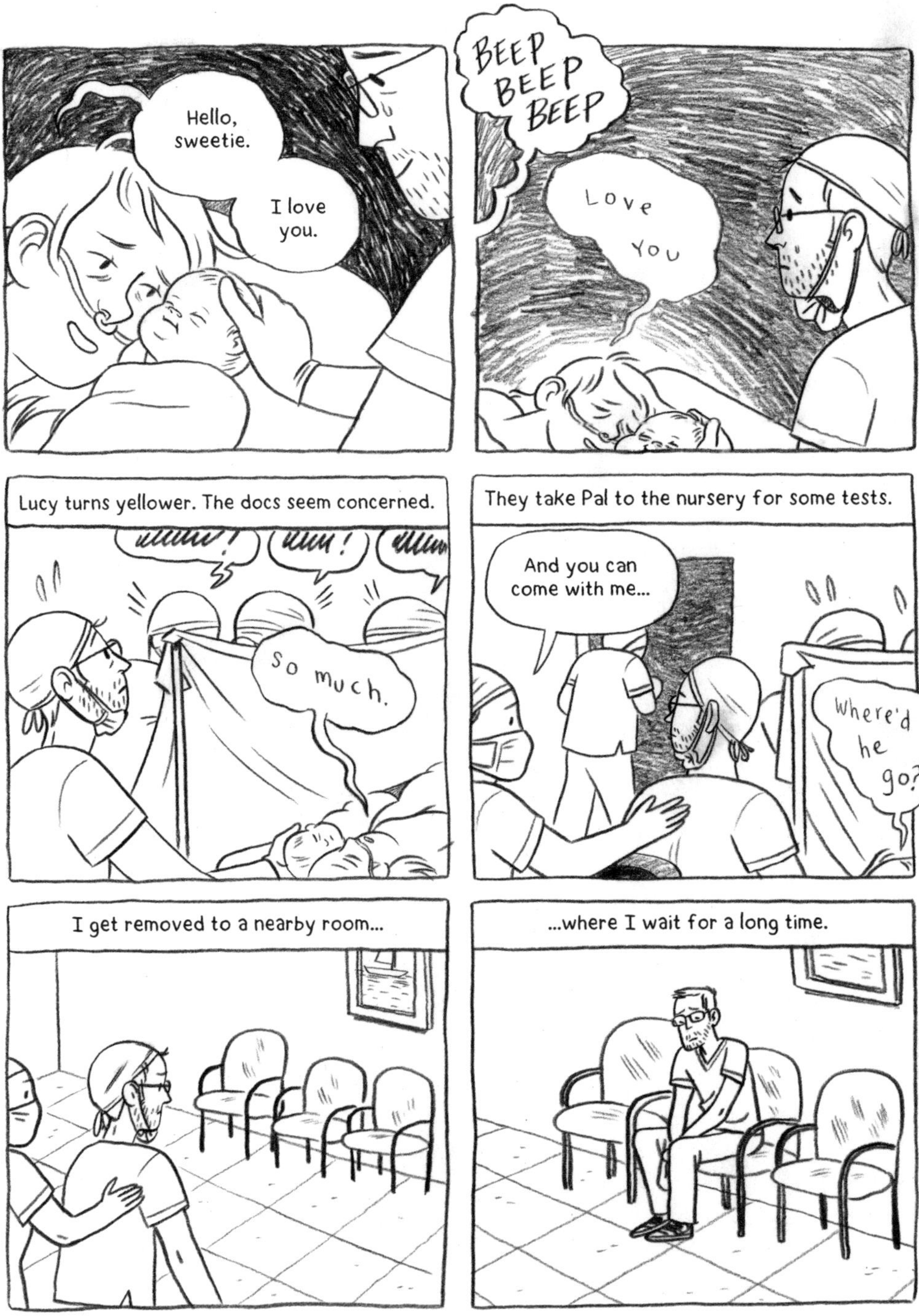
Hello, sweetie.
I love you.
BEEP BEEP BEEP
Love you
Lucy turns yellower. The docs seem concerned.
so much.
They take Pal to the nursery for some tests.
And you can come with me...
Where'd he go?
I get removed to a nearby room...
...where I wait for a long time.

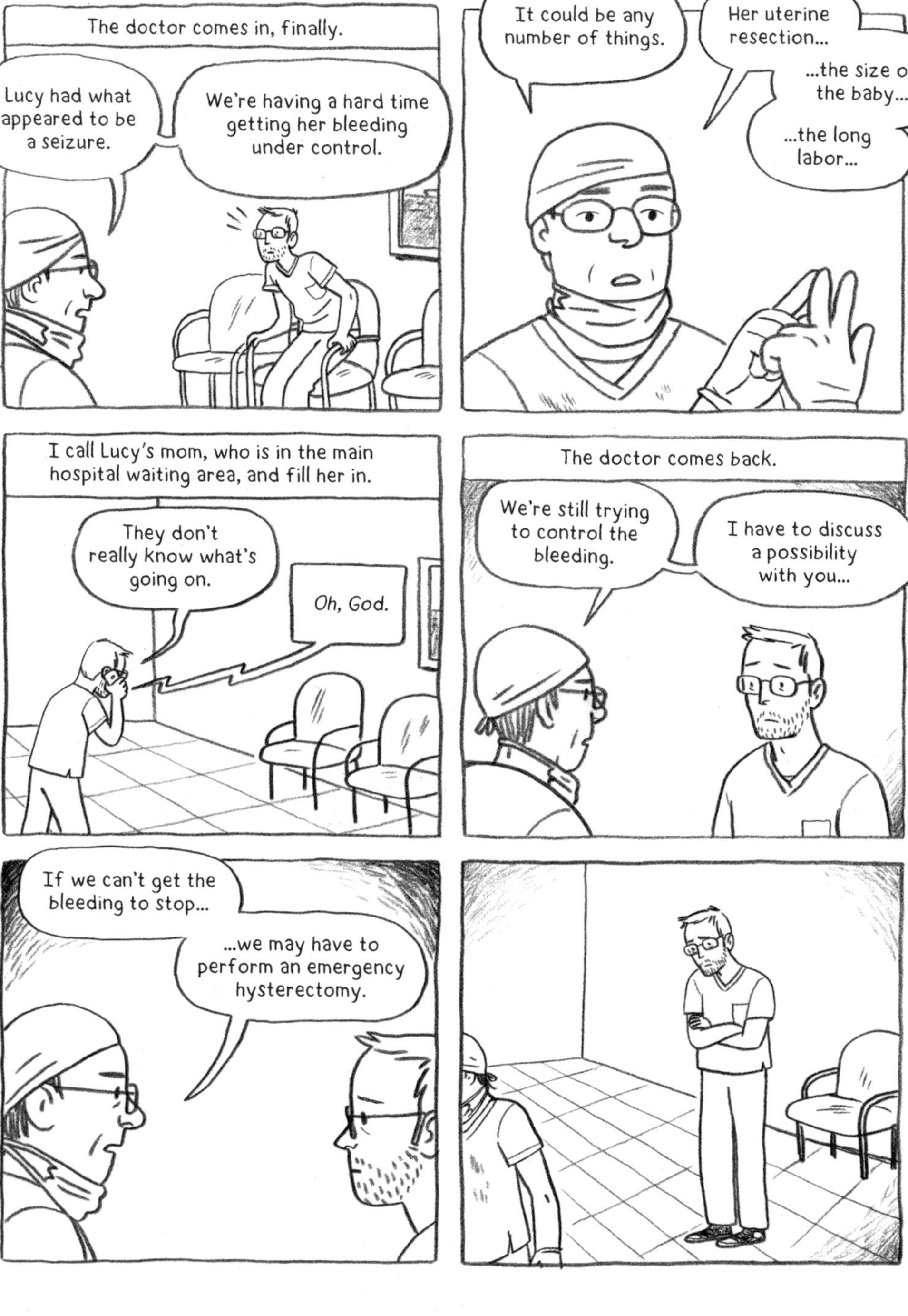
The doctor comes in, finally.
Lucy had what appeared to be a seizure.
We're having a hard time getting her bleeding under control.
It could be any number of things.
Her uterine resection...
...the size of the baby...
...the long labor...
I call Lucy's mom, who is in the main hospital waiting area, and fill her in.
They don't really know what's going on.
Oh, God.
The doctor comes back.
We're still trying to control the bleeding.
I have to discuss a possibility with you...
If we can't get the bleeding to stop...
...we may have to perform an emergency hysterectomy.

After a long time...

She's stable, but she's on a breathing tube and she's heading to the surgical ICU.

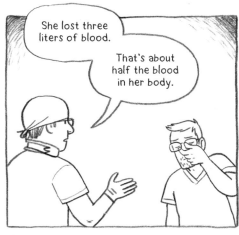

She lost three liters of blood.

That's about half the blood in her body.

I meet up with our parents in the waiting room.

And I take them to the nursery to meet Pal...

...then to the ICU to see Lucy, but when we arrive, the ward is locked.

Hello?

Is anyone there?

A nurse eventually emerges.

We're settling her into her room.

I'll let you know when you can come in.

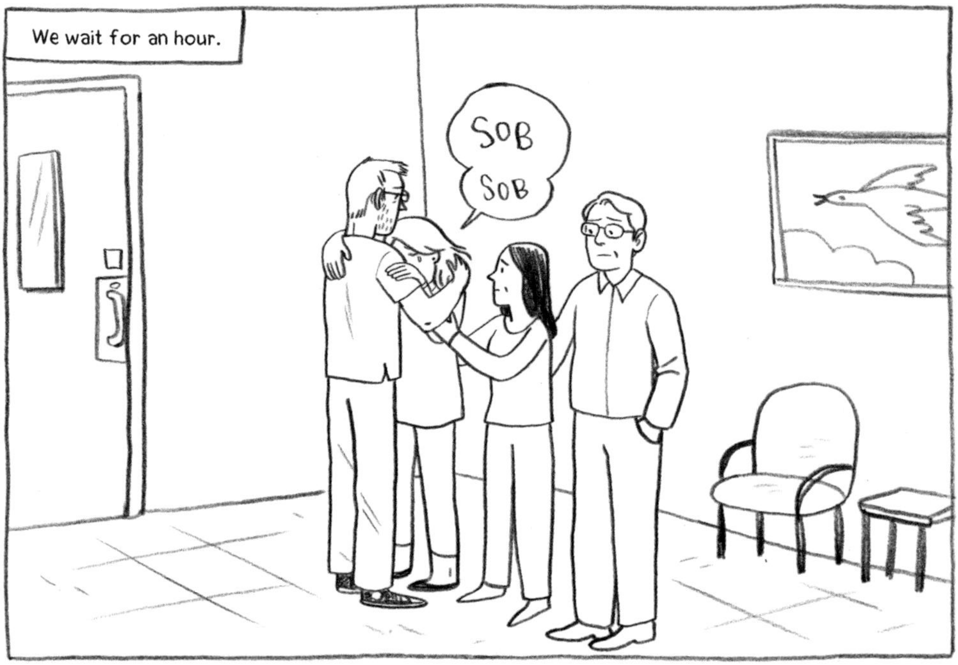
We wait for an hour.
SOB
SOB

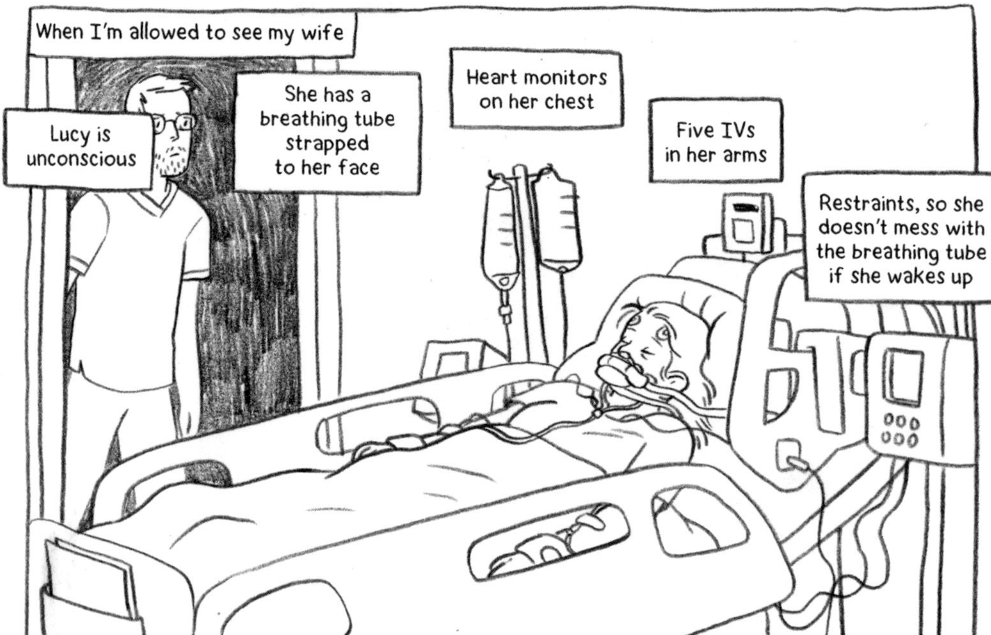
When I'm allowed to see my wife
Lucy is unconscious
She has a breathing tube strapped to her face
Heart monitors on her chest
Five IVs in her arms
Restraints, so she doesn't mess with the breathing tube if she wakes up

A respiratory technician comes in to stabilize the the CO_2 in Lucy's blood.

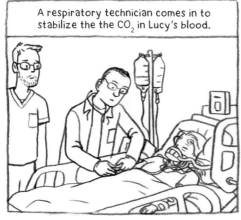

They change out her IV to fix her high levels (or was it low levels?) of potassium.

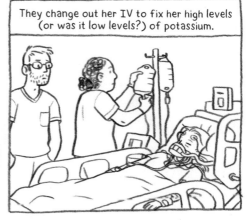

They listen to her breathing, to test how much fluid she has in her lungs.

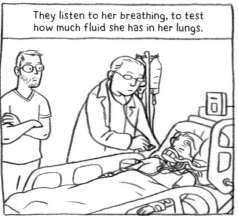

Neurologists come to examine her to try to discern the cause of her seizures.

The working theory is eclampsia.*

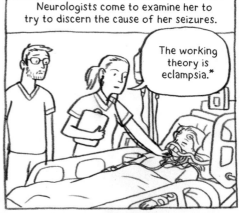

*Remember when Lucy asked her doctor about this and he ignored her?!

I stay up all night watching my family.

201

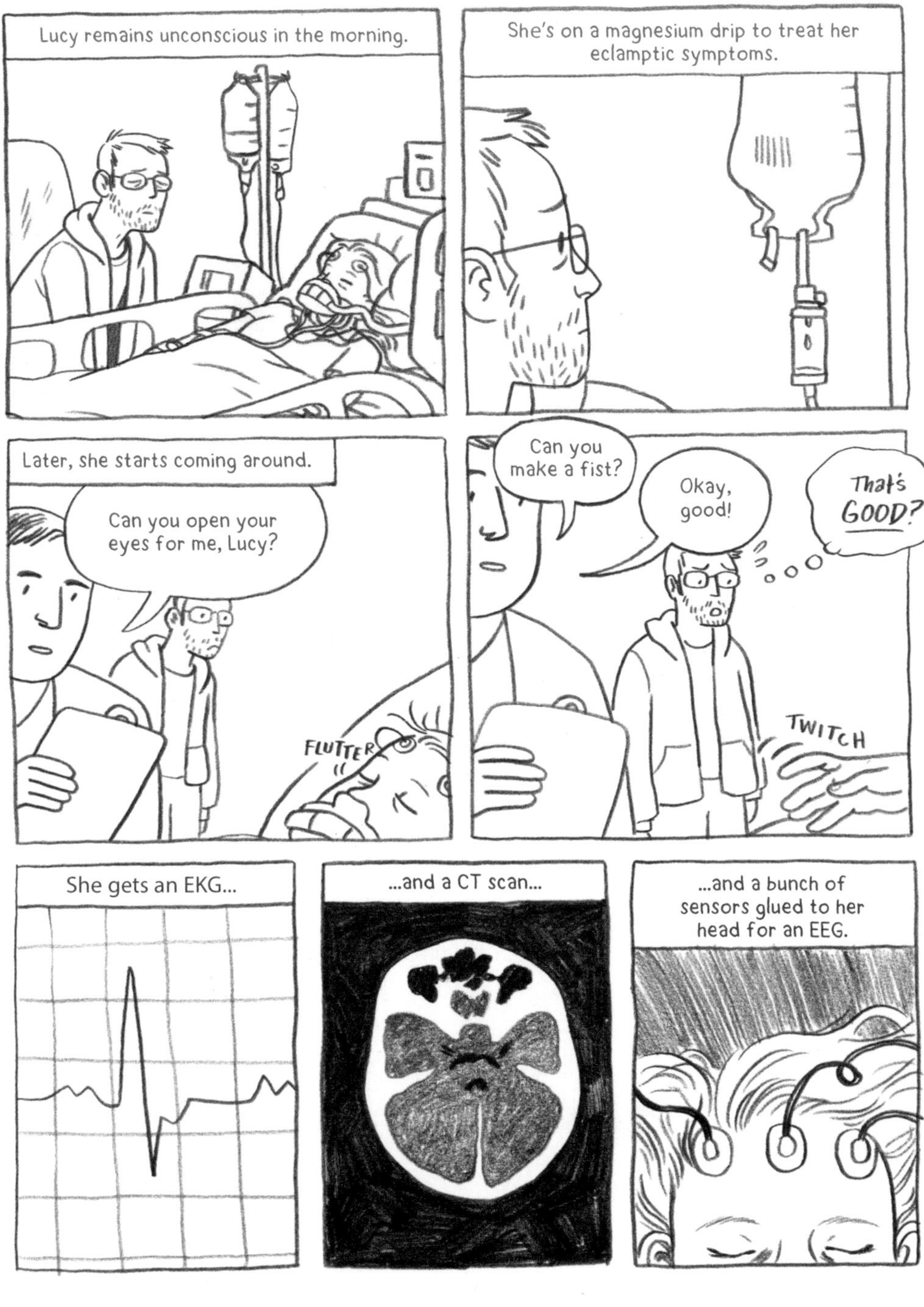
Lucy remains unconscious in the morning.
She's on a magnesium drip to treat her eclamptic symptoms.
Later, she starts coming around.
Can you open your eyes for me, Lucy?
FLUTTER
Can you make a fist?
Okay, good!
That's GOOD?
TWITCH
She gets an EKG...
...and a CT scan...
...and a bunch of sensors glued to her head for an EEG.

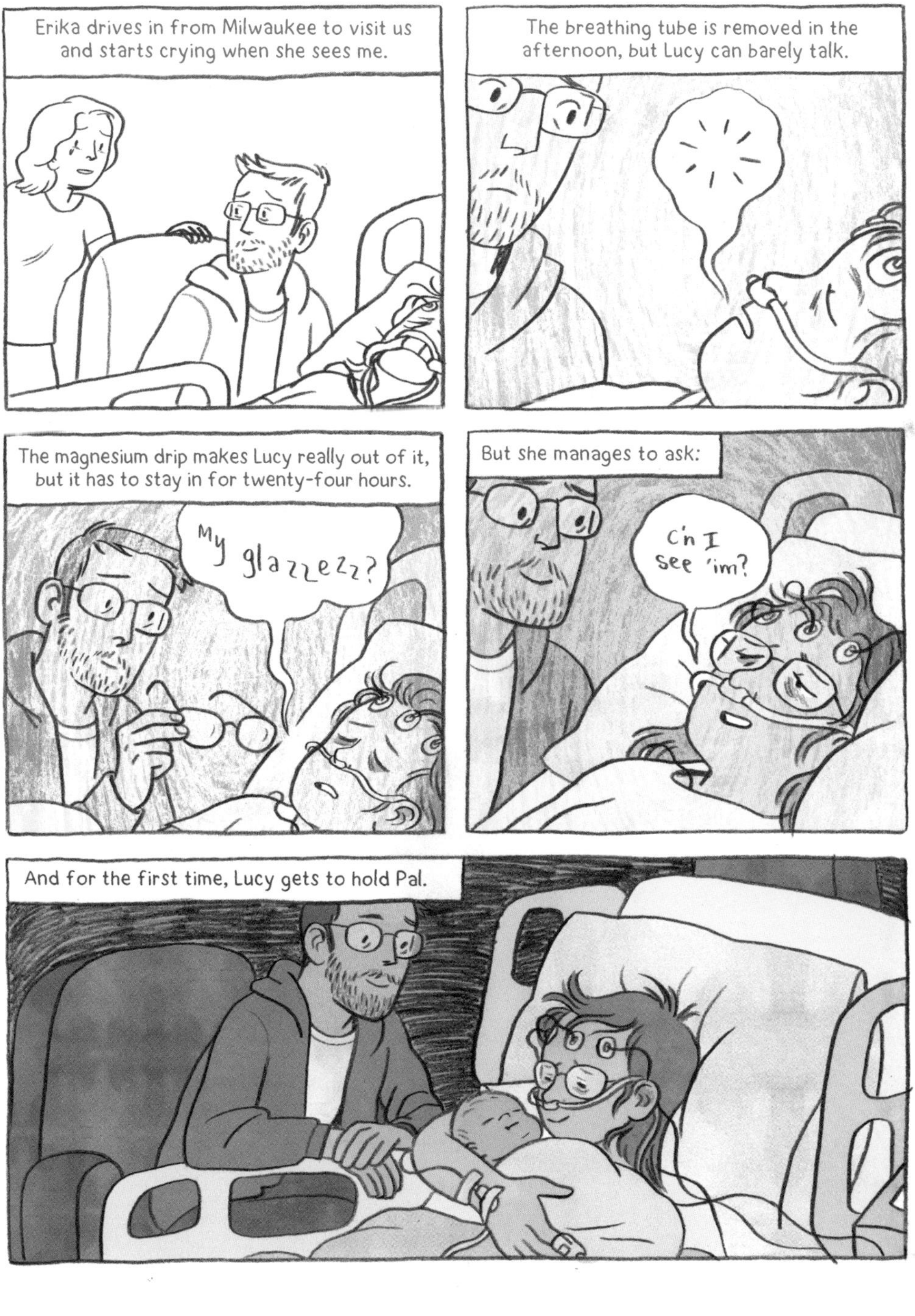
Erika drives in from Milwaukee to visit us and starts crying when she sees me.
The breathing tube is removed in the afternoon, but Lucy can barely talk.
The magnesium drip makes Lucy really out of it, but it has to stay in for twenty-four hours.
My glazzezz?
But she manages to ask:
C'n I see 'im?
And for the first time, Lucy gets to hold Pal.

ONCE AGAIN WITH THE PREGNANCY RESEARCH

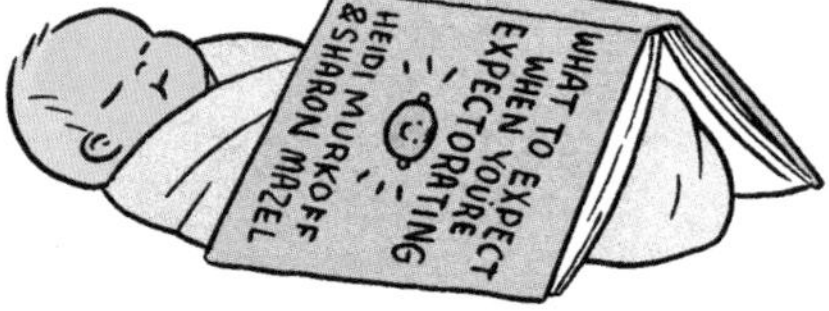
WHAT TO EXPECT WHEN YOU'RE EXPECTORATING
HEIDI MURKOFF & SHARON MAZEL

BIRTH CLASS

BUT FIRST, A DISCLAIMER

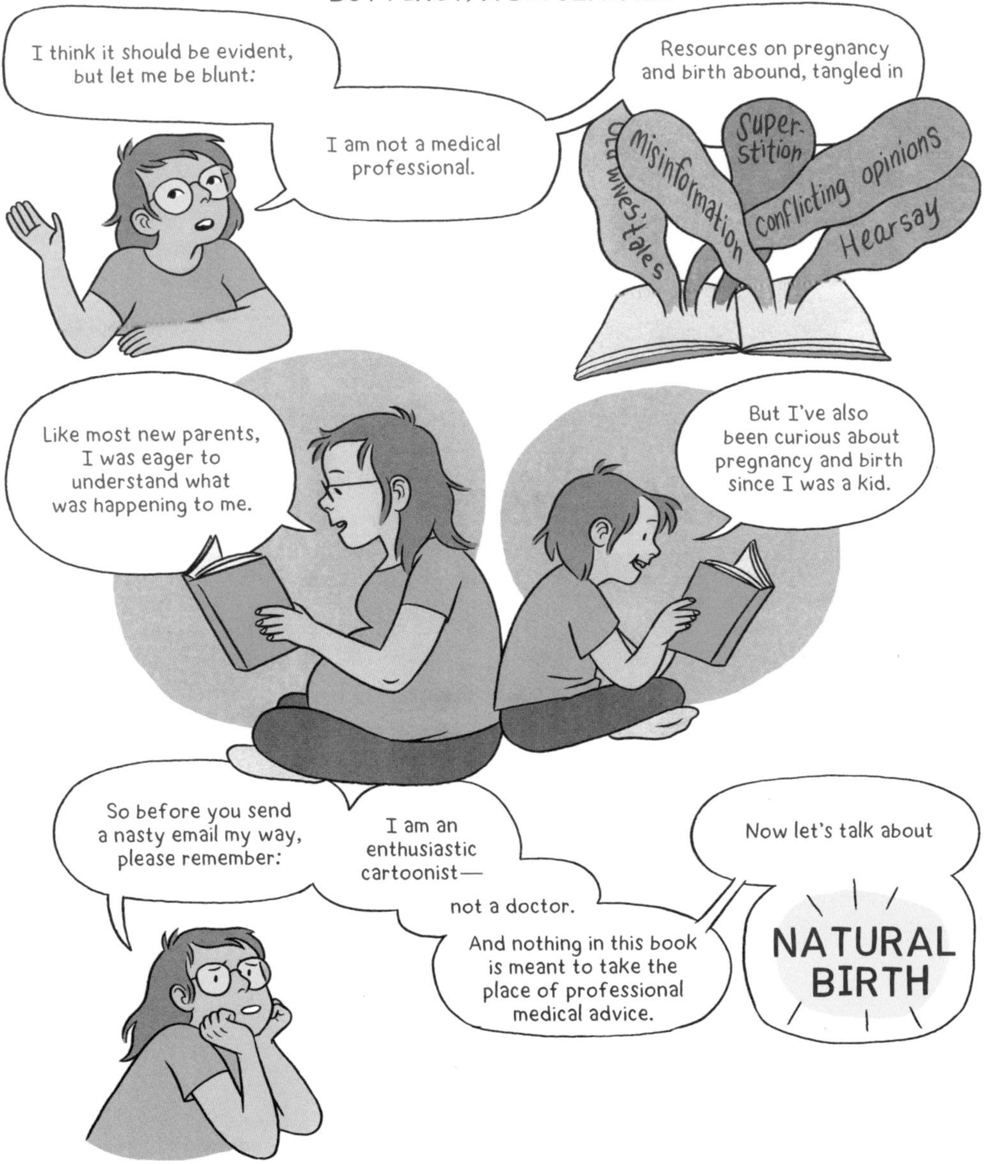
I think it should be evident, but let me be blunt:
I am not a medical professional.
Resources on pregnancy and birth abound, tangled in
Old wives' tales
Misinformation
Superstition
Conflicting opinions
Hearsay
Like most new parents, I was eager to understand what was happening to me.
But I've also been curious about pregnancy and birth since I was a kid.
So before you send a nasty email my way, please remember:
I am an enthusiastic cartoonist—
not a doctor.
And nothing in this book is meant to take the place of professional medical advice.
Now let's talk about
NATURAL BIRTH

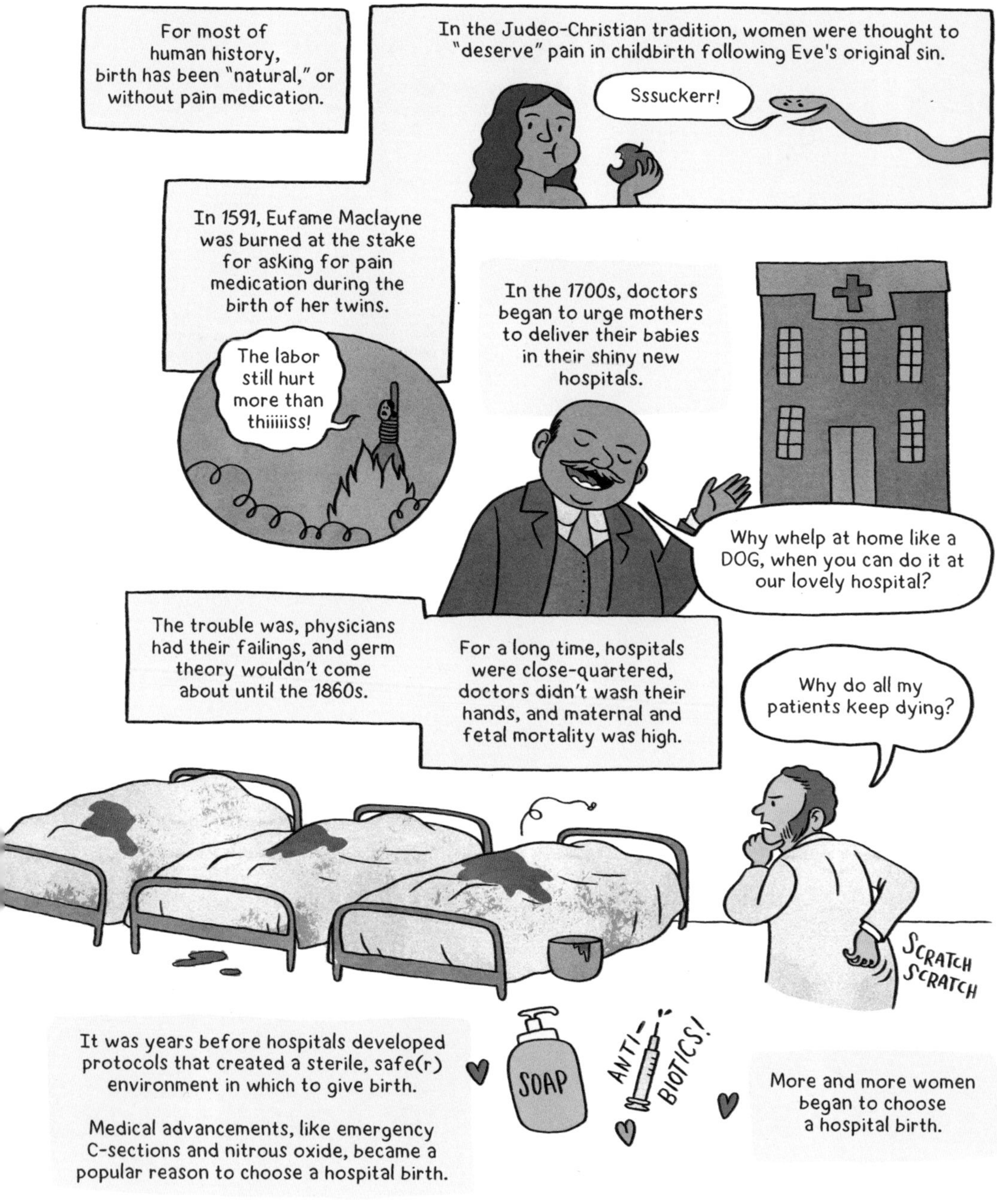
For most of human history, birth has been "natural," or without pain medication.
In the Judeo-Christian tradition, women were thought to "deserve" pain in childbirth following Eve's original sin.
Sssuckerr!
In 1591, Eufame Maclayne was burned at the stake for asking for pain medication during the birth of her twins.
The labor still hurt more than thiiiiiss!
In the 1700s, doctors began to urge mothers to deliver their babies in their shiny new hospitals.
Why whelp at home like a DOG, when you can do it at our lovely hospital?
The trouble was, physicians had their failings, and germ theory wouldn't come about until the 1860s.
For a long time, hospitals were close-quartered, doctors didn't wash their hands, and maternal and fetal mortality was high.
Why do all my patients keep dying?
SCRATCH SCRATCH
It was years before hospitals developed protocols that created a sterile, safe(r) environment in which to give birth.
Medical advancements, like emergency C-sections and nitrous oxide, became a popular reason to choose a hospital birth.
SOAP
ANTI-BIOTICS!
More and more women began to choose a hospital birth.

Queen Victoria was responsible for changing the stigma about pain relief in childbirth when she asked for a whiff of chloroform to ease her delivery of Prince Leopold in 1853.

This paved the way for women to follow her lead.

I am much gratified with the effect of the drug.

Developments in the field of obstetrics meant that women no longer needed to just be grateful to survive, but could choose different ways to enhance their experience of birth.

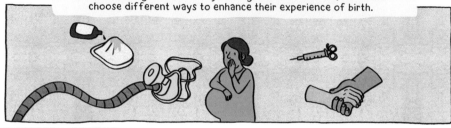

Early in the 1900s, doctors developed the technique known as "twilight sleep."

Morphine and scopolamine were combined to create an analgesic, but also an amnesiac mother, who would barely be conscious while giving birth and would remember none of it.

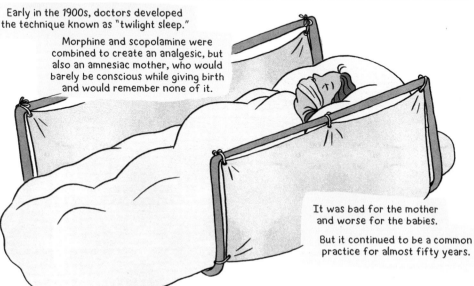

It was bad for the mother and worse for the babies.

But it continued to be a common practice for almost fifty years.

209

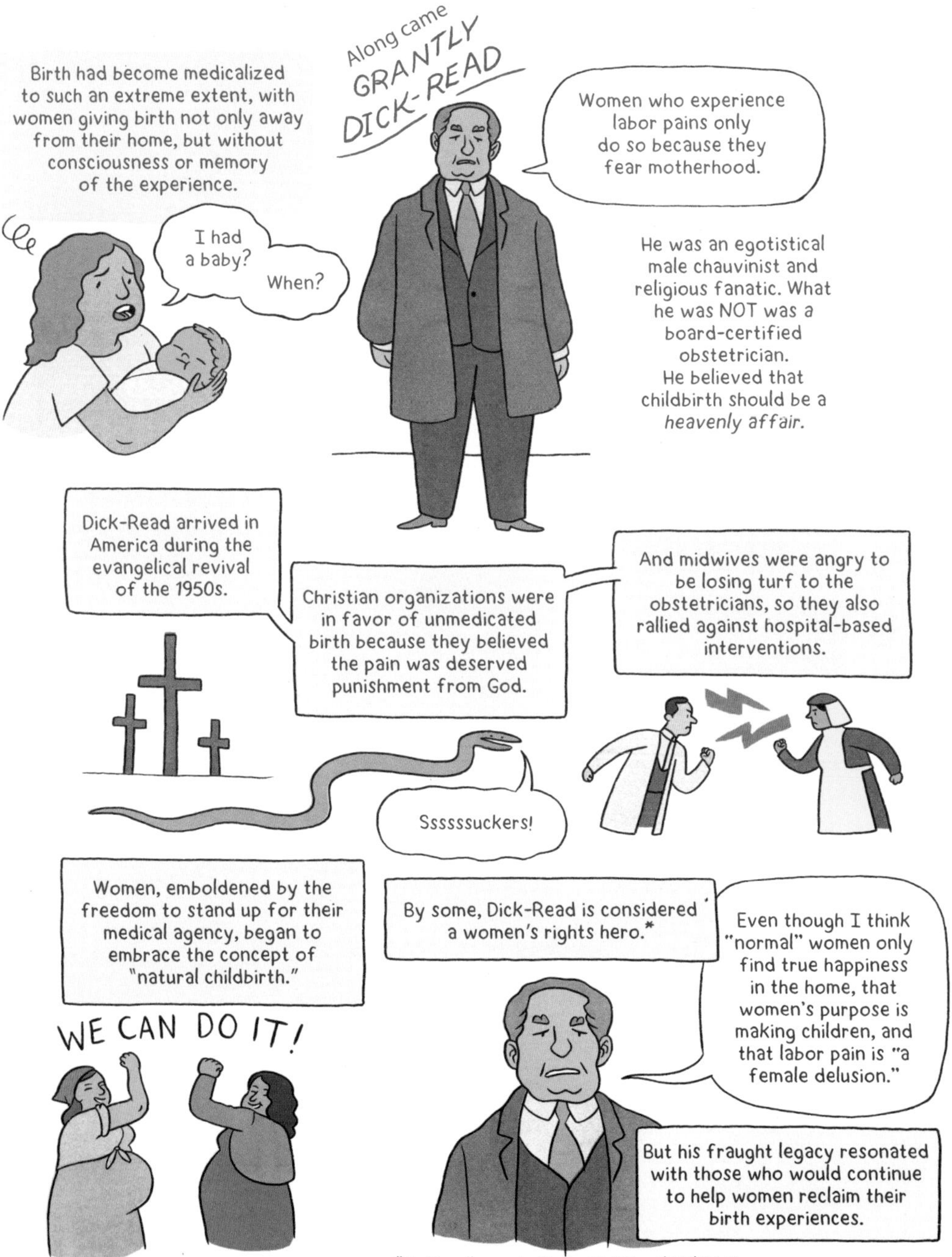

Birth had become medicalized to such an extreme extent, with women giving birth not only away from their home, but without consciousness or memory of the experience.
I had a baby?
When?
Along came
GRANTLY DICK-READ
Women who experience labor pains only do so because they fear motherhood.
He was an egotistical male chauvinist and religious fanatic. What he was NOT was a board-certified obstetrician.
He believed that childbirth should be a *heavenly affair.*
Dick-Read arrived in America during the evangelical revival of the 1950s.
Christian organizations were in favor of unmedicated birth because they believed the pain was deserved punishment from God.
And midwives were angry to be losing turf to the obstetricians, so they also rallied against hospital-based interventions.
Ssssssuckers!
Women, emboldened by the freedom to stand up for their medical agency, began to embrace the concept of "natural childbirth."
WE CAN DO IT!
By some, Dick-Read is considered a women's rights hero.*
Even though I think "normal" women only find true happiness in the home, that women's purpose is making children, and that labor pain is "a female delusion."
But his fraught legacy resonated with those who would continue to help women reclaim their birth experiences.

*He literally wrote the book *Natural Childbirth.*

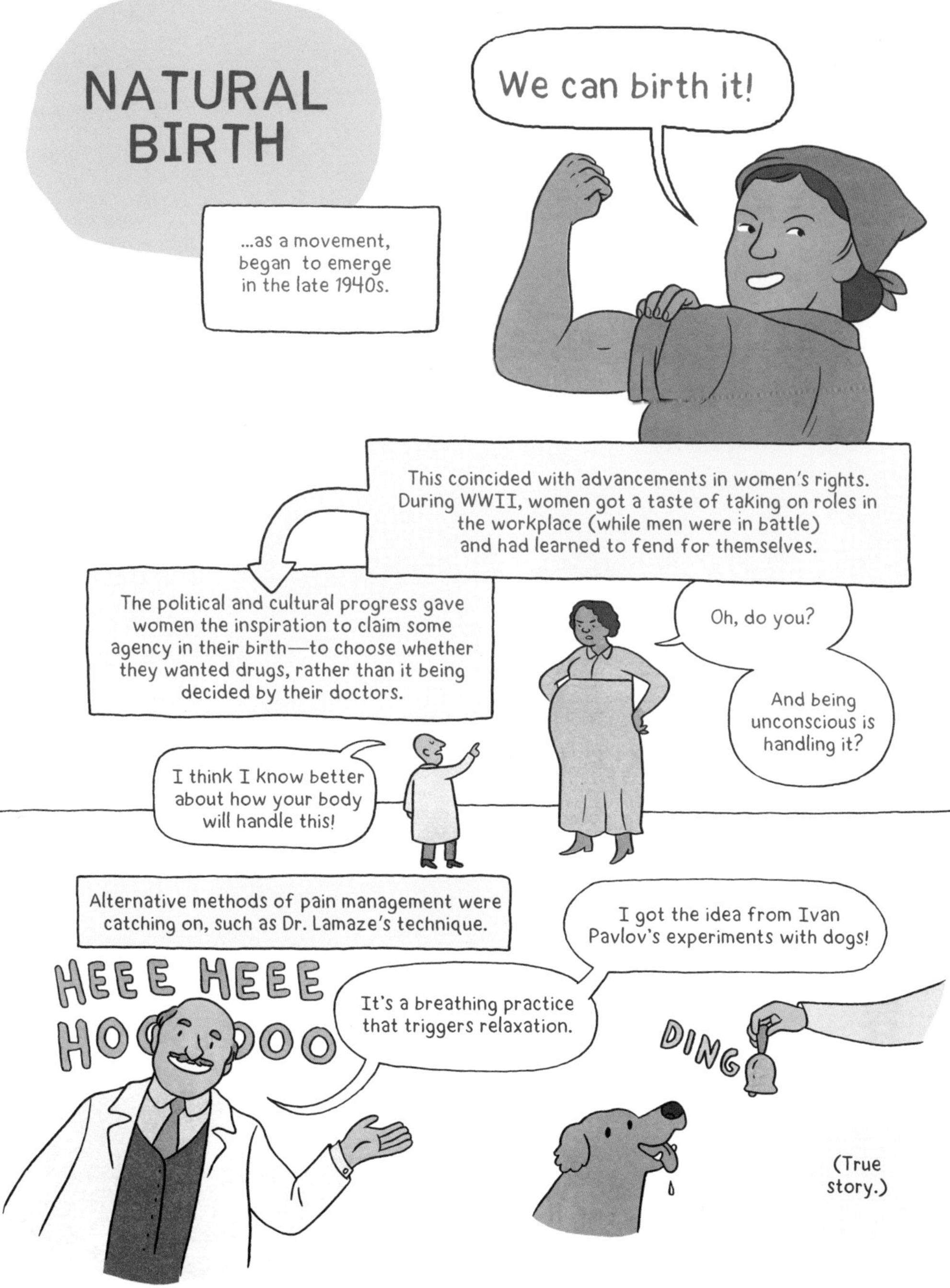
NATURAL BIRTH
We can birth it!
...as a movement, began to emerge in the late 1940s.
This coincided with advancements in women's rights. During WWII, women got a taste of taking on roles in the workplace (while men were in battle) and had learned to fend for themselves.
The political and cultural progress gave women the inspiration to claim some agency in their birth—to choose whether they wanted drugs, rather than it being decided by their doctors.
I think I know better about how your body will handle this!
Oh, do you?
And being unconscious is handling it?
Alternative methods of pain management were catching on, such as Dr. Lamaze's technique.
HEEE HEEE HOOOOOO
It's a breathing practice that triggers relaxation.
I got the idea from Ivan Pavlov's experiments with dogs!
DING
(True story.)

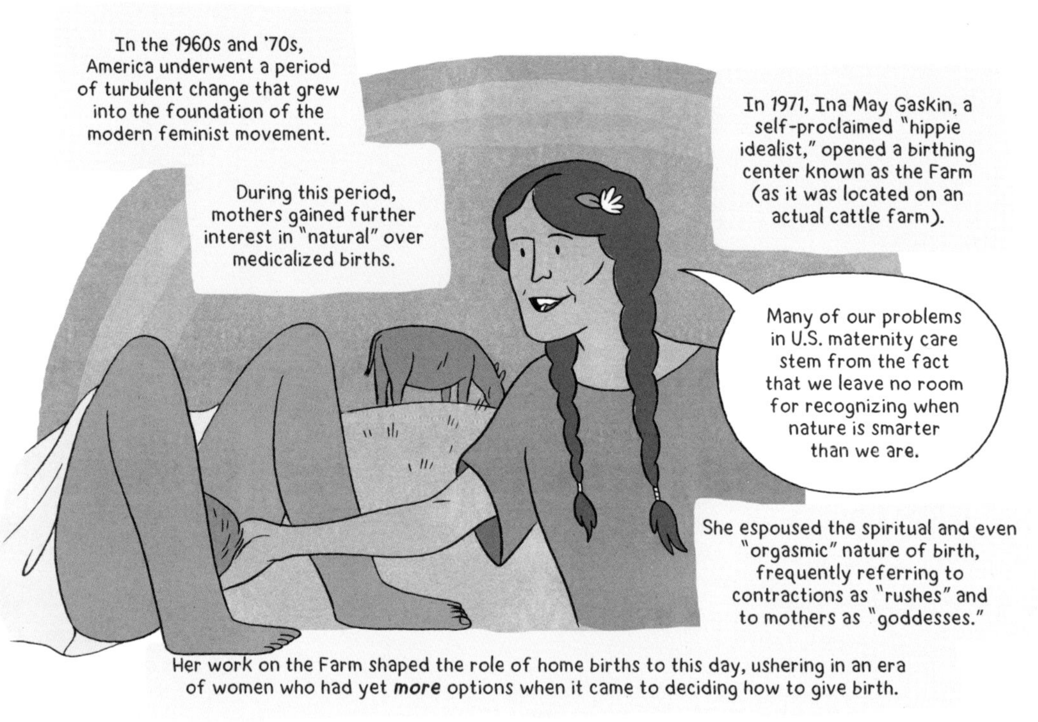
In the 1960s and '70s, America underwent a period of turbulent change that grew into the foundation of the modern feminist movement.
During this period, mothers gained further interest in "natural" over medicalized births.
In 1971, Ina May Gaskin, a self-proclaimed "hippie idealist," opened a birthing center known as the Farm (as it was located on an actual cattle farm).
Many of our problems in U.S. maternity care stem from the fact that we leave no room for recognizing when nature is smarter than we are.
She espoused the spiritual and even "orgasmic" nature of birth, frequently referring to contractions as "rushes" and to mothers as "goddesses."
Her work on the Farm shaped the role of home births to this day, ushering in an era of women who had yet ***more*** options when it came to deciding how to give birth.

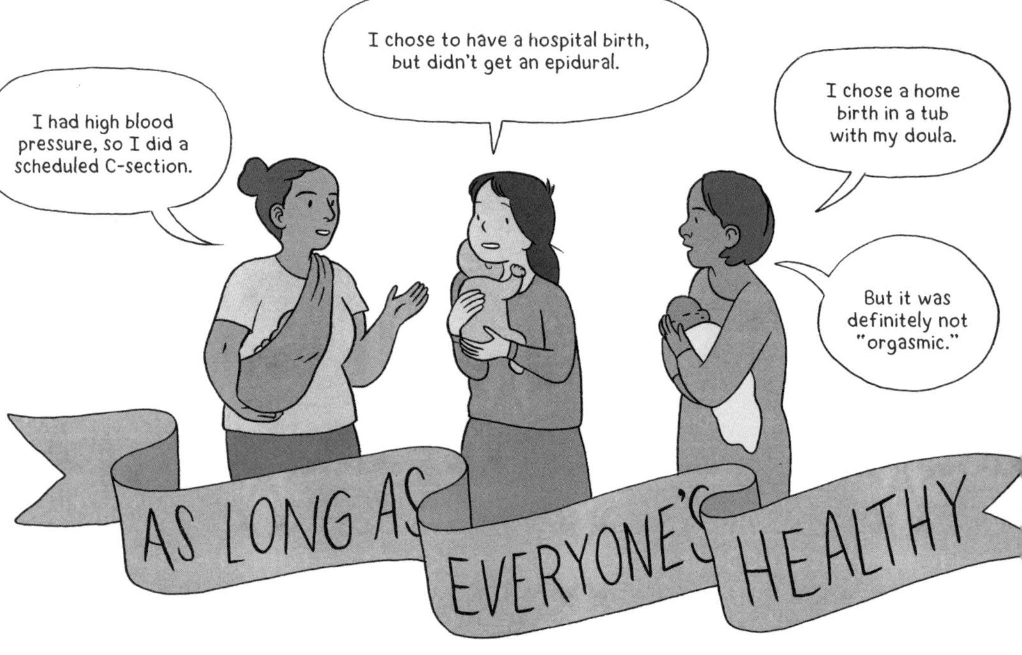
I had high blood pressure, so I did a scheduled C-section.
I chose to have a hospital birth, but didn't get an epidural.
I chose a home birth in a tub with my doula.
But it was definitely not "orgasmic."
AS LONG AS EVERYONE'S HEALTHY

Today, a pregnant person is deluged with options and opinions regarding their "birth plan."

MEDICATED DOULA UNMEDICATED
HOSPITAL HOME CLINIC
LAMAZE

But the debates still rage around what constitutes a "natural" birth.

Is it unnatural to want to avoid pain?

The assumed modern definition of a "natural birth" generally means "to go without an epidural."

Epidurals were first used in surgical procedures in the early 1900s, but weren't very effective in childbirth due to the fact that half the time they slowed contractions and brought labor to a halt.

But in the 1970s, researchers developed synthesized oxytocin, otherwise known as Pitocin. This meant that doctors could speed up contractions again.

Electronic fetal monitoring was also made commercially available in 1968, which allowed doctors to keep better tabs on the babies while treating the mother.

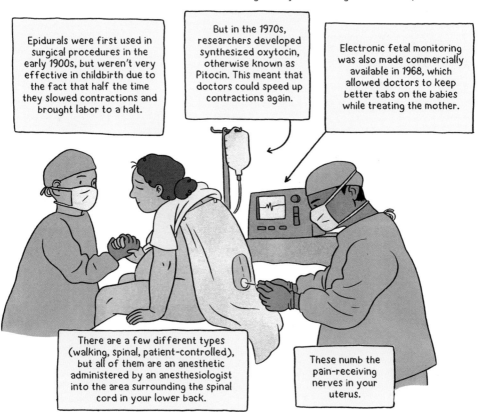

There are a few different types (walking, spinal, patient-controlled), but all of them are an anesthetic administered by an anesthesiologist into the area surrounding the spinal cord in your lower back.

These numb the pain-receiving nerves in your uterus.

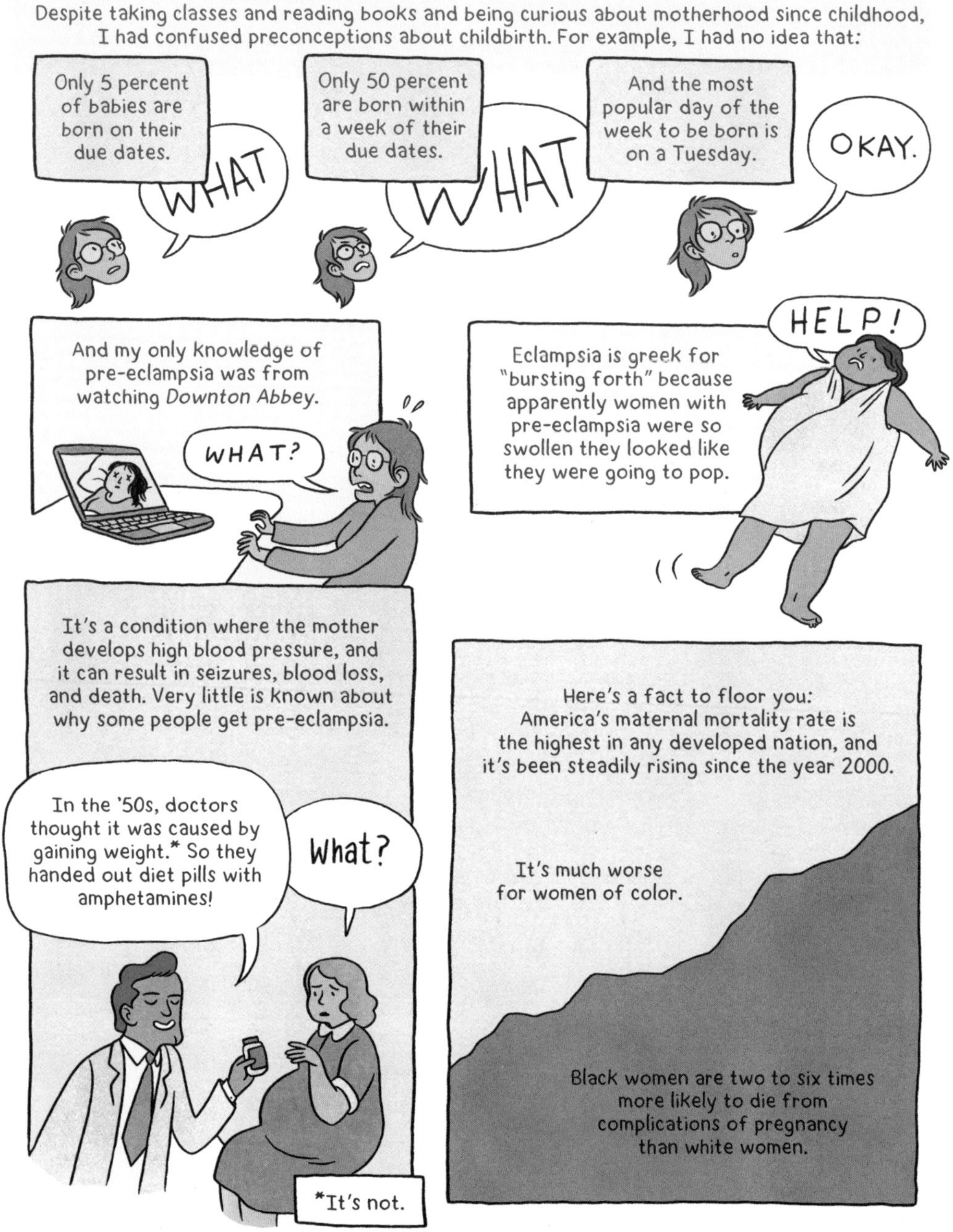
Despite taking classes and reading books and being curious about motherhood since childhood, I had confused preconceptions about childbirth. For example, I had no idea that:
Only 5 percent of babies are born on their due dates.
WHAT
Only 50 percent are born within a week of their due dates.
WHAT
And the most popular day of the week to be born is on a Tuesday.
OKAY.
And my only knowledge of pre-eclampsia was from watching Downton Abbey.
WHAT?
Eclampsia is greek for "bursting forth" because apparently women with pre-eclampsia were so swollen they looked like they were going to pop.
HELP!
It's a condition where the mother develops high blood pressure, and it can result in seizures, blood loss, and death. Very little is known about why some people get pre-eclampsia.
In the '50s, doctors thought it was caused by gaining weight.* So they handed out diet pills with amphetamines!
What?
*It's not.
Here's a fact to floor you: America's maternal mortality rate is the highest in any developed nation, and it's been steadily rising since the year 2000.
It's much worse for women of color.
Black women are two to six times more likely to die from complications of pregnancy than white women.

Federal and state funding show only 6 percent of funding for "maternal and child health" actually go to the care of mothers.

Many hospitals account for premature births (ICUs for premature infants, specialists on staff, etc.), but don't reserve nearly as much for maternal emergencies.

Even after hundreds of years of research and medical advancements, mothers are still dying in childbirth. In the USA, more every year.

But the good news is that smart, caring people are working on the problem, and I am grateful every day for their efforts in saving the lives of enthusiastic cartoonists, like myself.

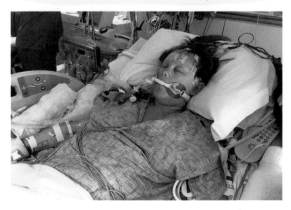

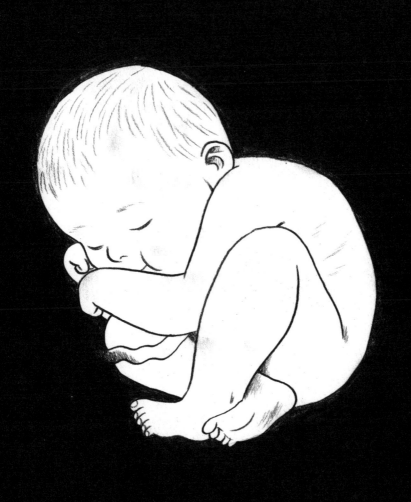

COMING HOME

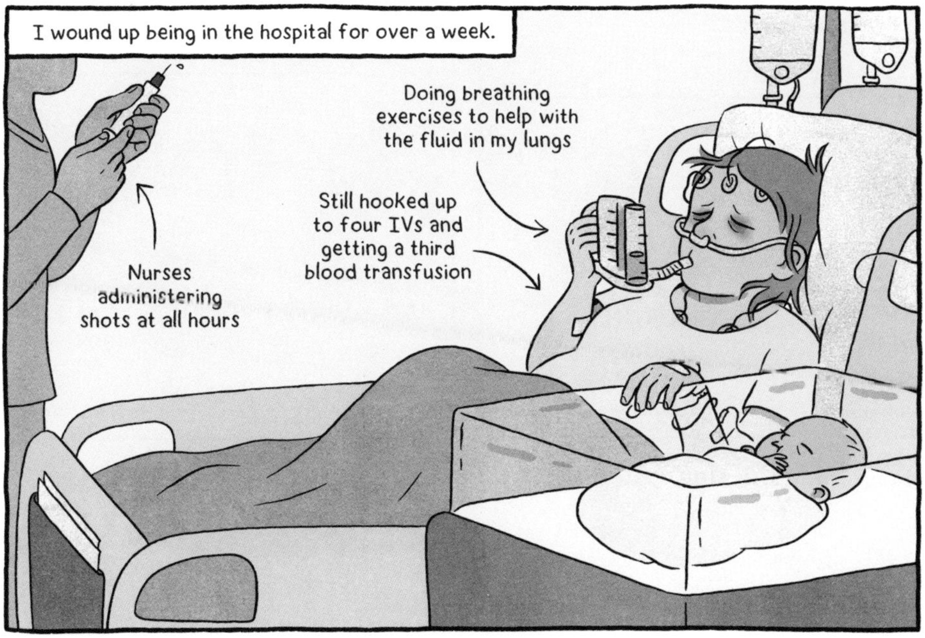
I wound up being in the hospital for over a week.
Doing breathing exercises to help with the fluid in my lungs
Still hooked up to four IVs and getting a third blood transfusion
Nurses administering shots at all hours

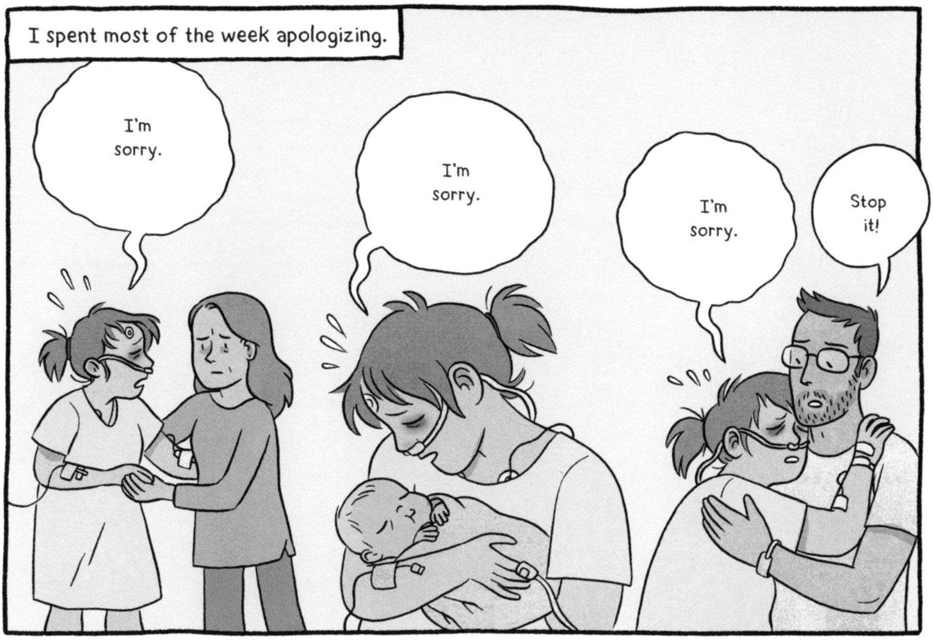
I spent most of the week apologizing.
I'm sorry.
I'm sorry.
I'm sorry.
Stop it!

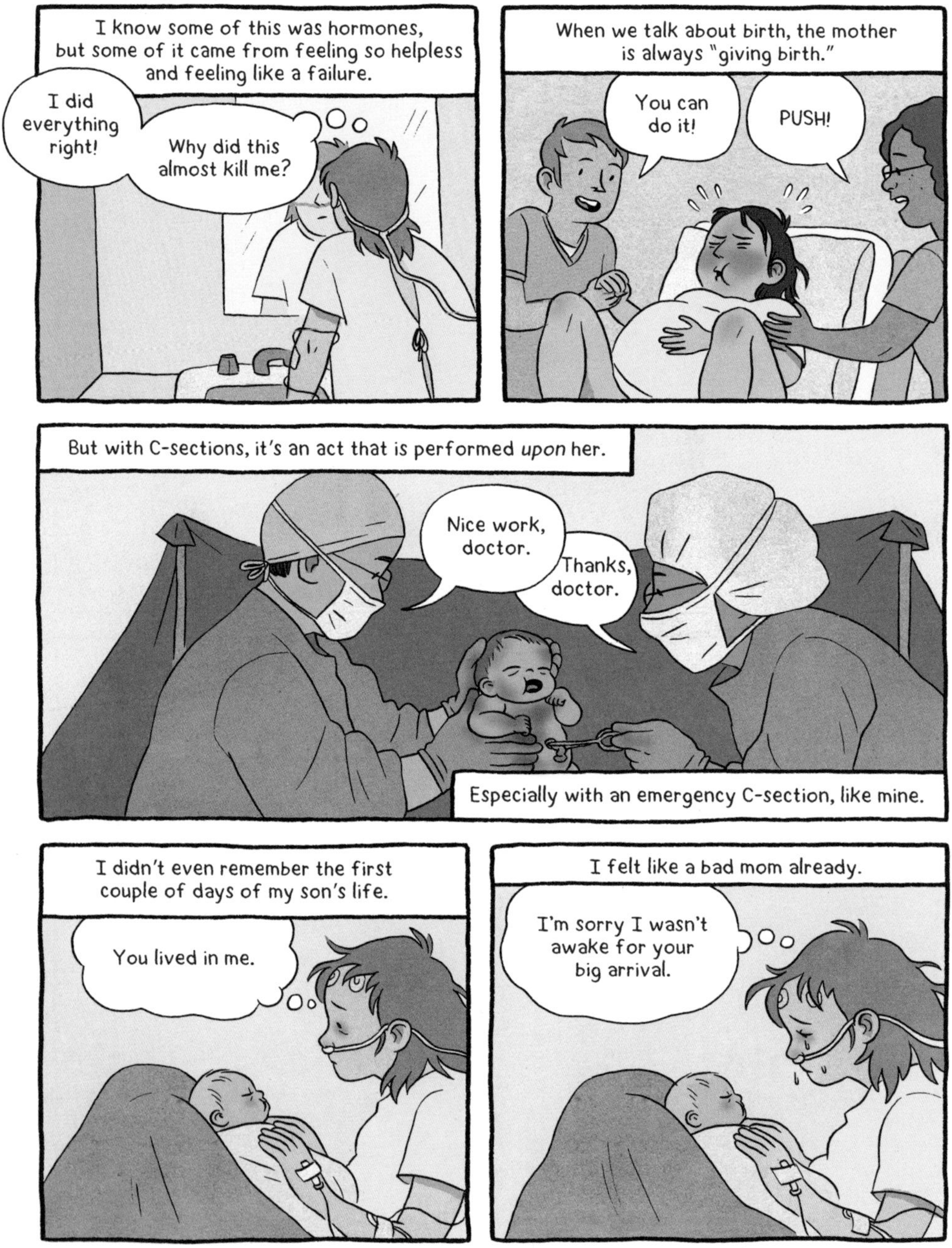
I know some of this was hormones, but some of it came from feeling so helpless and feeling like a failure.
I did everything right!
Why did this almost kill me?
When we talk about birth, the mother is always "giving birth."
You can do it!
PUSH!
But with C-sections, it's an act that is performed *upon* her.
Nice work, doctor.
Thanks, doctor.
Especially with an emergency C-section, like mine.
I didn't even remember the first couple of days of my son's life.
You lived in me.
I felt like a bad mom already.
I'm sorry I wasn't awake for your big arrival.

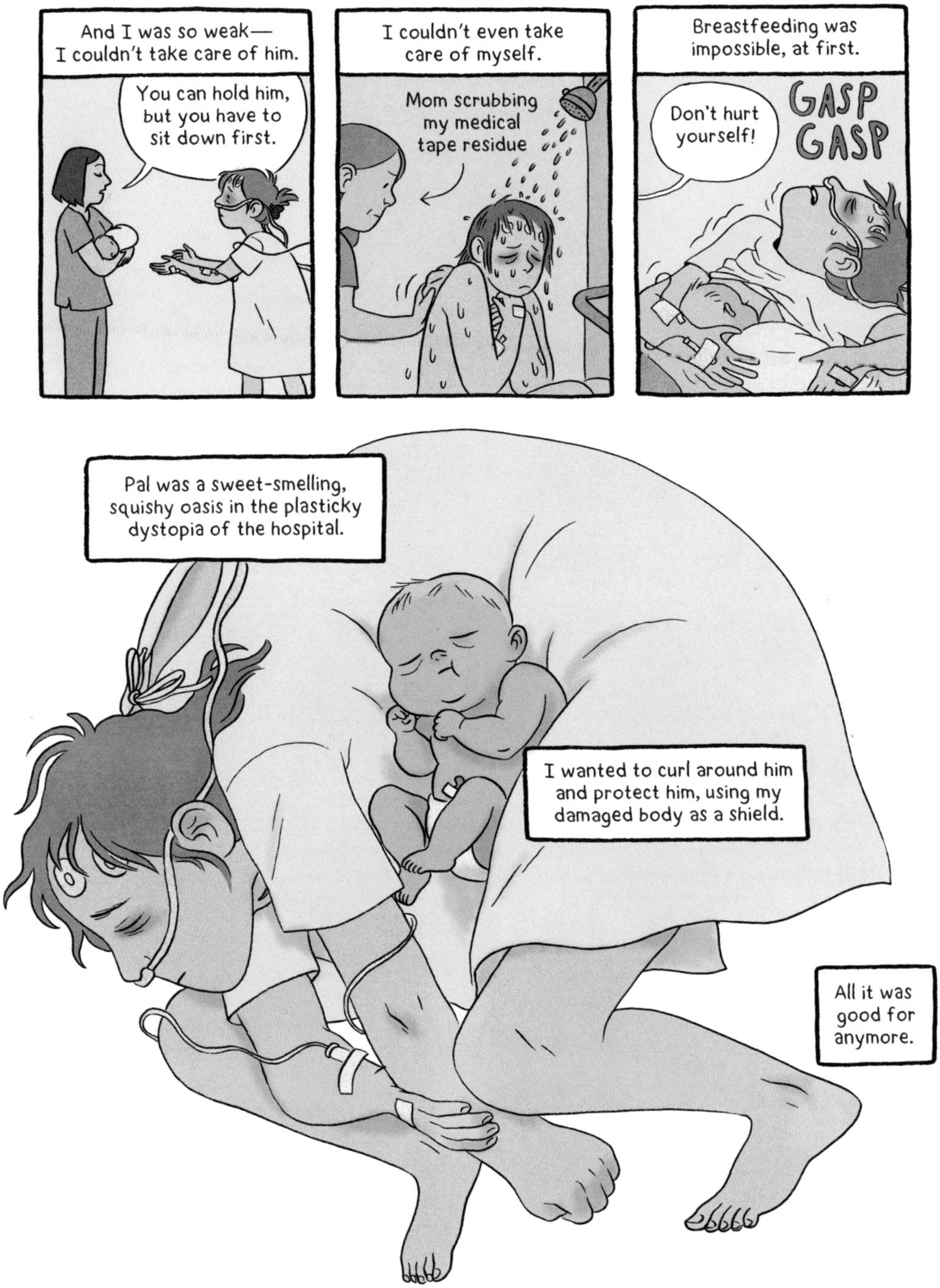
And I was so weak—
I couldn't take care of him.
You can hold him, but you have to sit down first.
I couldn't even take care of myself.
Mom scrubbing my medical tape residue
Breastfeeding was impossible, at first.
Don't hurt yourself!
GASP GASP
Pal was a sweet-smelling, squishy oasis in the plasticky dystopia of the hospital.
I wanted to curl around him and protect him, using my damaged body as a shield.
All it was good for anymore.

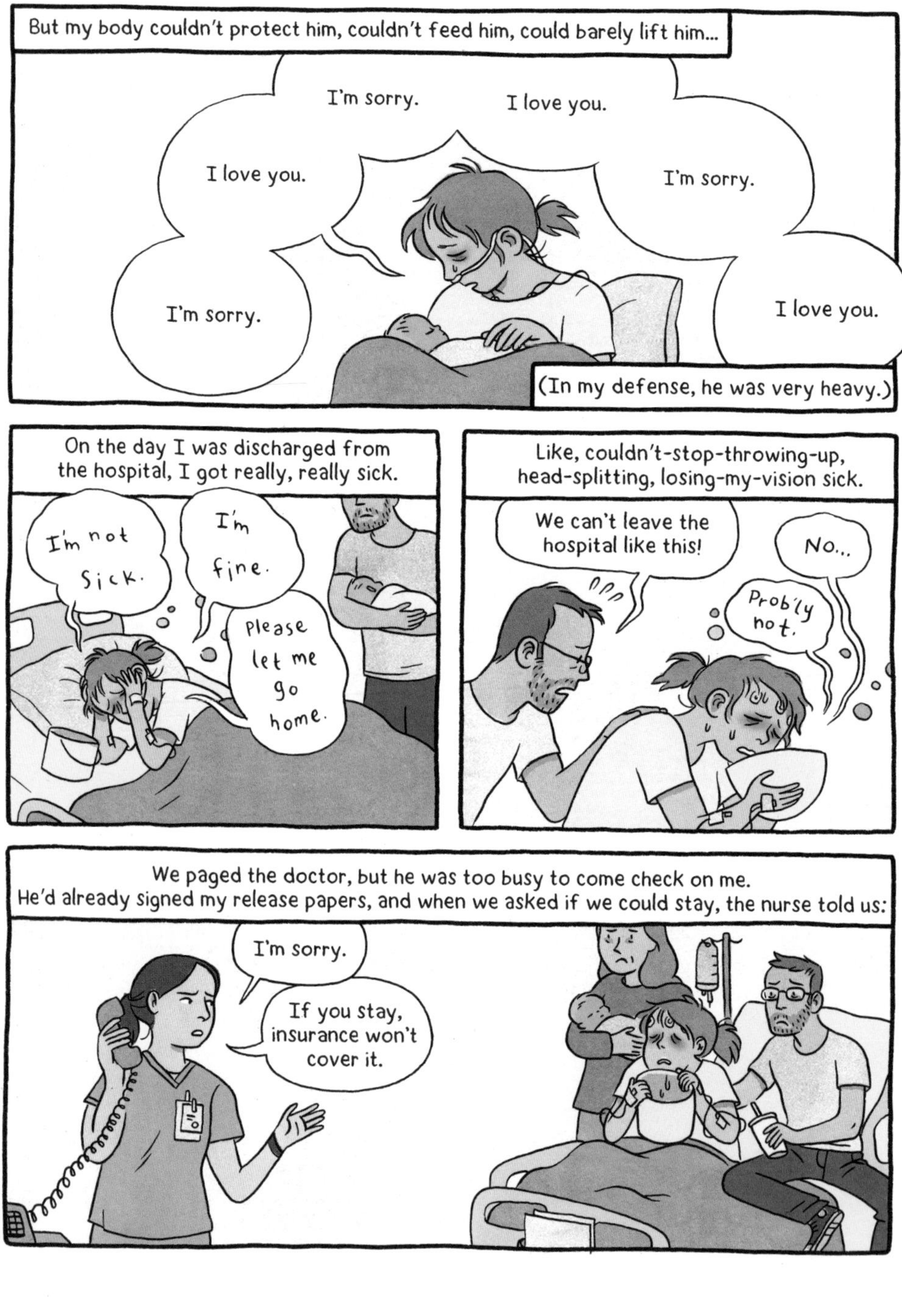

But my body couldn't protect him, couldn't feed him, could barely lift him...
I'm sorry.
I love you.
I love you.
I'm sorry.
I'm sorry.
I love you.
(In my defense, he was very heavy.)
On the day I was discharged from the hospital, I got really, really sick.
I'm not sick.
I'm fine.
Please let me go home.
Like, couldn't-stop-throwing-up, head-splitting, losing-my-vision sick.
We can't leave the hospital like this!
No...
Prob'ly not.
We paged the doctor, but he was too busy to come check on me.
He'd already signed my release papers, and when we asked if we could stay, the nurse told us:
I'm sorry.
If you stay, insurance won't cover it.

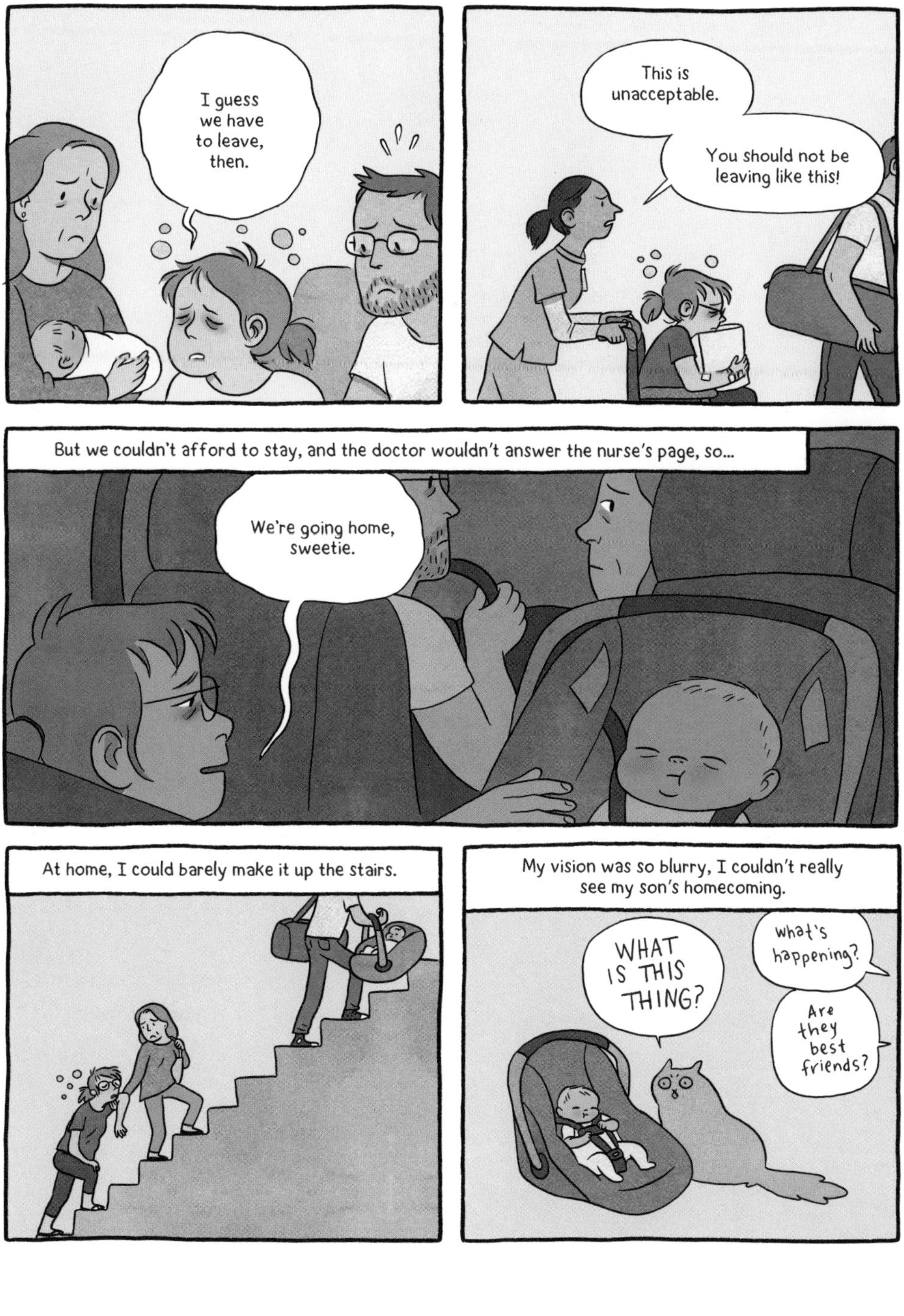

I guess we have to leave, then.
This is unacceptable.
You should not be leaving like this!
But we couldn't afford to stay, and the doctor wouldn't answer the nurse's page, so...
We're going home, sweetie.
At home, I could barely make it up the stairs.
My vision was so blurry, I couldn't really see my son's homecoming.
WHAT IS THIS THING?
what's happening?
Are they best friends?

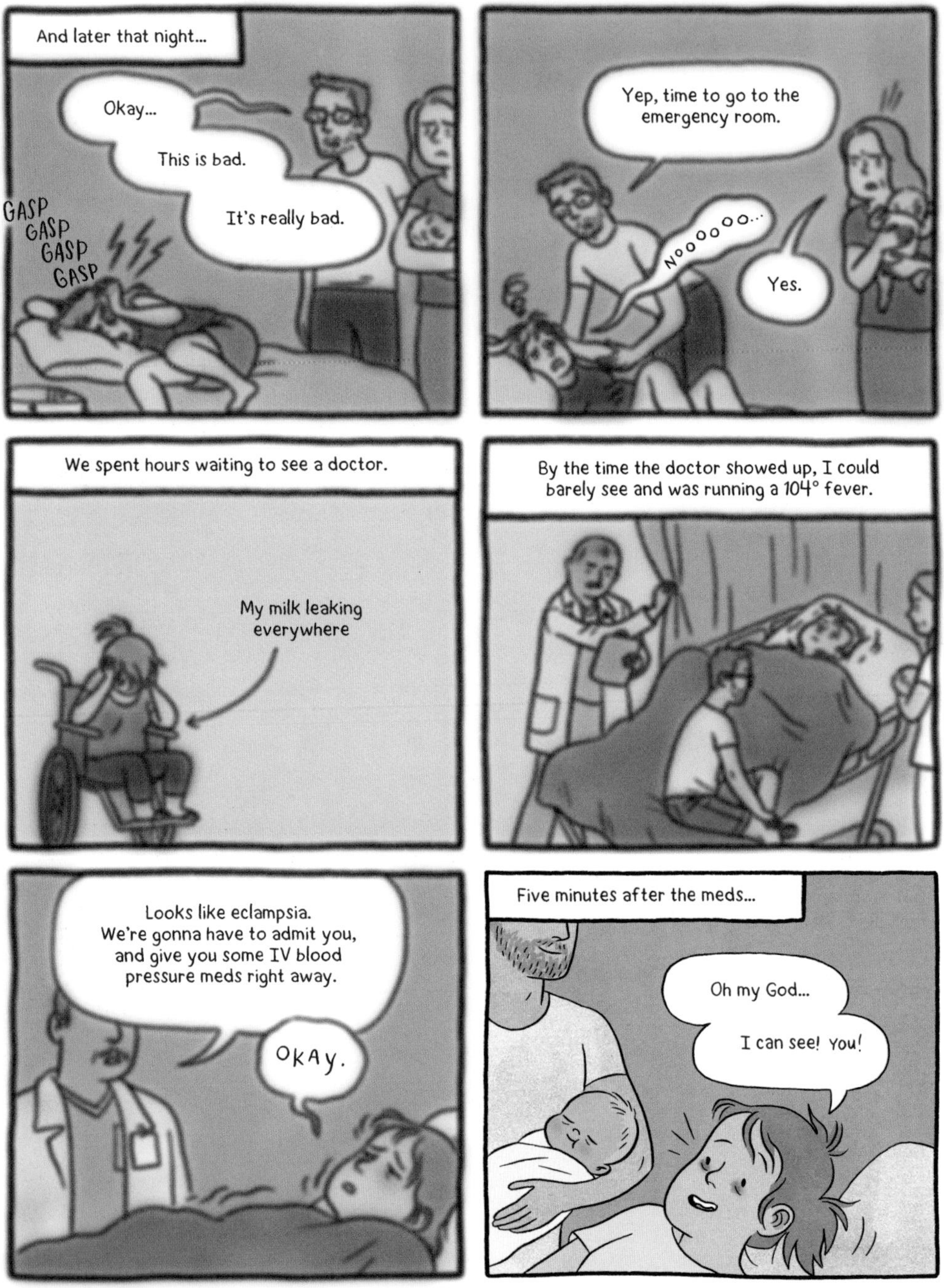
And later that night...
Okay...
This is bad.
It's really bad.
GASP
GASP
GASP
GASP
Yep, time to go to the emergency room.
Noooooo...
Yes.
We spent hours waiting to see a doctor.
My milk leaking everywhere
By the time the doctor showed up, I could barely see and was running a 104° fever.
Looks like eclampsia. We're gonna have to admit you, and give you some IV blood pressure meds right away.
OKAY.
Five minutes after the meds...
Oh my God...
I can see! You!

My second stay in the hospital was worse than the first.

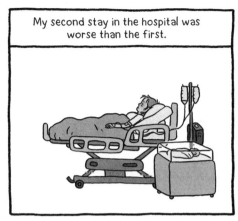

I had PTSD from the emergency surgery, and my new-mom hormones made it worse.

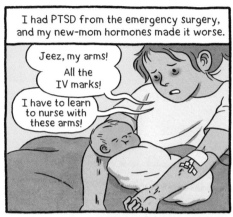

Jeez, my arms! All the IV marks!

I have to learn to nurse with these arms!

I worried about Pal constantly.

ARE YOU OKAY?

I didn't sleep.

The only thing that saved me was John, holding me together while I felt like I was flying apart.

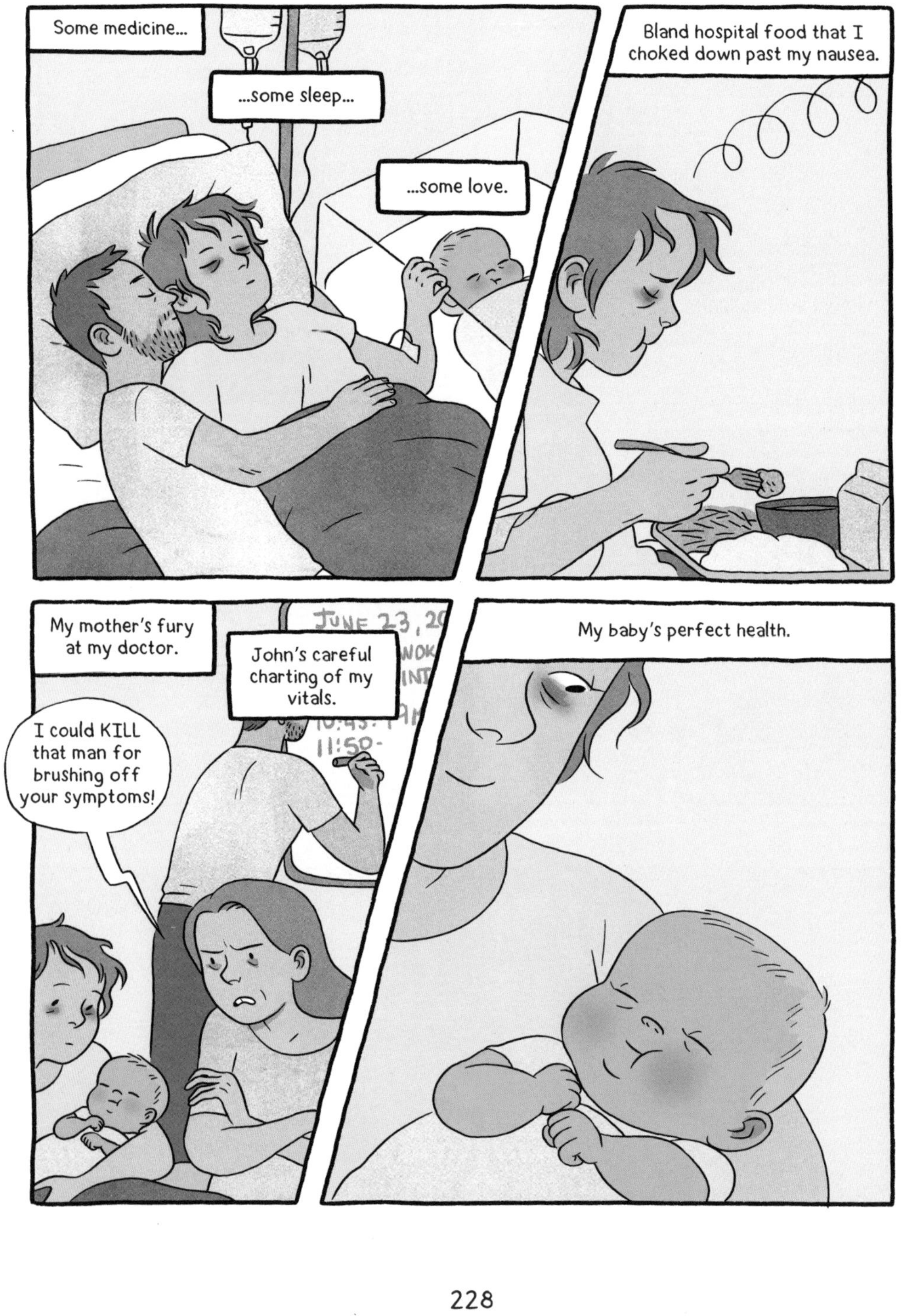
Some medicine...
...some sleep...
...some love.
Bland hospital food that I choked down past my nausea.
My mother's fury at my doctor.
John's careful charting of my vitals.
I could KILL that man for brushing off your symptoms!
My baby's perfect health.

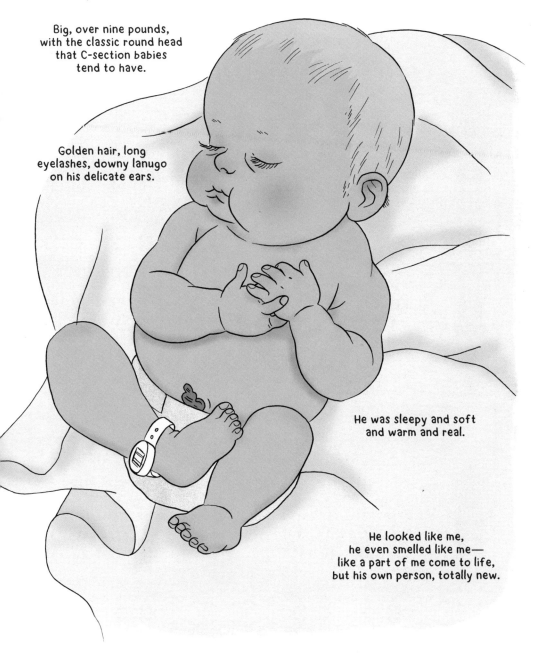

And he was perfect.

Big, over nine pounds,
with the classic round head
that C-section babies
tend to have.

Golden hair, long
eyelashes, downy lanugo
on his delicate ears.

He was sleepy and soft
and warm and real.

He looked like me,
he even smelled like me—
like a part of me come to life,
but his own person, totally new.

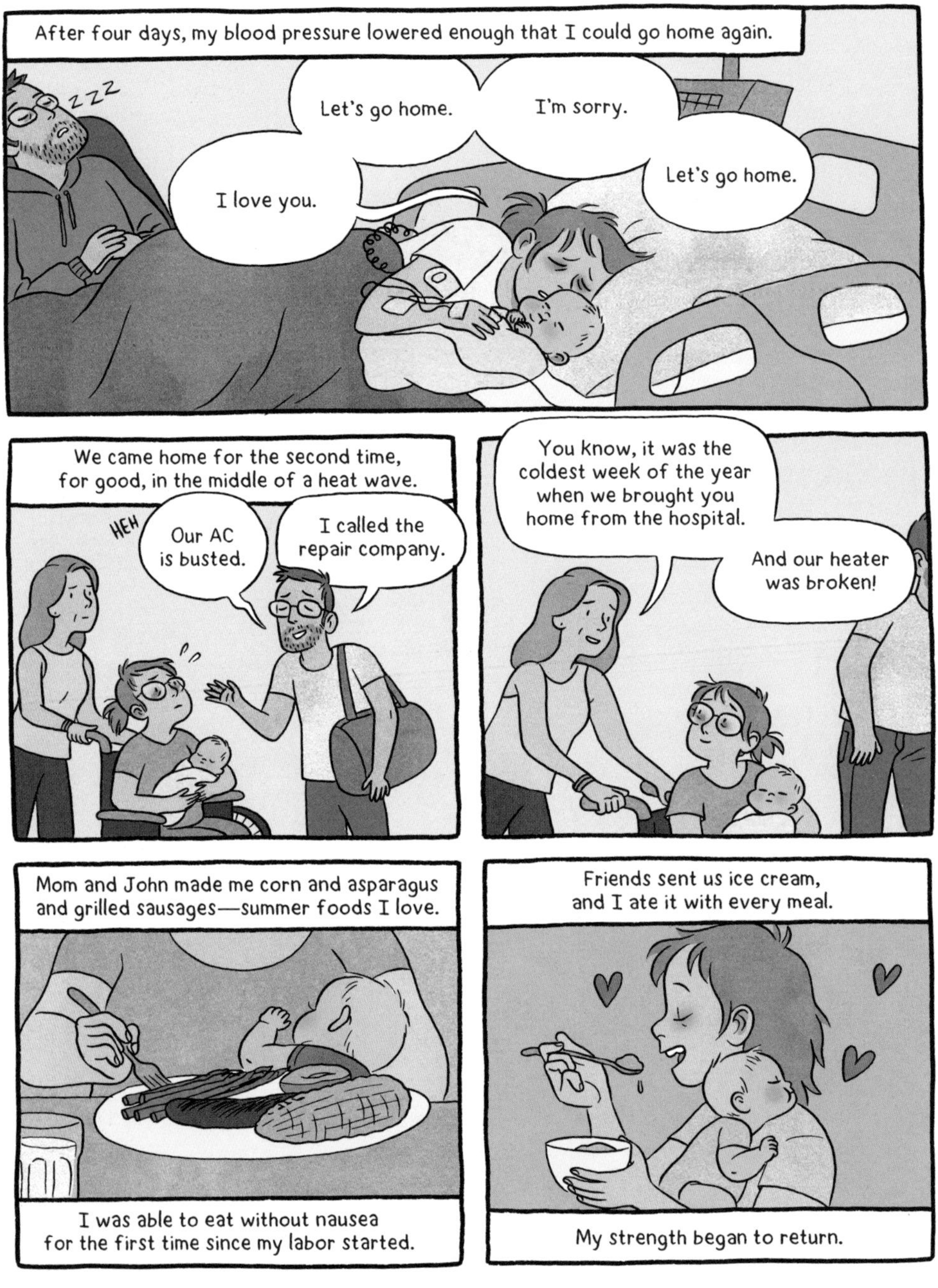
After four days, my blood pressure lowered enough that I could go home again.
ZZZ
I love you.
Let's go home.
I'm sorry.
Let's go home.
We came home for the second time, for good, in the middle of a heat wave.
HEH
Our AC is busted.
I called the repair company.
You know, it was the coldest week of the year when we brought you home from the hospital.
And our heater was broken!
Mom and John made me corn and asparagus and grilled sausages—summer foods I love.
I was able to eat without nausea for the first time since my labor started.
Friends sent us ice cream, and I ate it with every meal.
My strength began to return.

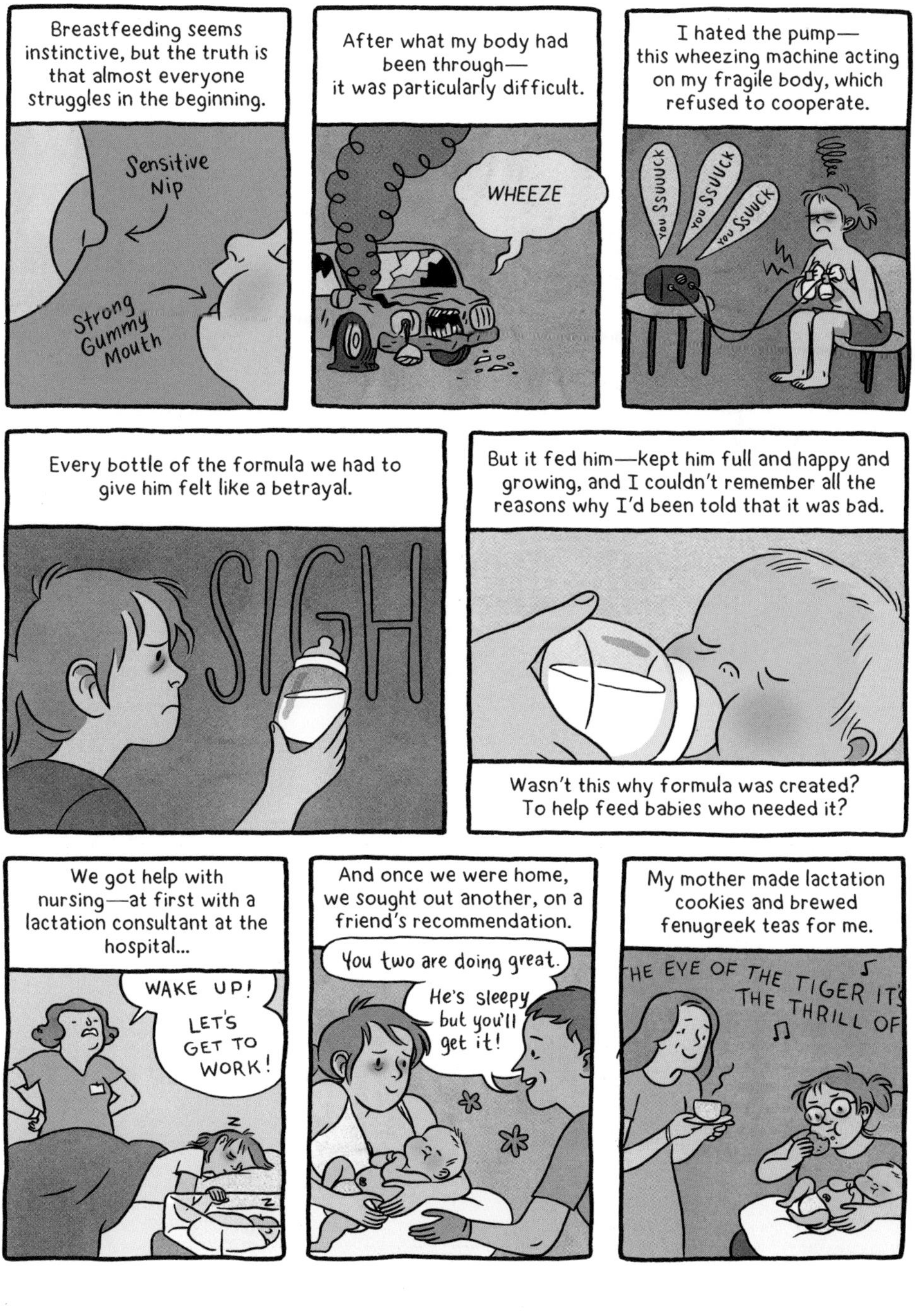
Breastfeeding seems instinctive, but the truth is that almost everyone struggles in the beginning.
Sensitive Nip
Strong Gummy Mouth
After what my body had been through— it was particularly difficult.
WHEEZE
I hated the pump— this wheezing machine acting on my fragile body, which refused to cooperate.
YOU SSUUUCK
YOU SSUUCK
YOU SSUUCK
Every bottle of the formula we had to give him felt like a betrayal.
SIGH
But it fed him—kept him full and happy and growing, and I couldn't remember all the reasons why I'd been told that it was bad.
Wasn't this why formula was created? To help feed babies who needed it?
We got help with nursing—at first with a lactation consultant at the hospital...
WAKE UP!
LET'S GET TO WORK!
Z
Z
And once we were home, we sought out another, on a friend's recommendation.
You two are doing great.
He's sleepy but you'll get it!
My mother made lactation cookies and brewed fenugreek teas for me.
THE EYE OF THE TIGER IT'S THE THRILL OF

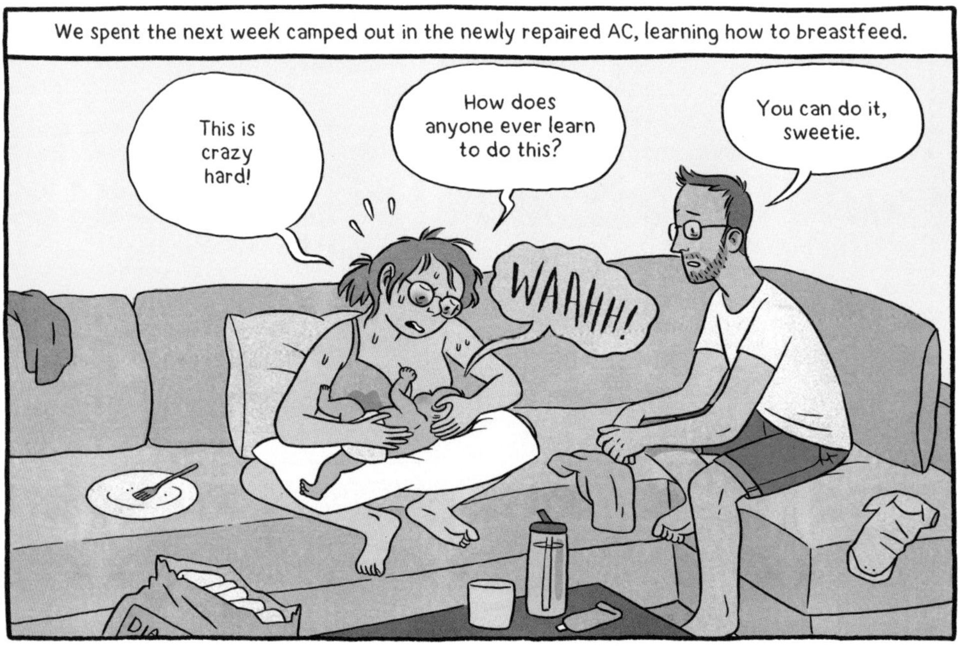
We spent the next week camped out in the newly repaired AC, learning how to breastfeed.
This is crazy hard!
How does anyone ever learn to do this?
WAAHH!
You can do it, sweetie.

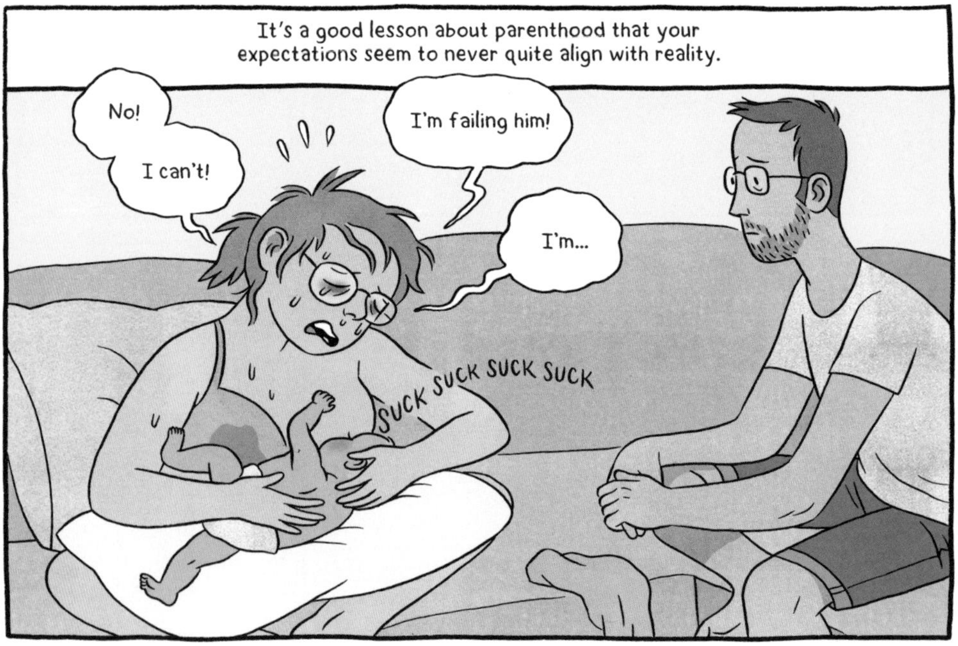
It's a good lesson about parenthood that your expectations seem to never quite align with reality.
No!
I can't!
I'm failing him!
I'm...
SUCK SUCK SUCK SUCK

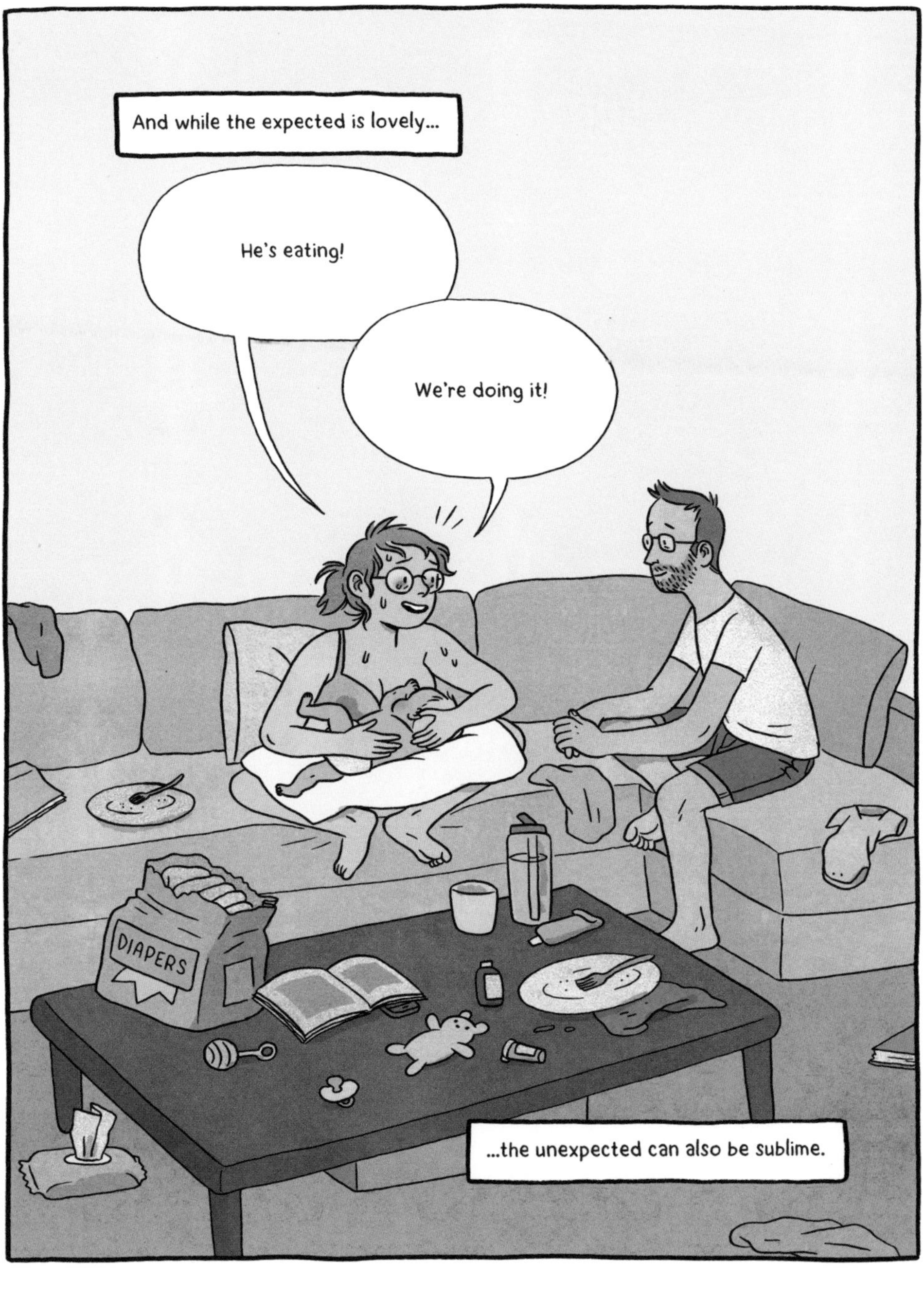
And while the expected is lovely...
He's eating!
We're doing it!
DIAPERS
...the unexpected can also be sublime.

AFTERWORD

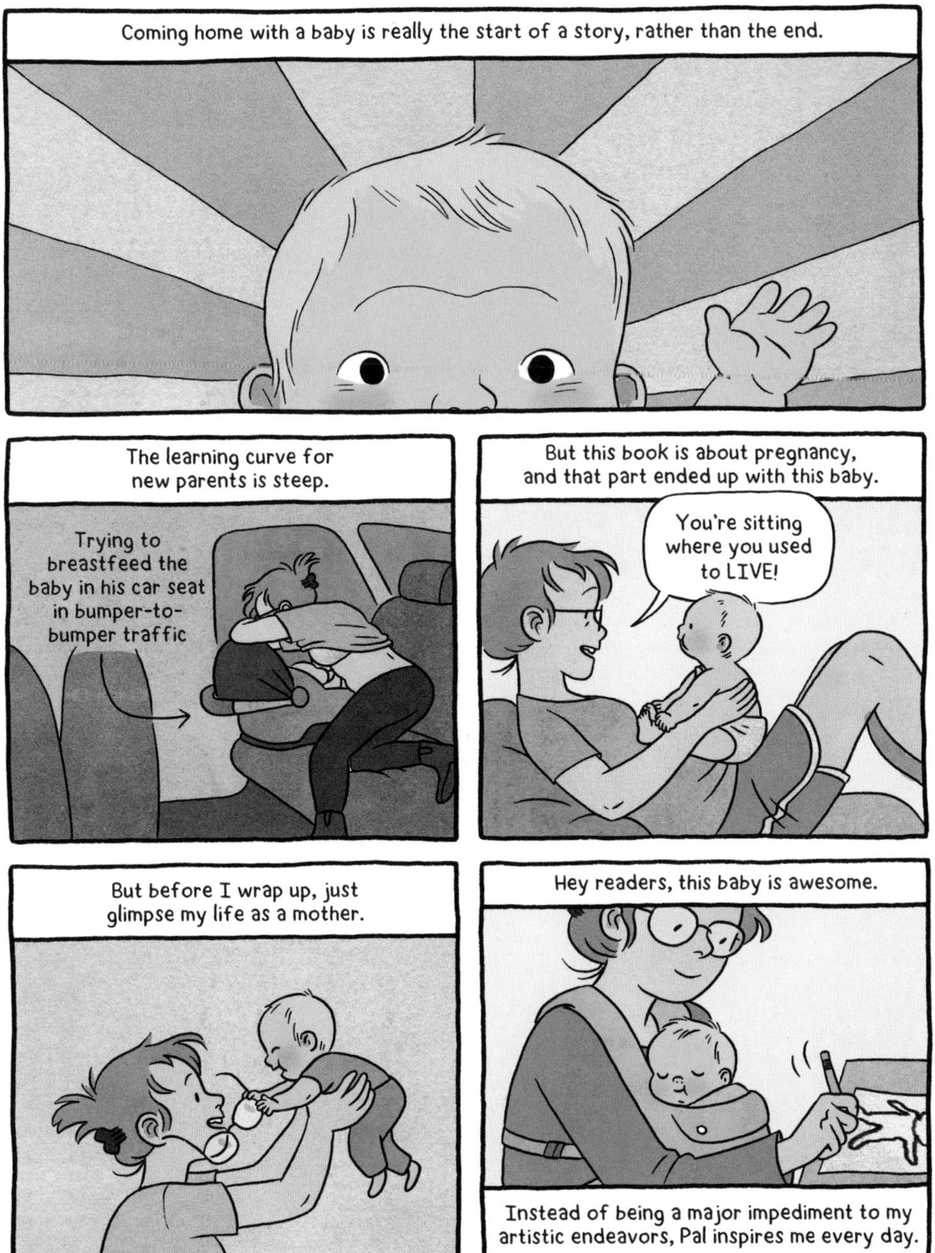
Coming home with a baby is really the start of a story, rather than the end.
The learning curve for new parents is steep.
Trying to breastfeed the baby in his car seat in bumper-to-bumper traffic
But this book is about pregnancy, and that part ended up with this baby.
You're sitting where you used to LIVE!
But before I wrap up, just glimpse my life as a mother.
Hey readers, this baby is awesome.
Instead of being a major impediment to my artistic endeavors, Pal inspires me every day.

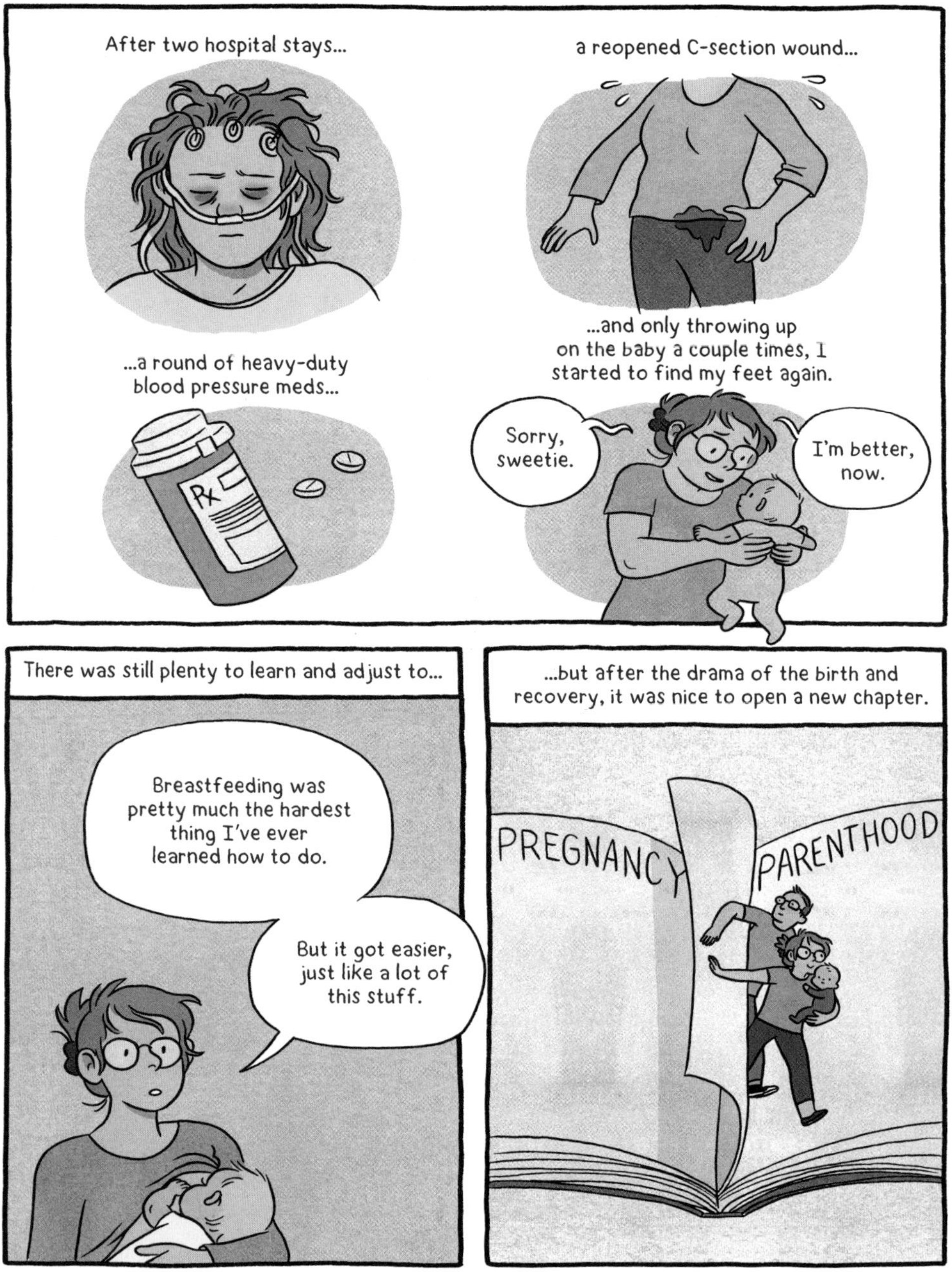
After two hospital stays...
a reopened C-section wound...
...a round of heavy-duty blood pressure meds...
...and only throwing up on the baby a couple times, I started to find my feet again.
Sorry, sweetie.
I'm better, now.
There was still plenty to learn and adjust to...
Breastfeeding was pretty much the hardest thing I've ever learned how to do.
But it got easier, just like a lot of this stuff.
...but after the drama of the birth and recovery, it was nice to open a new chapter.
PREGNANCY
PARENTHOOD

John is a natural dad.

He handled a very sick wife and very new baby with levelheaded gentleness.

After the frantic and terrifying birth, both of us are kind with each other.

Take a break.

WAAAH!

We do our best to give each other the patience and fortitude new parents need when dealing with a newborn on precious little sleep.

We have both been pooped on multiple times.

It seems to get easier with every poop.

But those are all stories for another book!

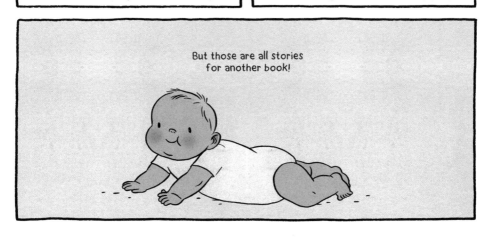

This has been a story about what came before:

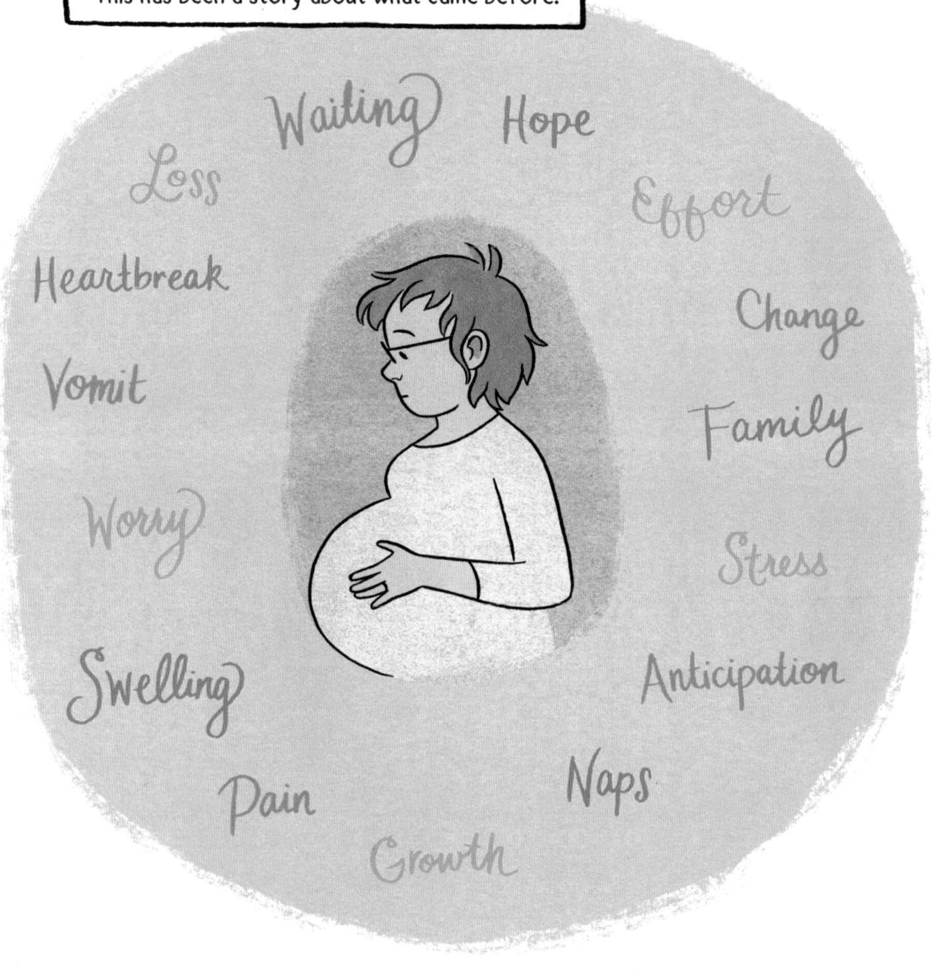
Waiting
Hope
Loss
Effort
Heartbreak
Change
Vomit
Family
Worry
Stress
Swelling
Anticipation
Naps
Pain
Growth

And love.

It all ends, for now, with a new beginning.

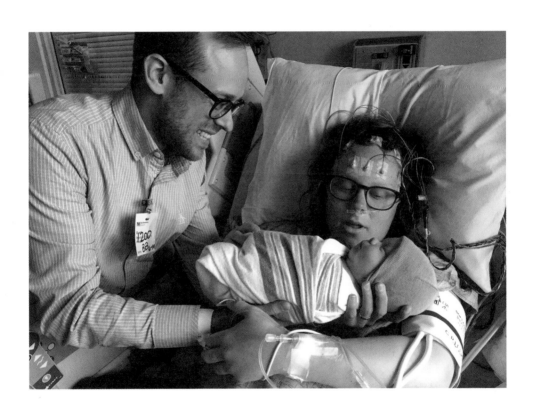

FURTHER RECOMMENDATIONS

READING

BABY BEHAVIOR
BABY BEHAVIOR

- *HOW TO ROCK YOUR BABY* (ERIN BRIED)
- *PREGNANT BUTCH* (A. K. SUMMERS)
- *ABOUT WHAT WAS LOST* (JESSICA BERGER GROSS)
- *OF THIS MUCH I'M SURE* (NADINE KENNEY JOHNSTONE)
- *LET'S PANIC ABOUT BABIES!* (ALICE BRADLEY AND EDEN M. KENNEDY)
- *MAMA TRIED* (EMILY FLAKE)
- *A USER'S GUIDE TO NEGLECTFUL PARENTING* (GUY DELISLE)
- *LITTLE LABORS* (RIVKA GALCHEN)
- *WOMEN IN CLOTHES* (SHEILA HETI, HEIDI JULAVITS, AND LEANNE SHAPTON)
- *STRANGERS IN PARADISE* (TERRY MOORE)
- *GET ME OUT* (RANDI HUTTER EPSTEIN, M.D.)
- *WRITING MOTHERHOOD: A CREATIVE ANTHOLOGY* (EDITED BY CAROLYN JESS-COOKE)

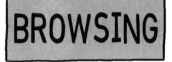

BROWSING

- "MONSTROUS BIRTHS" (SARAH BLACKWOOD FOR *THE HAIRPIN*)
- "THE LAST PERSON YOU'D EXPECT TO DIE IN CHILDBIRTH" (NINA MARTIN FOR *PROPUBLICA* AND RENEE MONTAGNE FOR NPR)
- "ON FERTILITY" (EILEEN FAVORITE)
- *CARRIERS* (LAUREN R. WEINSTEIN FOR *NAUTILUS*)
- *MOM BODY* (REBECCA ROHER FOR *GUTS* MAGAZINE)

LISTENING

- "NOT PERFECT" (TIM MINCHIN)

- "HAVE A BABY" (JEFFREY LEWIS)

- "THIS YEAR" (THE MOUNTAIN GOATS)

- "STAY UP LATE" (TALKING HEADS)

- "LANDING GEAR" (ANI DIFRANCO)

- "ST. JUDY'S COMET" (PAUL SIMON)

- "MIDDLE OF THE NIGHT" (LOUDON WAINWRIGHT III)

- "I WANNA BE SEDATED" (THE RAMONES)

- "SHE USED TO BE MINE" (SARAH BAREILLES)

- "RAISING THE DEAD" (JOHNNY FLYNN)

- "INDIANA JONES THEME" (JOHN WILLIAMS)

GO TO WWW.LUCYKNISLEY.COM/KGTUNES FOR THE PLAYLIST

GESTATING

- A PREGNANCY PILLOW

- LUSH "CHUB RUB" POWDER
  FOR SUMMERTIME PREGGOS

- JENI'S ICE CREAM
  (SALTY CARAMEL IS MY FAVORITE)

245

ACKNOWLEDGMENTS

You would not be holding this book in your hands if not for the aid of Angelika, our part-time Pal-wrangler and nanny extraordinaire. For three days a week, I can sit in my studio and draw while I listen to her calm voice from the other room, reading to my laughing kid. Thank you for your kindness, patience, and care, and for being the only person I talk to other than my kid and husband, most days.

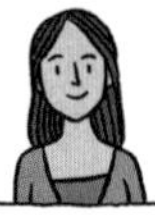

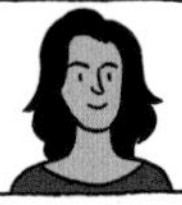

Thank you to the wonderful Holly Bemiss, without whom I wouldn't have this amazing career. I am so grateful to you for being my agent and friend for the better part of a decade.

Many thanks to my editor and preggo-buddy, Calista, who is the Ina May of this book's conception and delivery. I'm very glad to work with someone who gets me so well and who believes in my books.

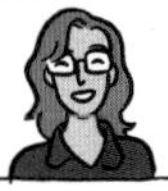

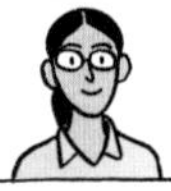

Thanks also to Gina Gagliano, for her stellar publicity work and for spreading my books near and far! The team at First Second Books has been so good to me.

I am also very grateful to Meg Lemke, who stepped in to give this book the polish and fixes it needed at the end. It's so nice to connect to someone through both work and motherhood.

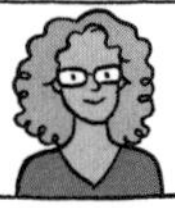

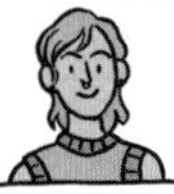

Big thanks to Stephanie Mided, who flatted every page of this tome. Her help made this book come together much more quickly and with far less stress than it might normally have taken, and I appreciate her hard work so much.

Thank you to my mom friends, who have reached out an incredible hand in mom-solidarity to me, through support and advice and shared annoyance. Thanks to Britt Wilson, Alex Graves, Marion Vitus, Lindsay Verstegen, and Renee Bailey, in particular, for their incredible help and friendship.

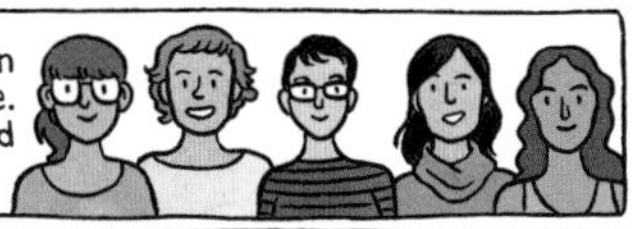

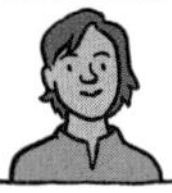

Thank you to Jane O'Conner, for helping me and Pal learn how to breastfeed. I honestly wasn't sure I'd ever get the hang of it, and you were so patient. Thanks also to Robin Frees for her further support.

Overwhelming thanks to the nurses on floor 15 at Prentice Hospital. Particularly Lindsey, who took such wonderful care of me and Pal.

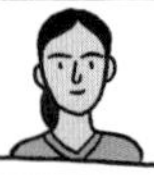

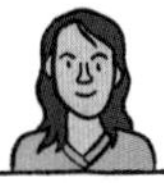

Thanks also to Amanda Criner, who is a nurse, a friend, and a mom (triple threat) who helped me understand what happened to me and to put it all in perspective.

Thank you to Shachar and Amy and their darling girls and boy, for more parenting advice and also the ice cream that saved my life at the beginning of Pal's.

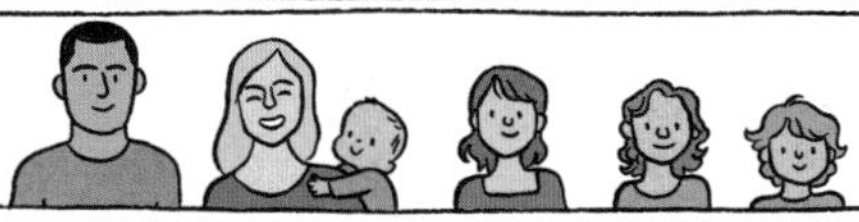

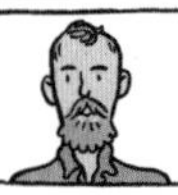

Big thank-you to Tony Breed, who came over and cooked for us at the beginning.

Thank you to all the parents and nonparents who follow me on Instagram, who lent their recommendations and support, especially in the early, rough days, and who continue to read my sketchbook comics about parenting and tell me how cute my kid is.

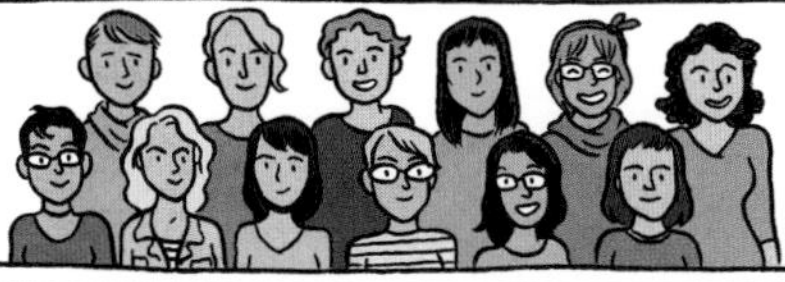

To my comics ladies, who have always shown me that being a woman who makes comics can look however you choose, and whom I am so proud to know and love: Dylan Meconis, Erika Moen, Hope Larson, Danielle Corsetto, Ming Doyle, Lucy Bellwood, Vera Brosgol, Jen Wang, Raina Telgemeier, Sarah Becan, Faith Erin Hicks, and Corrine Mucha.

Thank you to Ashley Van Buren, who took me to one of my favorite musicals as my first outing after Pal was born and who continues to be one of Pal's all-time favorite people.

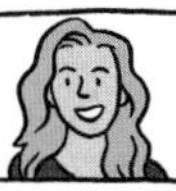

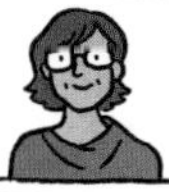

Thank you to Ruth Mills, whose brilliant mental health support has guided me through the medical trauma and emotional roller coaster of the last few years and made parenthood a saner, happier experience. Thank you for aiding me in titling this book.

Thanks to Erika and Greg, for being such wonderful siblings-in-law and for leading the way, machete in hand, through the jungle of parenting while we follow close behind. Our niece and nephew are perfect and amazing, and we love them.

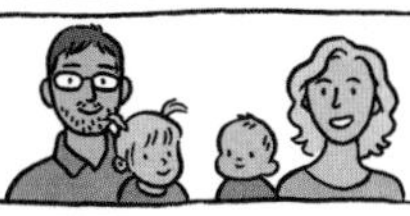

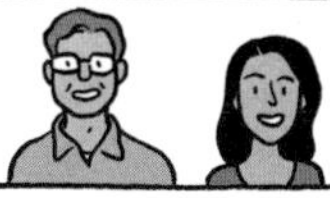

Thank you to my amazing parents-in-law, James and Jinx, for coming over every week to hang out with Pal and eat dinner and do laundry and fix cabinets. How did anyone ever survive having a kid without you two around?

Thanks to all of Pal's grands, including Jeffy and Susan and my dear old dad, who so adore my tiny dude and all he does. Thank you for lending your love and support; without you this book and that baby would not have been possible.

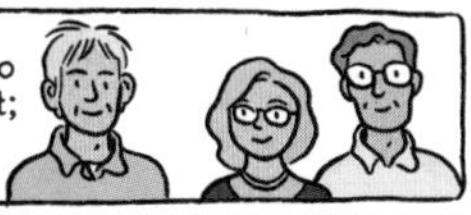

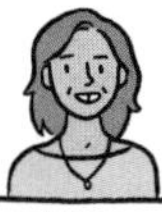

Thank you to my mother, who was by my side for every step of my traumatic experience giving birth to Pal. She was there rubbing my back, scrubbing off my surgical tape residue, and making cookies for the nurses through the whole ugly and beautiful nightmare/dream. I don't know how I'll ever thank her enough for her help in those early days, but I'll try to never put her through that kind of drama again.

My gratitude and solidarity go out to those of you who have suffered a pregnancy or infant loss and were brave enough to reach out and share your story. I am grateful every day for the understanding and empathy I gained from the stories of others who had lived through this heartbreak. I don't know how I could have pulled myself out of the pit if not for shared stories.

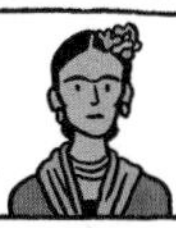

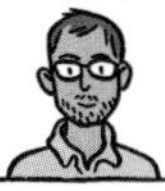

Thank you to John, the only dude I'd ever want to do this with. Thanks for helping me make the best possible baby of all time and taking such good care of him and of me.

Thank you to Pal for putting up with a mom who draws loving cartoons about your every waking moment, including this whole book about how you came to be.

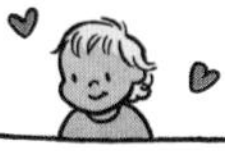

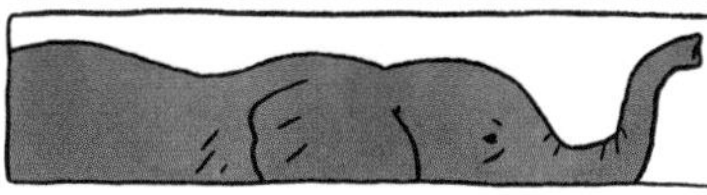

Finally, well done, elephants, on that two-year pregnancy. Elephants deserve to be worshipped like deities, and I love them very much.